IMAGES
of America

THE MISSISSIPPI RIVER FESTIVAL

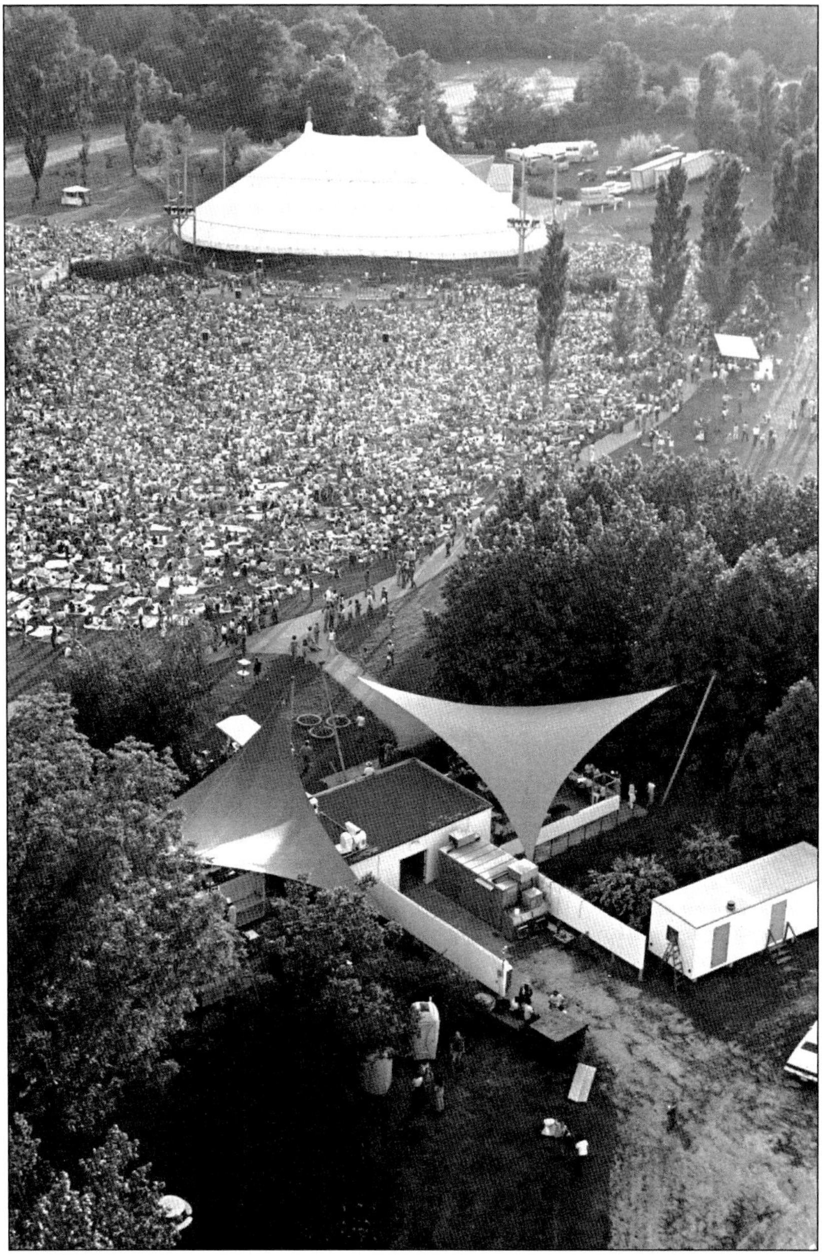

Not Far Down to Paradise. This aerial photograph looks down on the Mississippi River Festival site from the east to the west. It provides a view of the "sails" near the entrance area, the crowd on the lawn, and the tent.

On the cover: **The Lawn Crowd.** During the initial Mississippi River Festival season of 1969, ticket prices ranged from $5.50 to $2.50 for seats underneath the tent. Lawn seating cost $1.50 for adults and $1 for children less than 12 years old. By 1977, prices had risen to $3.50 for general admission and for certain events a range of $5 to $7 was charged for reserved seats. Because of price and for a variety of other reasons, many young people preferred to enjoy the performances seated on a blanket in a location of their choice on the long, sloping lawn. (Southern Illinois University Edwardsville.)

IMAGES
of America

THE MISSISSIPPI RIVER FESTIVAL

Amanda Bahr-Evola and Stephen Kerber

ARCADIA
PUBLISHING

ISBN 978-0-7385-4132-7

Published by Arcadia Publishing
Charleston, South Carolina

Printed in the United States of America

Library of Congress Catalog Card Number: 2006933894

For all general information contact Arcadia Publishing at:
Telephone 843-853-2070
Fax 843-853-0044
E-mail sales@arcadiapublishing.com
For customer service and orders:
Toll-Free 1-888-313-2665

Visit us on the Internet at www.arcadiapublishing.com

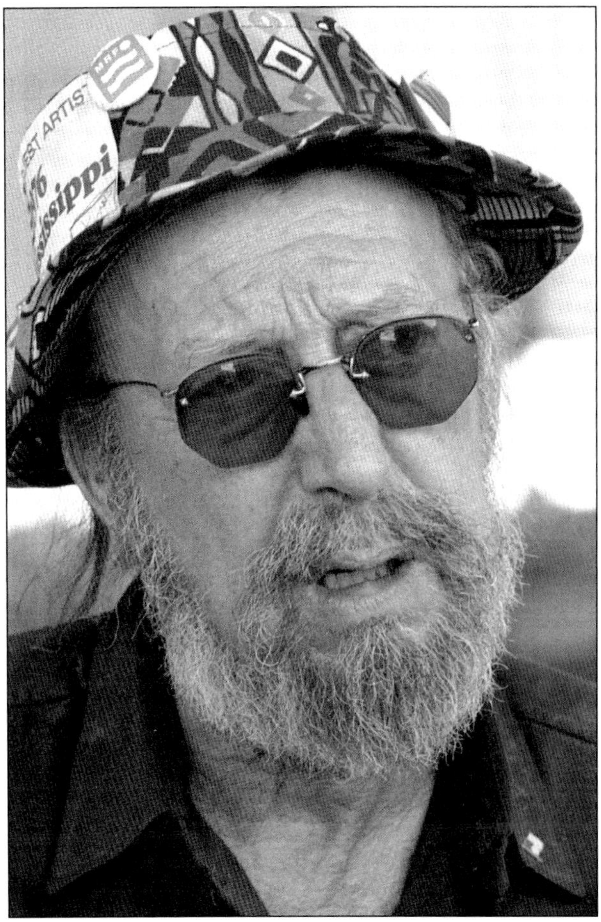

ROY "SKIP" MANLEY. Born in Illinois in 1903, Roy "Skip" Manley got started working with tents in the years following the conclusion of World War I. Manley began traveling around the West in order to gather information in preparation for his intended career as a cartoonist writing strips about cowboys. Manley soon discovered that he could obtain casual employment as a circus laborer. Eventually Manley encountered Curtis "Captain" Harris, who introduced him to the art of tent management.

Contents

ACKNOWLEDGMENTS

We are grateful to Chancellor Vaughn Vandegrift of Southern Illinois University Edwardsville for his official permission and encouragement to prepare this historical work and to make use of the terms Mississippi River Festival and MRF, the logos, and other intellectual property owned by the university. We are also grateful to Dean Jay Starratt of Library and Information Services for his official permission to make use of the documentary source materials and historic images that are reproduced in the book. We greatly appreciate the enthusiastic support and collaborative involvement of the university in this endeavor.

We would also like to thank the members of the Southern Illinois University Edwardsville 50th Anniversary Committee for designating this book as one of the official activities of the celebration.

Without the efforts of Louisa Bowen and John Abbott of Lovejoy Library, who preserved the records and photographic images, this book would not exist.

In the course of developing this project, we have accumulated many scholarly debts. Charlie Cox and his assistants deserve tremendous credit for their artistry in creating the wonderful photographs included here. We would especially like to thank Bill Brinson and Denise Macdonald for their assistance with the digitization of the photographs, Tony Leopold for his help with micro text and copies, and Matt Schmitz for his aid with information technology tools.

We are especially grateful to our families: Debbie Mann, Catherine Elizabeth Kerber, Rob Evola and Audrey Evola. Thank you for your endless patience and support.

Finally, we would like to thank and salute all those who played a role in creating the Mississippi River Festival for the heritage of excellence they left behind.

INTRODUCTION

In 1969, Southern Illinois University Edwardsville initiated a remarkable performing arts series called the Mississippi River Festival. Over 12 summer seasons, between 1969 and 1980, the festival presented 353 events showcasing performers in a variety of musical genres, including classical, chamber, vocal, ragtime, blues, folk, bluegrass, barbershop, country, and rock, as well as dance and theater. During those years, more than one million visitors flocked to the spacious Gyo Obata–designed campus in the countryside near St. Louis.

The Mississippi River Festival began as a partnership promoting regional cooperation in the realm of the performing arts. Southern Illinois University Edwardsville invited the St. Louis Symphony Orchestra to establish residence on campus and to offer a summer season. To host the symphony, the university created an outdoor concert venue within a natural amphitheater by installing a large circus tent, a stage and acoustic shell, and a sophisticated sound system. To appeal to the widest possible audience, the university included contemporary popular musicians in the series. The audacity of the undertaking, the charm of the venue, the popularity of the artists, the excellence of the performances, and the nostalgic memory of warm summer evenings have combined to endow the festival with legendary status among those who attended.

The history of the Mississippi River Festival may be considered in three phases. The first phase, 1967–1970, involved the planning and implementation of the original concept of a cultural partnership. The second phase, 1971–1977, covered the evolution of the festival beyond the original concept with increasing participation by popular musicians. The third phase, 1978–1980, involved an attempt to outsource the operation of the festival in a futile effort to save it from financial difficulties.

The St. Louis Symphony Society embraced the concept of a cultural partnership with another institution primarily for financial reasons. Handicapped by insufficient revenue, the symphony management desired to provide the additional employment for its artists that would come with a summer season. For its part, the young university coveted the publicity and prestige that it hoped would be generated by the presence on its brand-new campus of a cultural arts festival built around one of the finest symphony orchestras in the nation.

By the late 1960s, Pres. Delyte W. Morris had reached the pinnacle of his career as a university administrator. During two decades of significant public support for higher education, with the assistance of talented but frequently overlooked academic colleagues and with the support of influential business and political leaders, Morris had overseen the meteoric growth of one major educational institution and the establishment of another. His reputation as a powerful leader who had access to the substantial resources necessary to implement his vision convinced the leaders of the St. Louis Symphony Society to partner with the university in the audacious festival endeavor.

As a part of the agreement negotiated between the university and the St. Louis Symphony Society and signed on October 8, 1968, the university committed itself to construct both a temporary site for the upcoming 1969 season and also a permanent venue to house the symphony for the 1970, 1971, and subsequent seasons. The agreement envisioned a permanent outdoor music venue comparable to existing facilities such as Tanglewood (home of the Boston Symphony and Boston Pops), Meadow Brook (home of the Detroit Symphony), Blossum Center (home of the Cleveland Orchestra), and Saratoga (home of the Philadelphia Orchestra), including a stage and acoustic shell, some covered area for part of the audience, and space on the lawn for more than 10,000 listeners. The university's trustees approved the agreement on November 20, 1968.

Unfortunately when personal errors of judgment and forces of revolutionary societal change beyond his comprehension and control drove Morris out of office in 1970, the conditions that had promised well for the financial stability and success of the festival changed abruptly. The circumstances of Morris's sudden departure contributed to enhanced scrutiny of individual campus resource management decisions throughout the state of Illinois both by boards of trustees and by a more centralized resource allocation and oversight system for higher education. Of equal or greater significance, partly because of concern over campus activism, disorders, and opposition to the controversial war in Vietnam, public officials showed less inclination to support higher education financially throughout the decade of the 1970s than they had during the 1950s and 1960s.

Thus when the removal of Morris essentially cancelled the university's ability to create and maintain a permanent venue to house the symphony, everything changed. The festival struggled from year to year at the temporary site to generate sufficient revenue for operation. The university vigorously sought and obtained individual, philanthropic, and government subsidies to bolster ticket sales, but the symphony performances never proved self-supporting. As early as the 1971 season, the symphony made a decision to start cutting back its appearances from the projected 18 per year during 1969 and 1970 to only 12 per year during 1971 through 1974. The symphony appeared just six times in 1975 and five times in 1976. In addition, the symphony began to compete with itself by scheduling outdoor summer concerts back across the river in Missouri.

As the symphony reduced its involvement, the university increased the number of popular music events on the festival schedule. Although artistic excellence remained the criteria for scheduling choices and the hallmark of actual performances, financial success remained consistently elusive. Variables such as weather fluctuations, evolving musical trends and tastes, and increasing competition from other venues made it difficult for the festival to balance revenues with expenditures. It seemed almost impossible for the festival to become self-sustaining. Finally when Pres. Kenneth "Buzz" Shaw assumed office following the death of unwavering festival advocate John Rendleman, he made a very difficult decision to lease out the site to a private group that would assume all responsibility for financing and promoting the festival. The three-year experiment (1978, 1979, 1980) in outside management did not prosper and the festival ceased operation following the 1980 season.

Although financial issues ultimately undermined the continuing existence of the Mississippi River Festival, the enduring significance of the festival is to be found not in an analysis of finances but in the spectrum of excellent performances in multiple artistic genres woven within the fabric of the audacity of the original undertaking. Many of the most distinguished performing artists of their era participated in 353 diverse cultural events. Over a span of 12 years, more than a million spectators (many of whom lived far from major cities) enjoyed the rare opportunity of experiencing excellent entertainment in company with fellow enthusiasts in a very unique and charming venue. We trust that all those who participated in the Mississippi River Festival between 1969 and 1980 will enjoy it once again through the images included in this book.

One

ENCHANTMENT 1967–1970

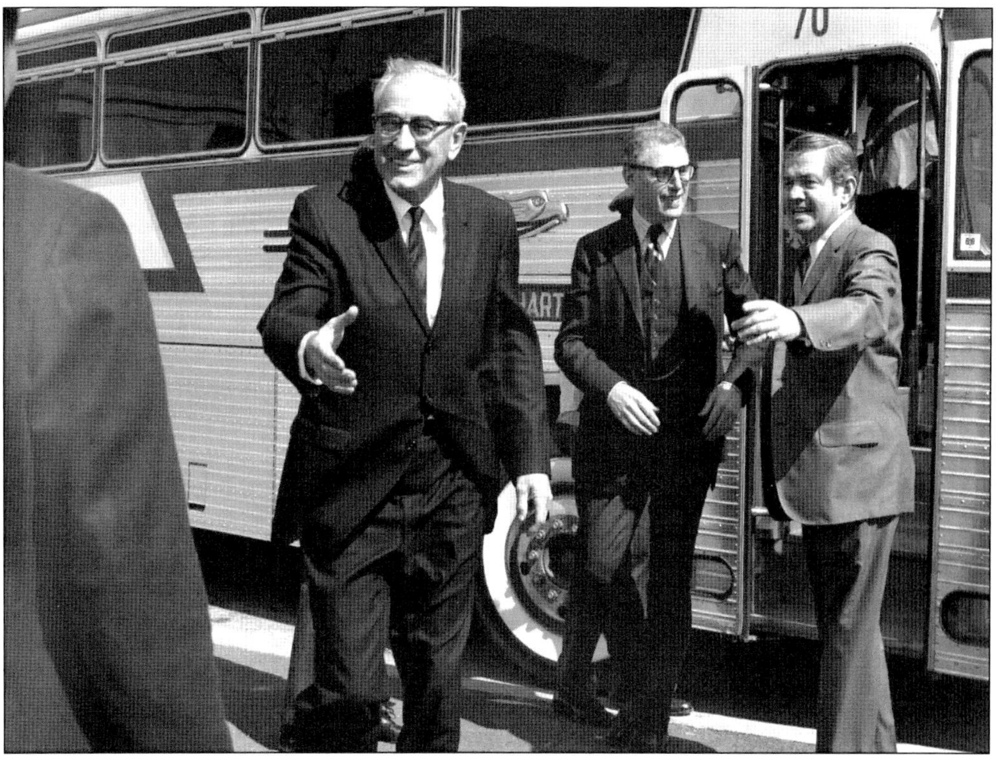

EXPECTATIONS. Pres. Delyte Morris, St. Louis Symphony Society president Stanley Goodman, and Chancellor John Rendleman exchanged greetings when members of the society visited Southern Illinois University Edwardsville (SIUE) on March 17, 1969. The group discussed festival plans, held a press conference, and climbed to the roof of Lovejoy Library to view the temporary festival location to the north and the permanent site to the south.

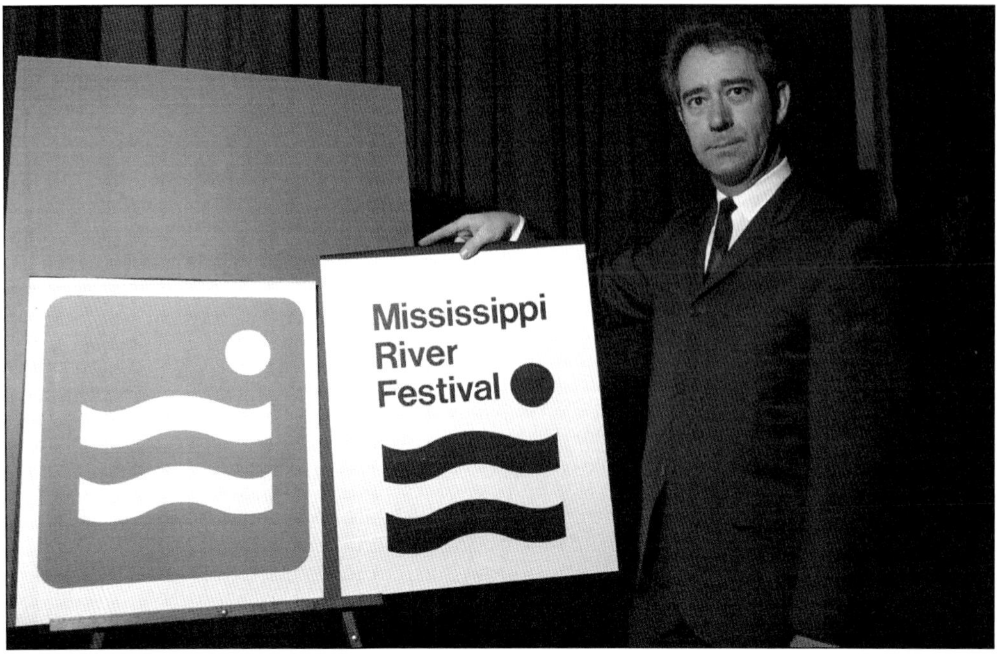

A. B. MIFFLIN. As the coordinator of university graphics, A. B. Mifflin designed the original Mississippi River Festival (MRF) logo. Mifflin placed two curving lines representing gentle waves in the Mississippi River beneath a sphere representing the summer moon shining high above the evening events.

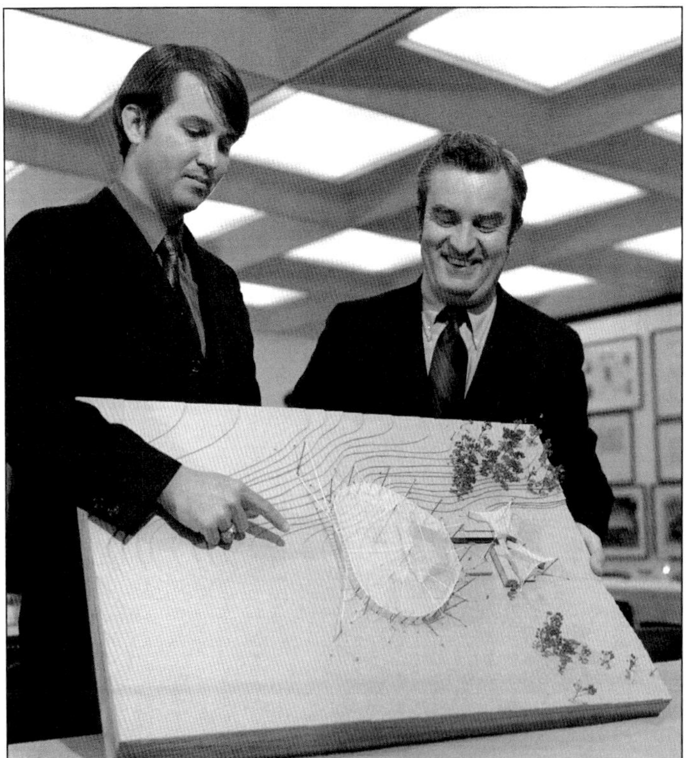

PROFESSIONAL CONSULTANTS. The university retained the services of the architectural firm of Anselevicius, Rupe and Larry Medlin of St. Louis to design the tent. Christopher Jaffe of Norwalk, Connecticut, served as acoustic consultant. David Mintz of New York City functioned as lighting expert for the project.

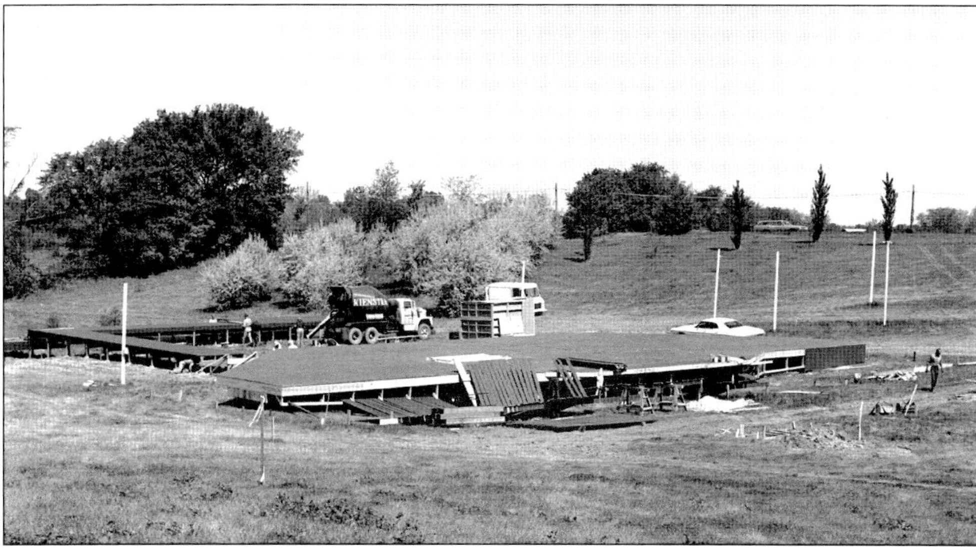

NATURAL AMPHITHEATER. Since 1963, commencement ceremonies had been held in a grassy natural amphitheater situated on the northern side of the campus. During 1965, a consultant prepared a report suggesting that a permanent outdoor multi-purpose facility could be constructed in the amphitheater for approximately $750,000. Therefore in the interval before a permanent concert venue for the MRF could be designed and built on the southern edge of campus, high atop the bluffs, the natural amphitheater seemed an obvious site for the festival's inaugural season.

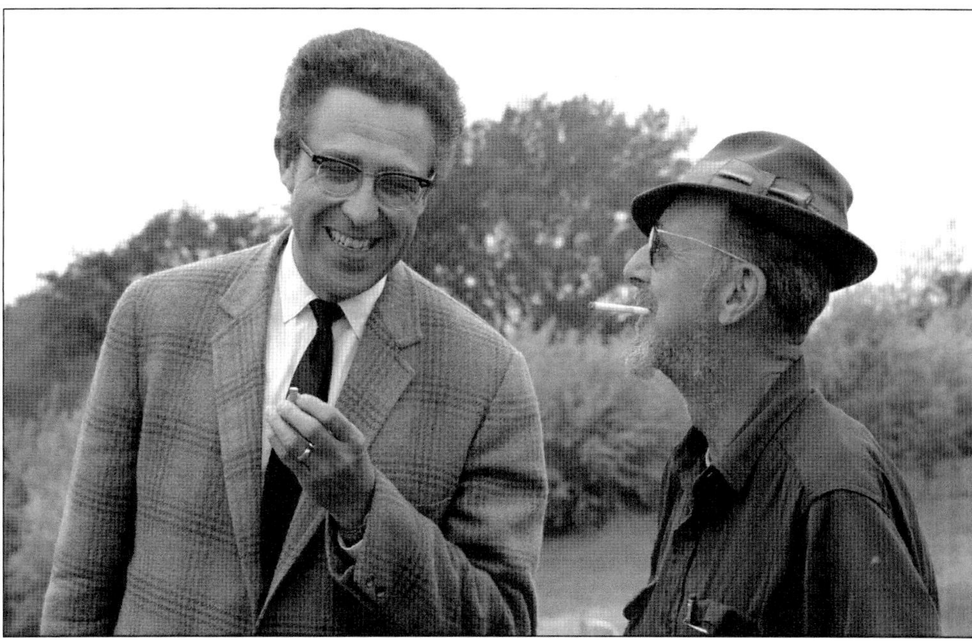

WILLIAM H. TARWATER. William H. Tarwater (left) and Skip Manley (right) enjoyed a joke at the site. Tarwater, a professor of music and gifted artist specializing in the French horn, played a major role in establishing the festival, in arranging for its first season, and sustaining it through the following years. Manley, a veteran circus tent master, contributed to the design of the original MRF tent, lived in a trailer at the site, and managed the tent during its several incarnations.

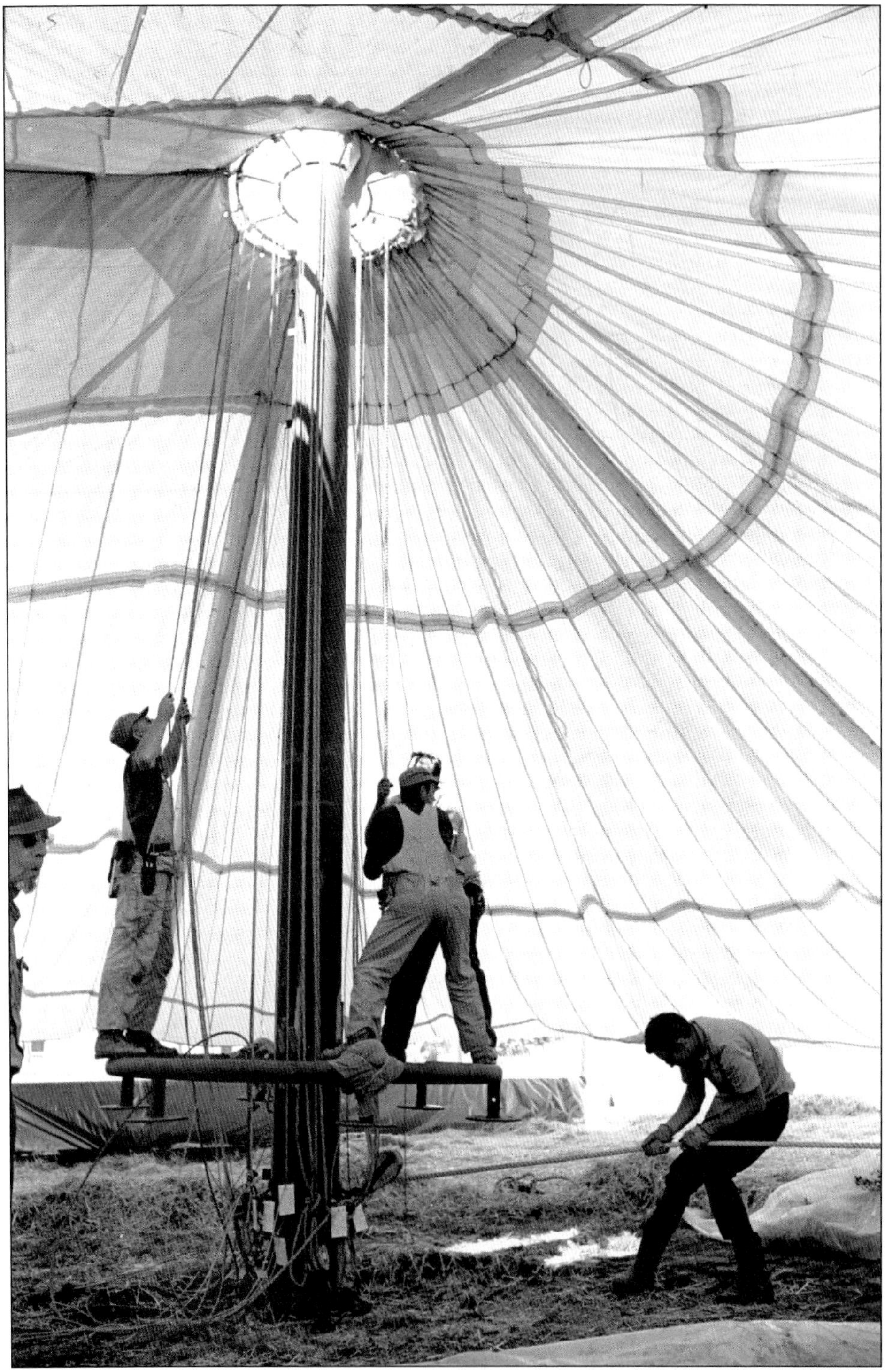

RAISING THE TENT. While closely following the verbal guidance provided by Skip Manley, university physical plant workers raised the original MRF tent for the first time on June 3, 1969. The crowd of spectators included Pres. Delyte Morris and Chancellor John Rendleman.

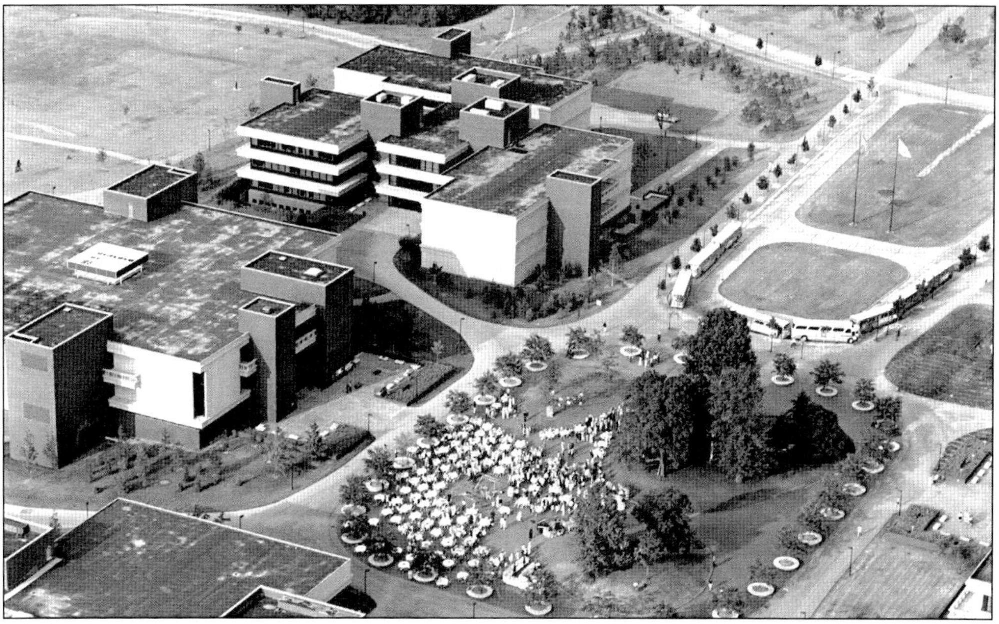

AERIAL OF "PICQUE NIQUE." This photograph provides an aerial view of the central mall of the campus on opening night of the festival, Friday, June 20, 1969. The Communications Building, Lovejoy Library, and the Peck Building are visible on the left of the image. The special buses used to transport symphony supporters and other special guests from St. Louis are parked along the Hairpin.

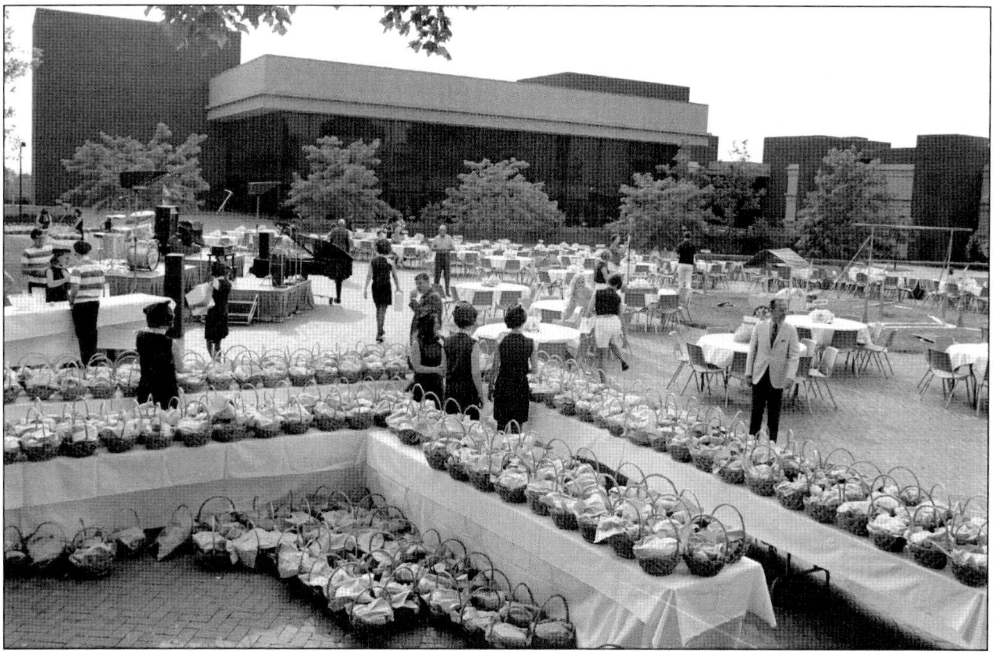

"PICQUE NIQUE" BUFFET. Chartered buses carried specially invited guests from gathering points at the prestigious John Burroughs School and at Powell Symphony Hall east across the Mississippi River from SIUE. The guests dined at an outdoor buffet encircled by the new Gyo Obata–designed buildings while being entertained by student gymnasts, fortune-tellers, and musicians.

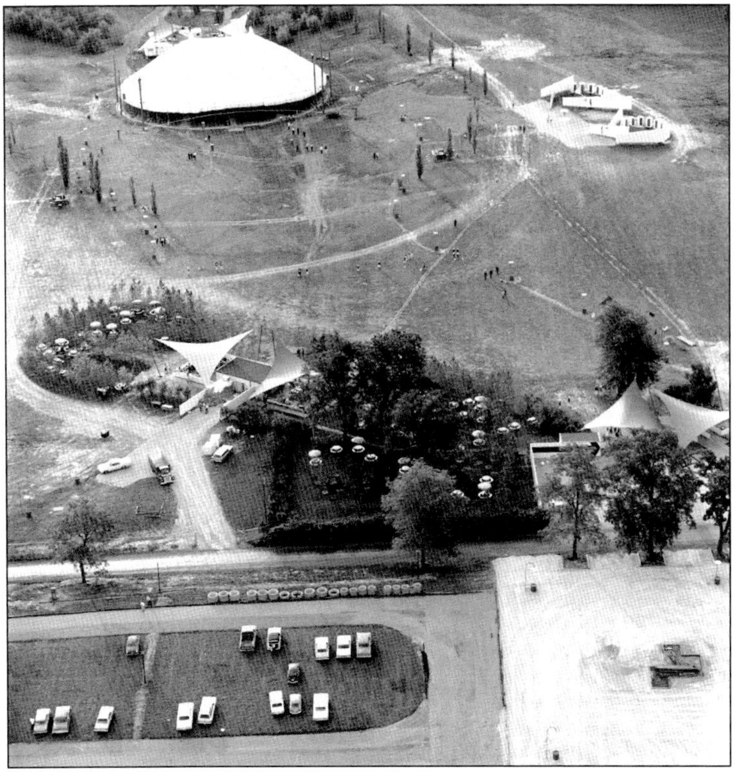

AERIAL OF OPENING NIGHT. Looking from the east to the west, this aerial photograph reveals the configuration of the front entrance to what had been the natural amphitheater used for commencement ceremonies. Visitors entered through the area at the bottom of this photograph, and could purchase food and drinks before walking down the sloping lawn toward the tent.

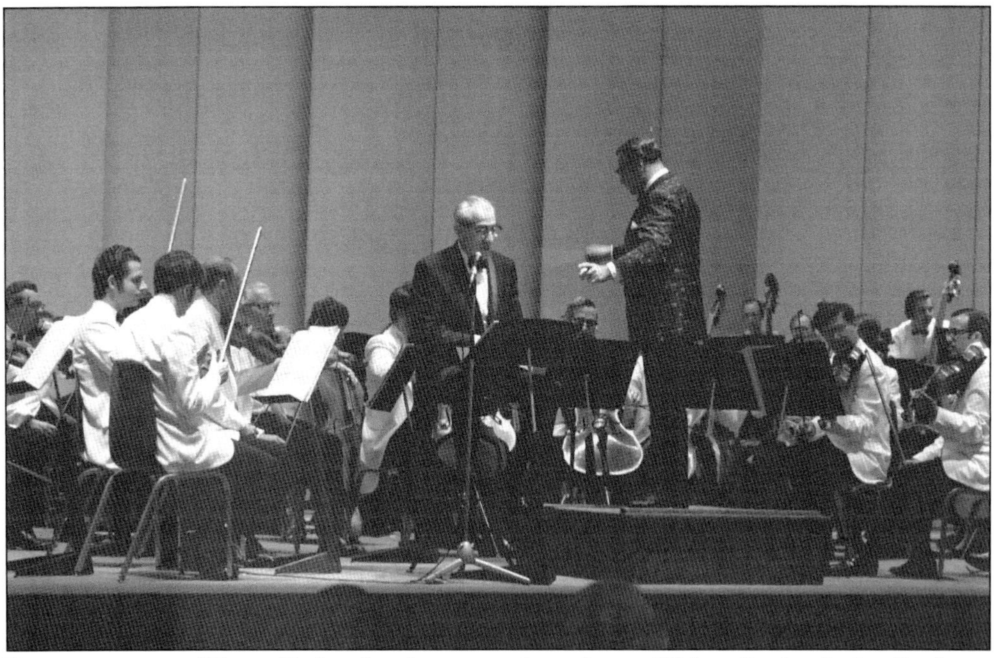

PETER AND THE WOLF. Under the direction of conductor Walter Susskind, the St. Louis Symphony Orchestra presented a program that included works by Tchaikovsky, Khachaturian, and Prokofiev on Sunday, June 22, 1969. Pres. Delyte Morris narrated Prokofiev's symphonic fairy tale *Peter and the Wolf.*

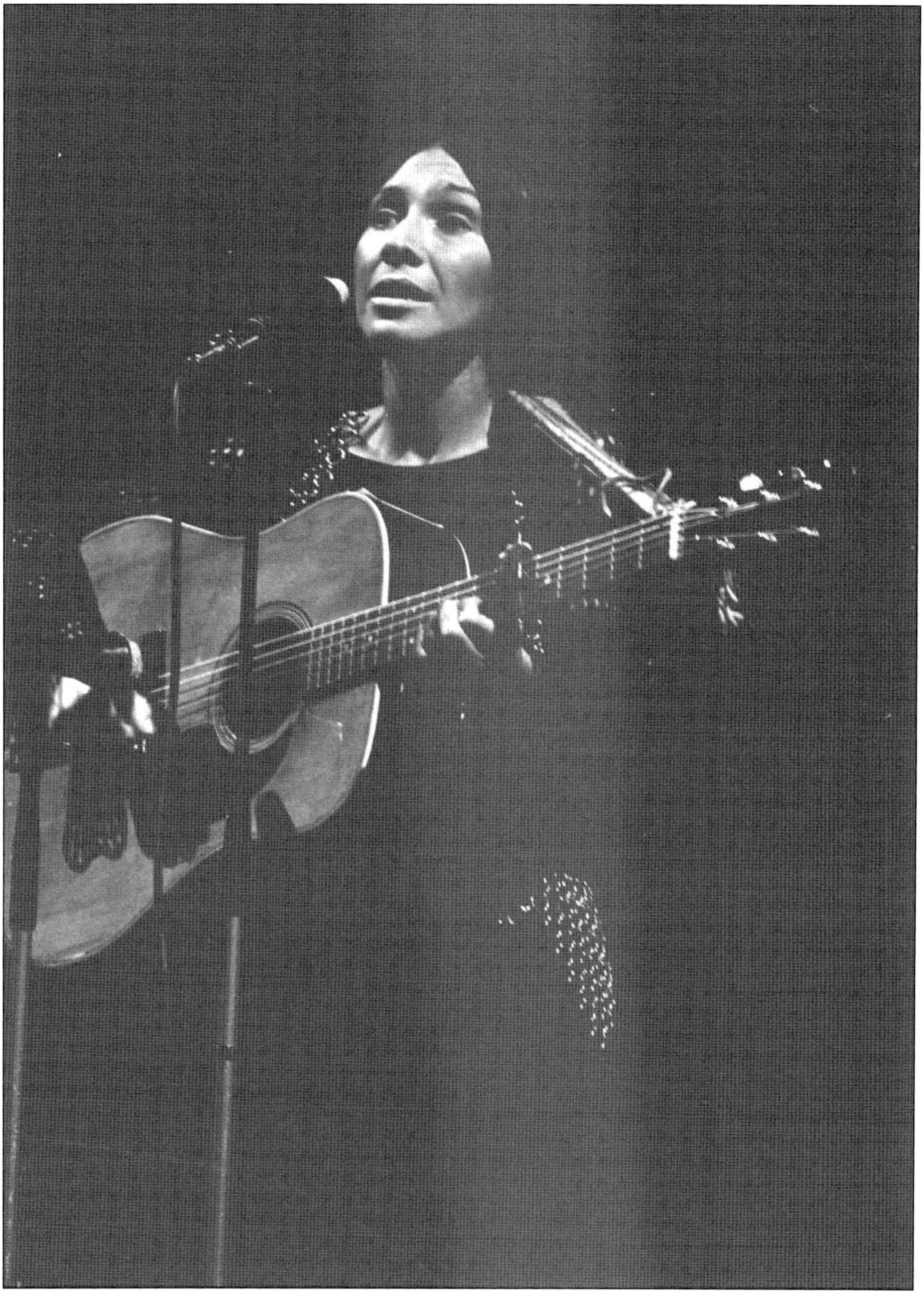

BUFFY SAINTE-MARIE. A Native American born in Canada but raised in New England, Buffy Sainte-Marie became the first popular music performer at the festival on Monday, June 23, 1969. She sang both protest songs like "The Universal Soldier" and gentler material such as "Until It's Time for You to Go" while playing the guitar and the mouth bow. The lawn audience outside the tent included one group that sat on the edge of a large, inflated rubber life raft.

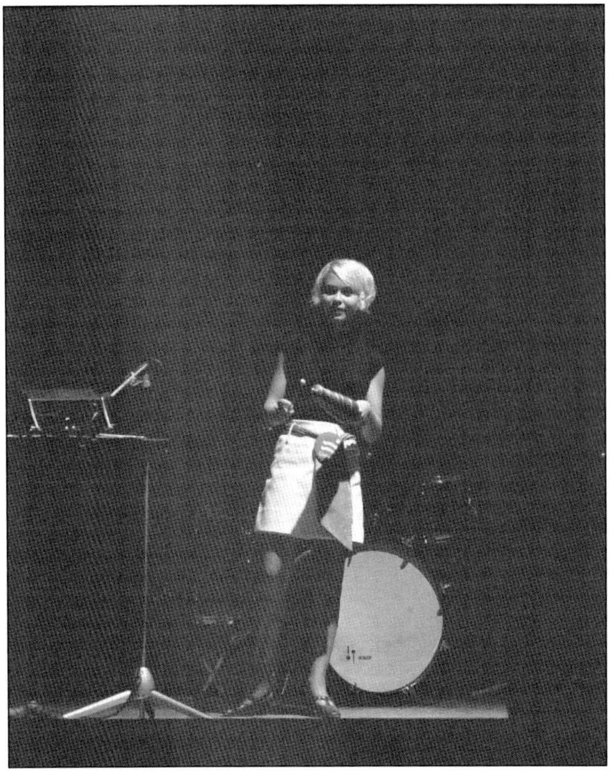

Dodie Ladd. A freshman who was working as an usher at the festival, Dodie Ladd achieved momentary fame as the official bell-tree ringer who summoned symphony audiences back to their seats after intermission. Student workers performed multiple tasks such as directing traffic, preparing and serving food, and seating ticket holders under the tent. During the 1969 season, the St. Louis Symphony Orchestra performed a total of 17 classical concerts at the MRF.

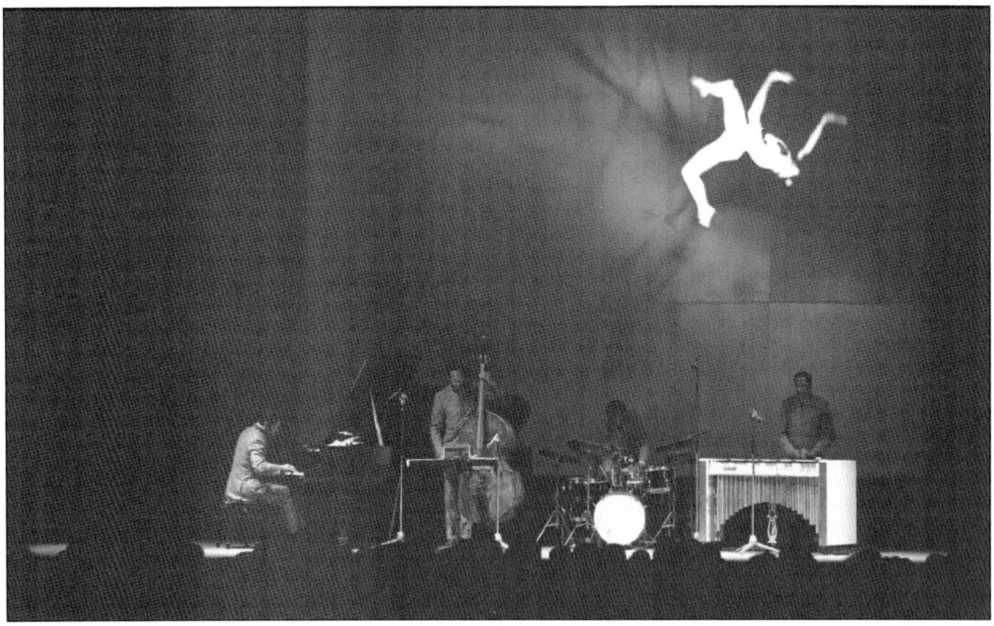

Modern Jazz Quartet. Milt Jackson (vibraphone), John Lewis (piano), Percy Heath (bass), and Connie Kay (drums) had been performing with distinction for years as the Modern Jazz Quartet. They followed Buffy Sainte-Marie on June 24, 1969, as the second popular music act at the festival. For their encore, the Modern Jazz Quartet played Lewis's "Golden Striker" from the score he had composed for the movie *No Sun in Venice*.

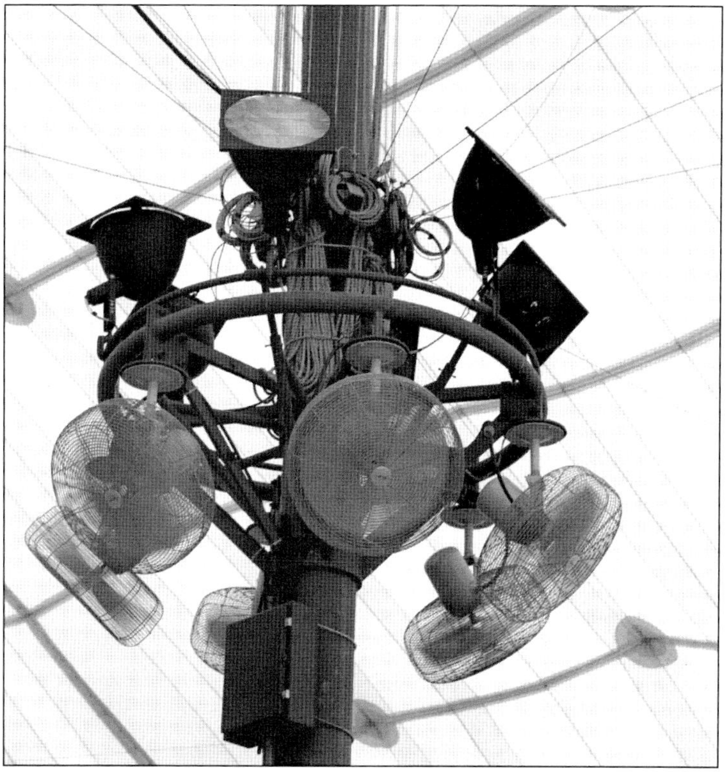

Masts in the Tent. The main masts that had been designed as part of the complex system that supported the Mississippi River Festival tent stood 65 feet high. In addition to providing support and a vertical pathway for workers, the masts contained large fans to circulate the air under the tent and powerful lights.

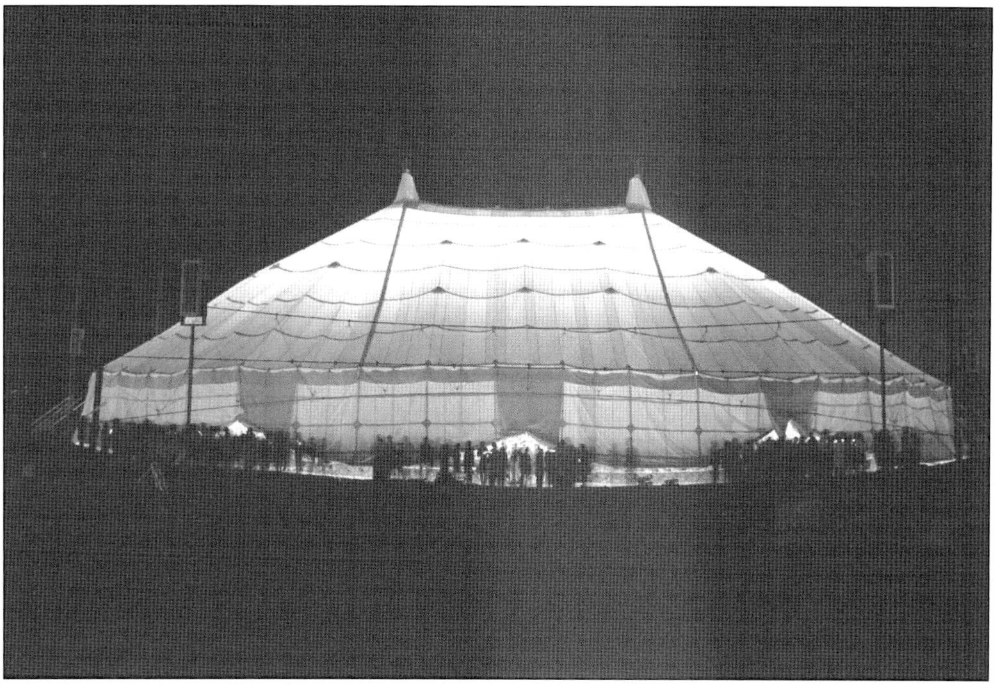

Tent After Dark. This photograph provides a view of the MRF tent after dark on the evening of July 3, 1969. Some of the speakers designed to help distribute the sound created during the performances are visible atop the tall, fork-shaped posts to the left and the right in this image.

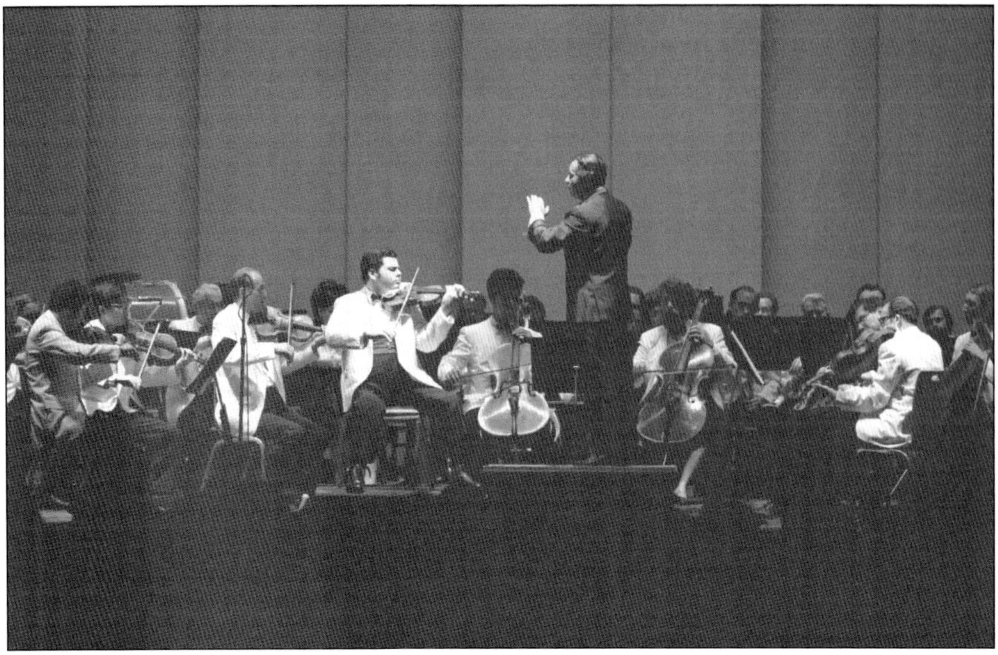

ITZHAK PERLMAN. A violent wind and rain storm forced cancellation of the first of two scheduled appearances by violinist Itzhak Perlman with the St. Louis Symphony Orchestra on July 3, 1969. The rain returned on July 5, but did not interfere with that evening's concert. Walter Susskind conducted the symphony and Perlman performed Beethoven's Concerto in D Major.

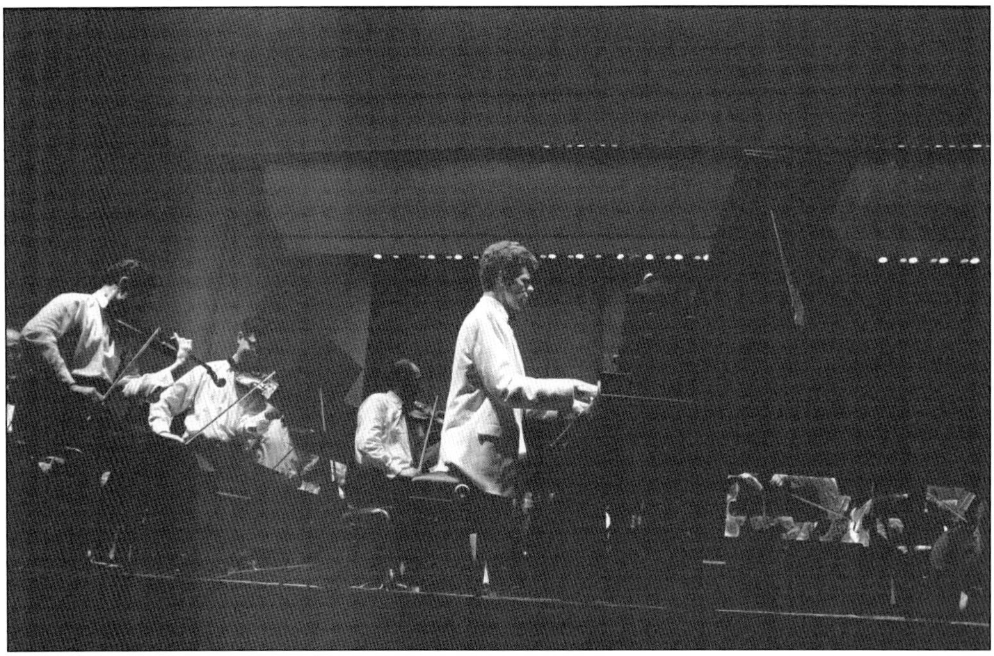

VAN CLIBURN. Pianist Van Cliburn made his first appearance at the MRF on July 11, 1969. The Texan played Rachmaninoff's Piano Concerto no. 3 as Walter Susskind conducted the St. Louis Symphony under the tent for the ninth time. The appreciative audience recalled Cliburn back to the stage four times.

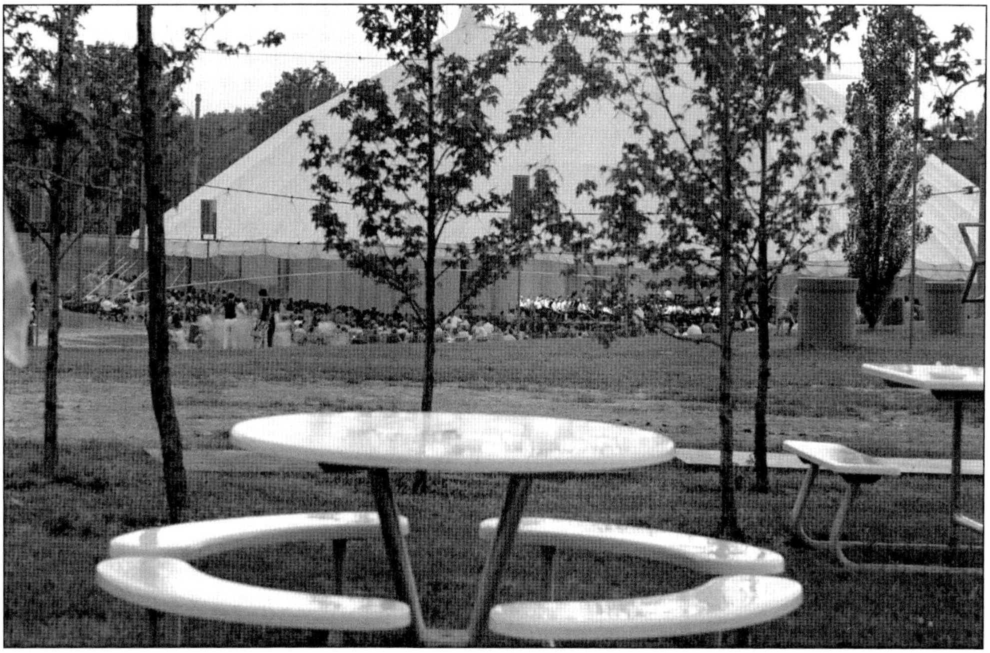

Dining Area. This photograph provides a view of the tent from the dining area. Pianist Alicia de Larrocha performed with the St. Louis Symphony Orchestra under the direction of Walter Susskind on July 18 and 19, 1969. She played Beethoven's Piano Concerto no. 2 the first night and Piano Concerto no. 4 on the second.

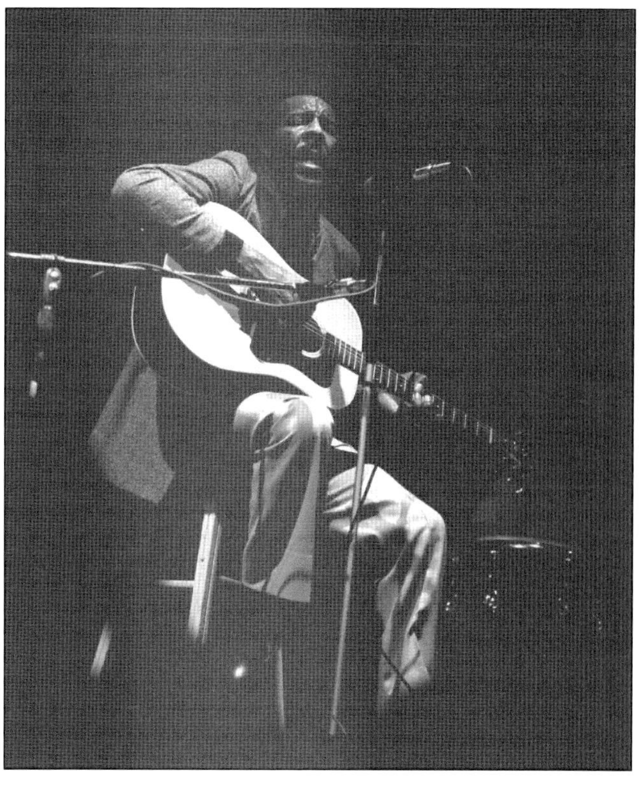

Richie Havens. The Eddie Fisher Trio of East St. Louis opened the program on July 22, 1969. The trio consisted of Eddie Fisher on guitar, William Dew on bass, and Jerome Harris on drums. The career of folksinger/guitarist Richie Havens benefited greatly from publicity regarding his subsequent appearance later in 1969 at the Woodstock festival in New York. Havens chatted to the audience a good deal during his Edwardsville visit.

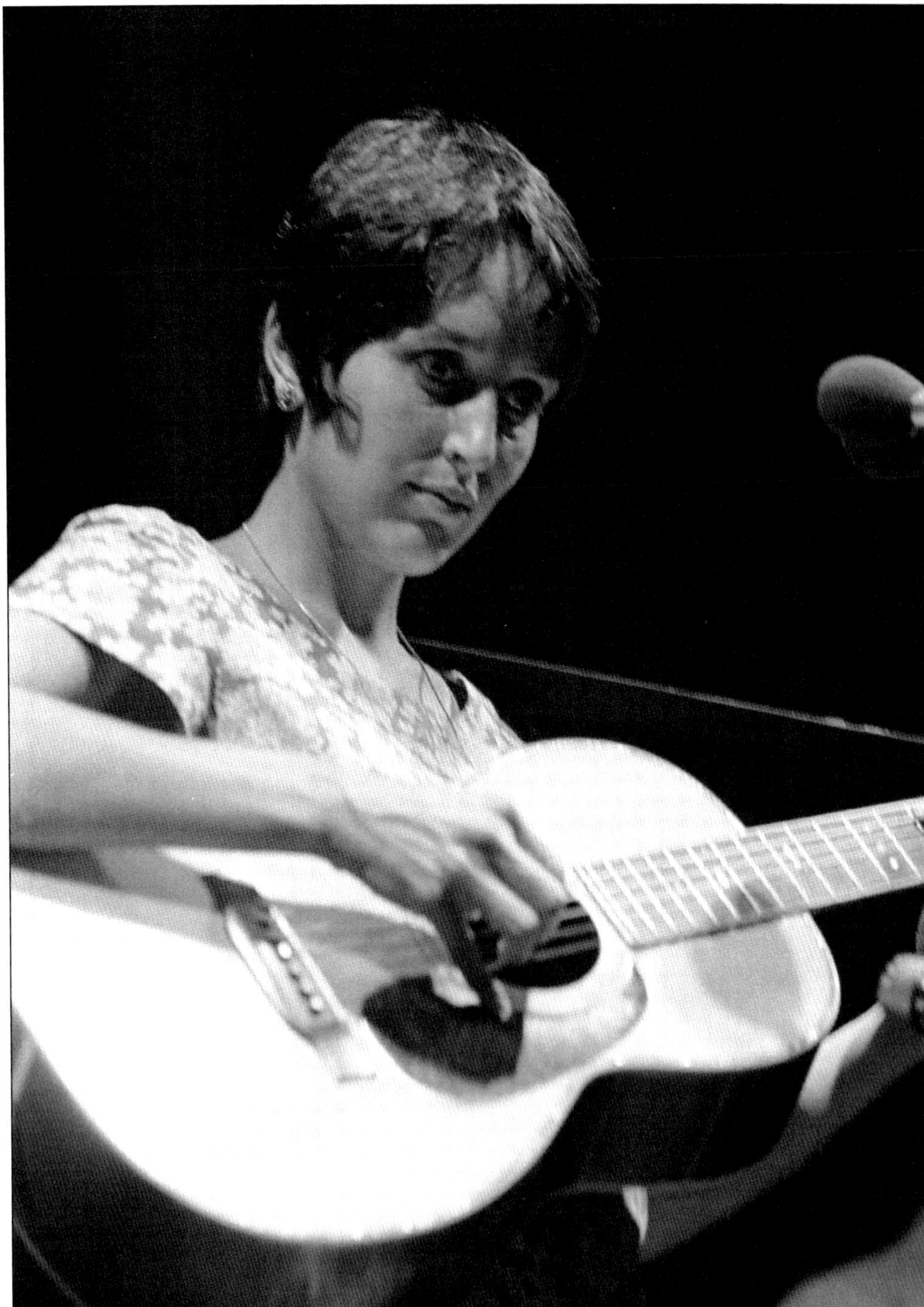

JOAN BAEZ. When she made her first MRF appearance on July 23, 1969, Walter Susskind praised Joan Baez as a vocalist "who has taste, talent, and can sing quietly." Baez personified the social and ethical concerns at the heart of folk music. At her request, festival officials reduced ticket prices for her concert to $2 for tent seats and $1 for lawn seating. Baez subsequently returned to the festival for a second performance on July 30, 1975.

MRF ENTRANCE. Passing underneath one of the distinctive sails at the entrance, visitors had a clear view of the tent situated in front of them at the bottom of the lawn. This photograph dates from the beginning of the second festival season in 1970.

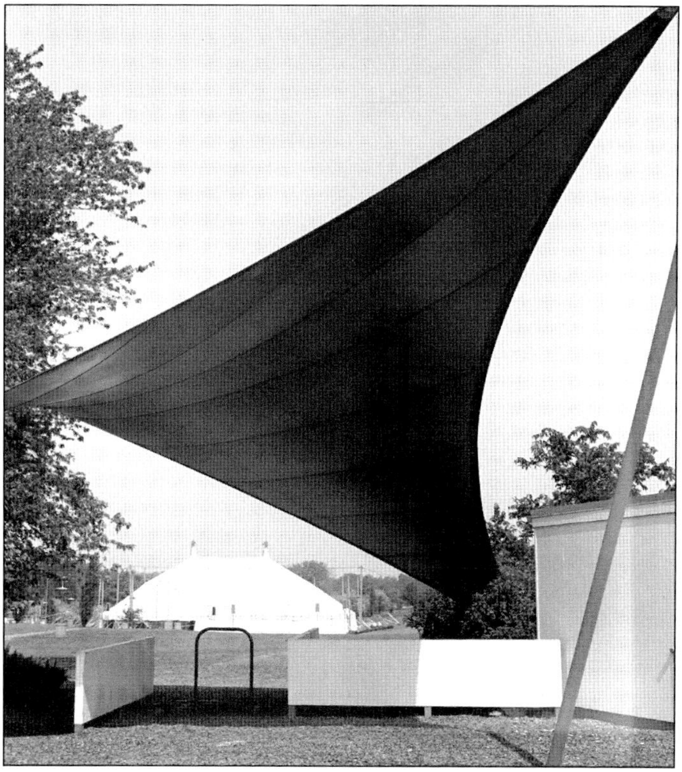

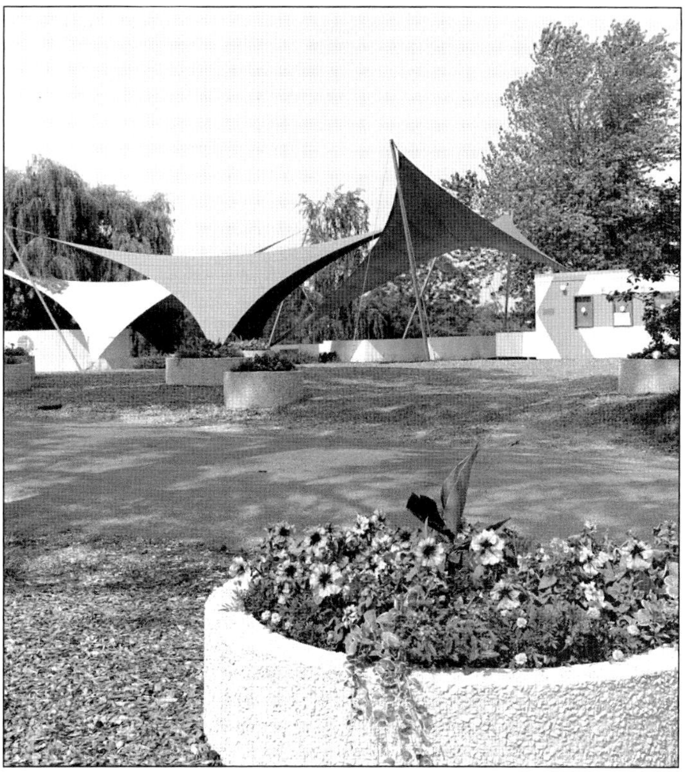

ENCHANTMENT. The planning for the temporary festival venue emphasized the natural beauty of the amphitheater and the entire campus. The sails reflect this harmony with the environment and the mood of summer. The hard-working physical plant crew did their best to enhance the area with flowers and other plantings as well as by cleaning the facility thoroughly following every concert.

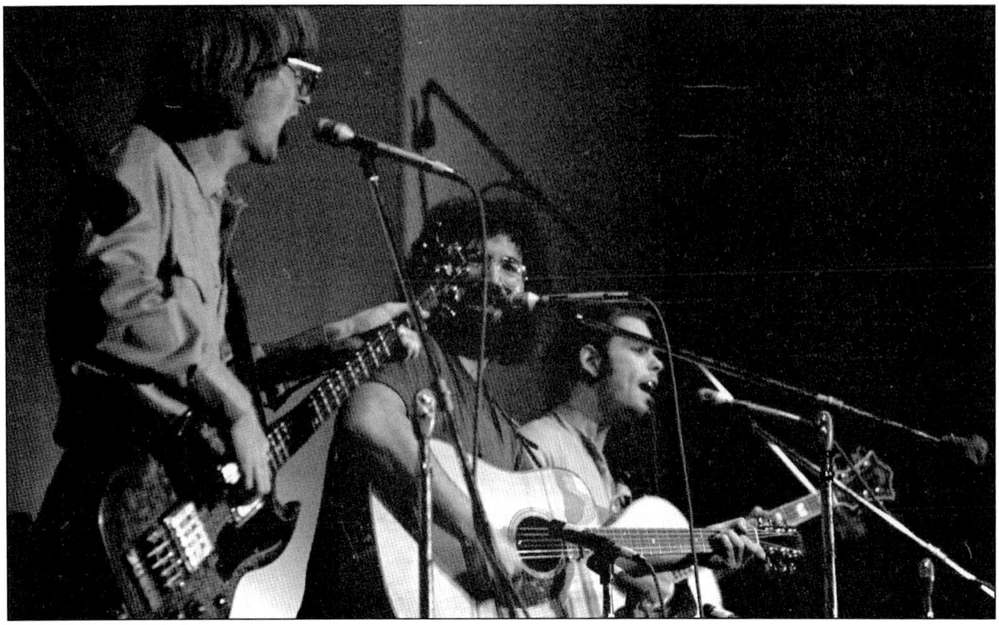

GRATEFUL DEAD. In one of the longest festival performances of any season, the Grateful Dead (featuring Jerry Garcia, Bob Weir, and Ron McKernan) performed for three hours before an extremely appreciative audience. Their first visit took place on July 8, 1970. Their song list included "Black Peter," "High Time," "Silver Threads and Golden Needles," and "Casey Jones." The band returned to the MRF a second time a full decade later on August 16, 1980.

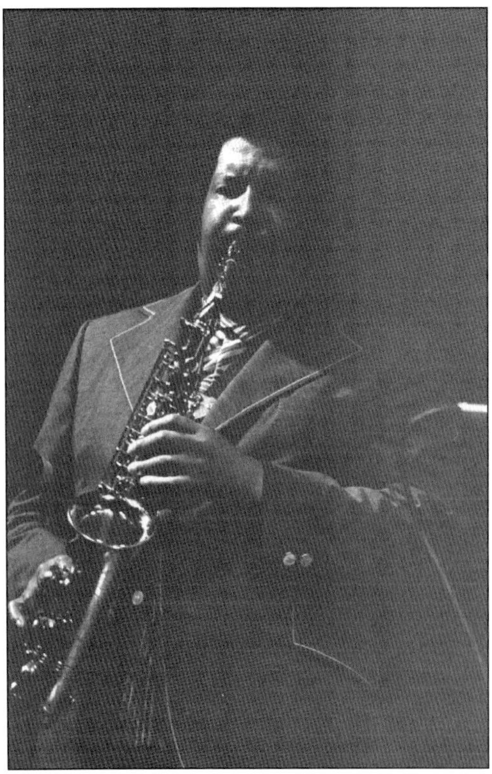

JULIAN "CANNONBALL" ADDERLEY. Julian "Cannonball" Adderley brought his saxophone to the festival for the only time on July 10, 1970. Joe Zawinul (piano), Roy McCurdy (drums), Walter Booker (bass), and his brother Nat Adderley (trumpet) provided accompaniment. Cannonball offered personal introductions and a solo to each of the artists in turn and provided a running commentary throughout the program.

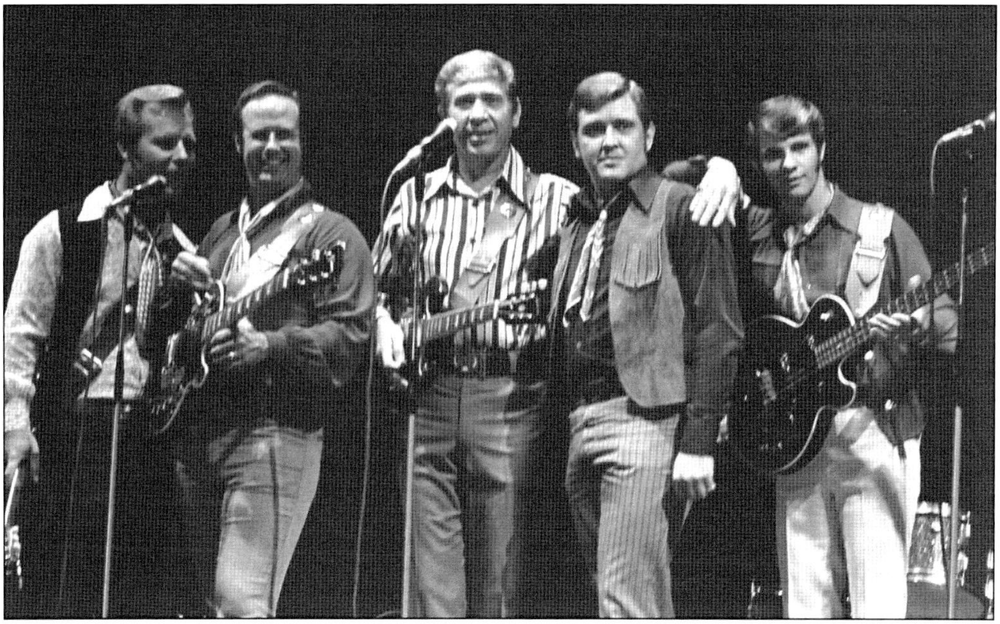

Buck Owens. Together with The Buckaroos (three guitarists and a drummer), Buck Owens demonstrated his brand of country music and humor at the festival on July 17, 1970. Jim and Jon Hager, Susan Raye, and Freddie Hart appeared on the bill as well. At the time, Owens had already begun an extended term as cohost of the long-lived television comedy show based on silly stereotypes of rural life, *Hee Haw.*

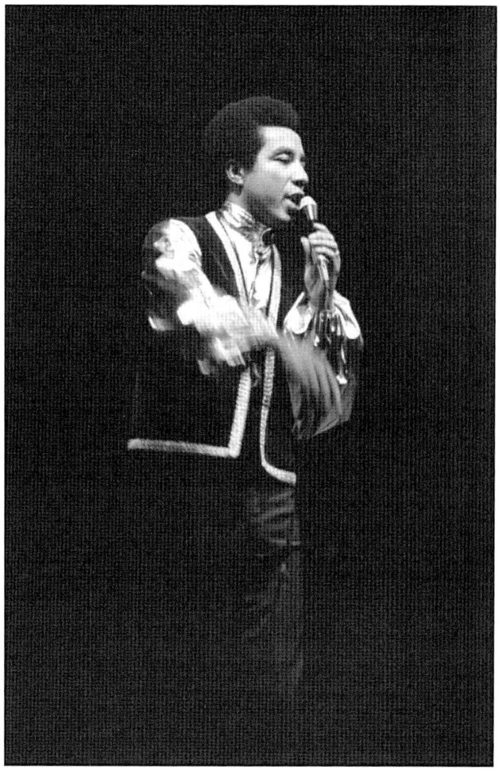

William "Smokey" Robinson. The Young Disciples and The Spinners opened the evening for William "Smokey" Robinson and the Miracles on July 20, 1970. Due to illness, Pete Moore did not appear with the headliners on this occasion, but Ronnie White and Bobby Rogers did perform. At one point during the show, a young woman jumped onto the stage and embraced Robinson, who continued performing until a policeman disentangled him from his admirer.

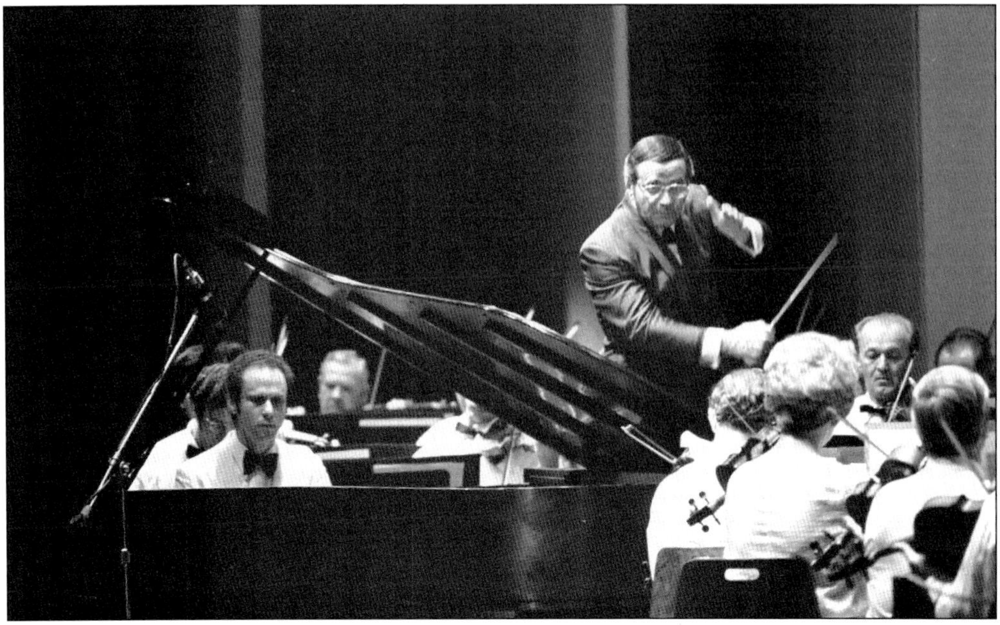

MALCOLM FRAGER. Pianist Malcolm Frager appeared as a soloist with conductor Walter Susskind and the St. Louis Symphony Orchestra on July 23, 1970. Frager performed Prokofiev's Piano Concerto no. 3. A native of St. Louis, Frager had first appeared with the St. Louis Symphony at the age of 10. Frager repeated his performance of the Prokofiev work two days later, on July 25. He later returned to the festival once more on August 12, 1972.

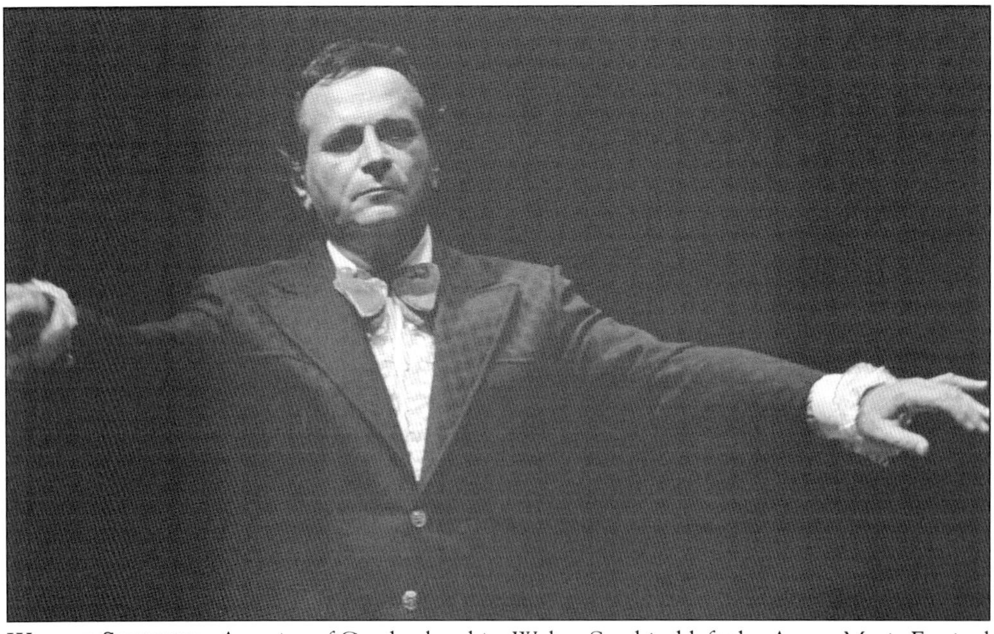

WALTER SUSSKIND. A native of Czechoslovakia, Walter Susskind left the Aspen Music Festival in 1968 to become conductor of the St. Louis Symphony Orchestra. In all, Susskind conducted the St. Louis Symphony 45 times at the festival. On the evening of August 4, 1973, Susskind led the symphony in a concert that included a solo performance of Beethoven's Piano Concerto no. 3 by guest pianist Gary Graffman.

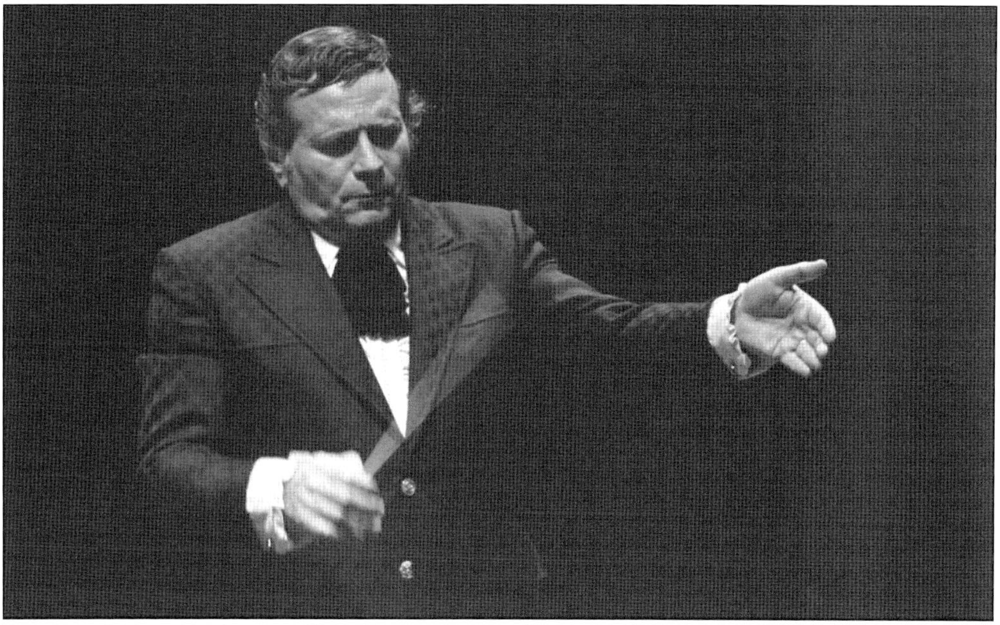

EUGENE ISTOMIN. Pianist Eugene Istomin performed Chopin's Piano Concerto no. 2 as guest soloist with the St. Louis Symphony Orchestra on August 3, 1974. Conductor Walter Susskind led the orchestra through a program that included works by Beethoven and Richard Wagner. Susskind conducted the St. Louis Symphony at the festival more times than any other artist.

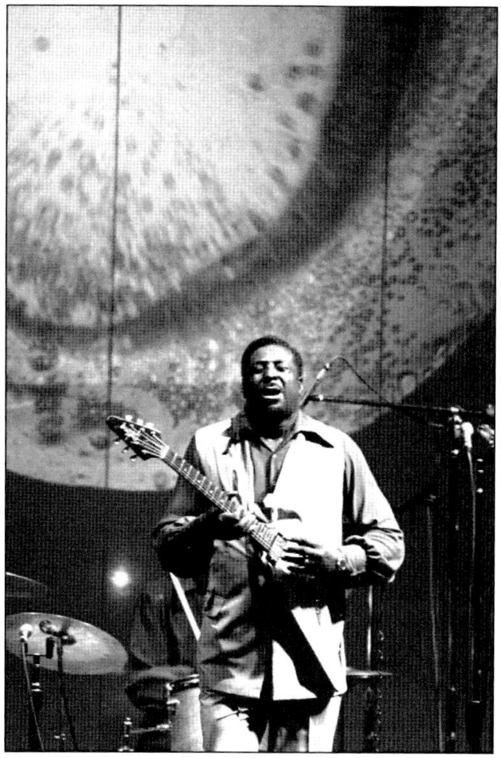

ALBERT KING. Blues guitarist Albert King opened for Delaney and Bonnie (Delaney Bramlett and Bonnie O'Farrell Bramlett) on July 29, 1970. King possessed a unique style and became a major influence on other guitar players. Unlike most, King played the guitar left-handed. For this concert, the Electric Rainbow put on a special light show that projected a tie-dye pattern on the tent and colored liquid shapes on a screen behind the performers.

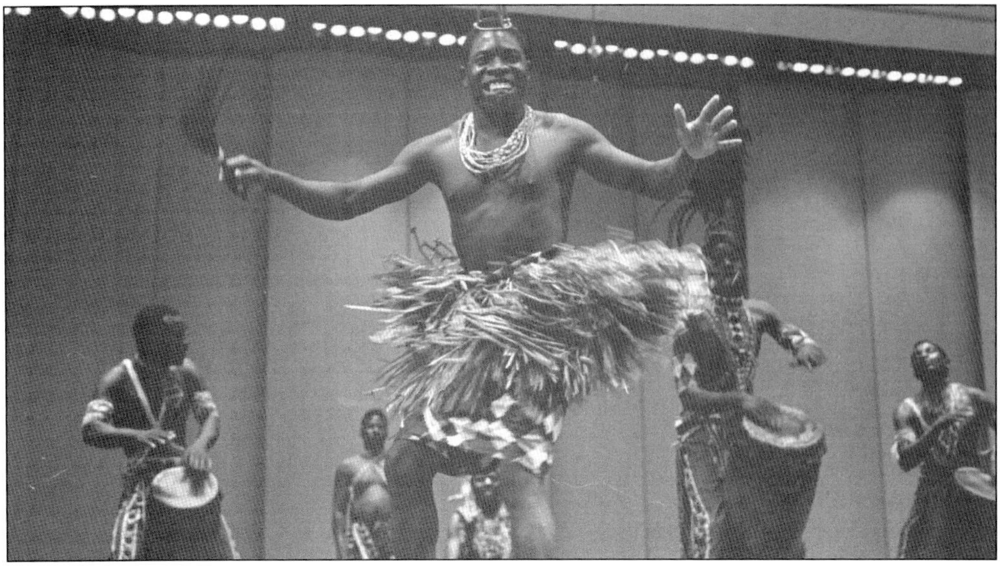

ZAMBIAN DANCERS. The National Dance Troupe of Zambia introduced the art of dance to the festival in its second season through their performance on July 31, 1970. The company consisted of 70 members between the ages of 15 and 57. The first part of the performance consisted of traditional Zambian dances portrayed in a village setting. The second part featured adaptations of contemporary music. Director Edwin K. Manda provided an English-language introduction for the benefit of the audience while the performers spoke only indigenous dialects as they sang and danced.

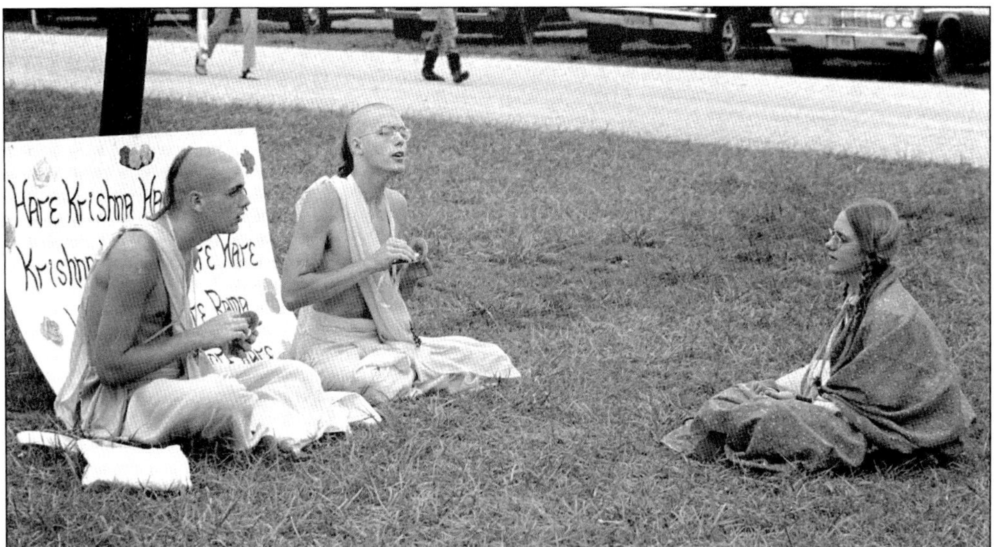

HARE KRISHNAS. One sign of the rise of a diverse counter-culture in an America deeply divided by racial animosity and by the war in Vietnam, Hare Krishnas appeared on many American campuses during the 1960s and 1970s. The persons in this photograph visited the MRF site when the Band (featuring Garth Hudson, Rick Danko, Levon Helm, Richard Manuel, and Robbie Robertson) made a second festival appearance on August 11, 1970. Their initial performance the previous year, on July 14, produced the greatest surprise in MRF history when close associate Bob Dylan unexpectedly joined the group for a four-number encore.

Two

Excitement
1971–1977

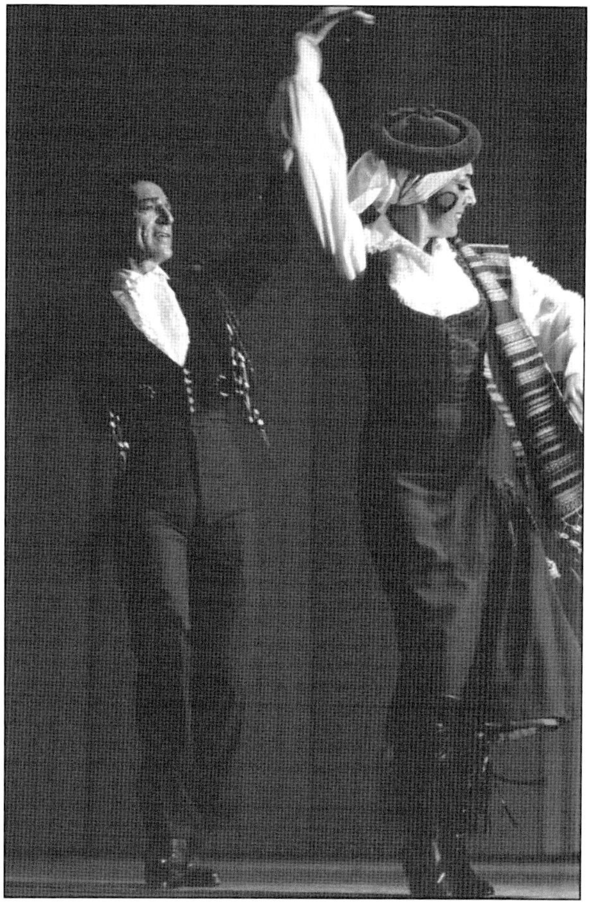

Jose Greco. On an evening marked by extreme humidity, master of Flamenco dance Jose Greco and his company, featuring Nana Lorca and Roberto Amaral, appeared at the festival on July 13, 1971. Greco's ensemble of 14 dancers, singers, and instrumentalists performed for two hours. One dance followed another without the benefit of introductions or commentaries of any kind.

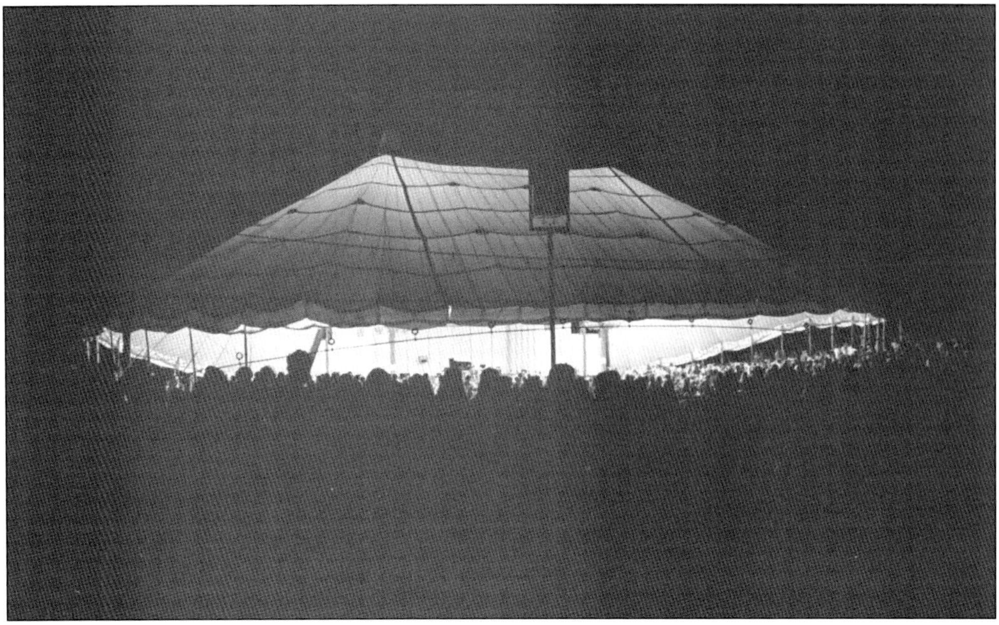

LAWN VIEW. This photograph of the illuminated tent shows the silhouettes of members of the lawn audience who enjoyed a direct view down into the tent toward the stage. On pleasant evenings, a place on the lawn provided fresh air and freedom of movement to visit the food and drink concessions and the restrooms. The parents of young children especially enjoyed the advantages of sitting on the lawn.

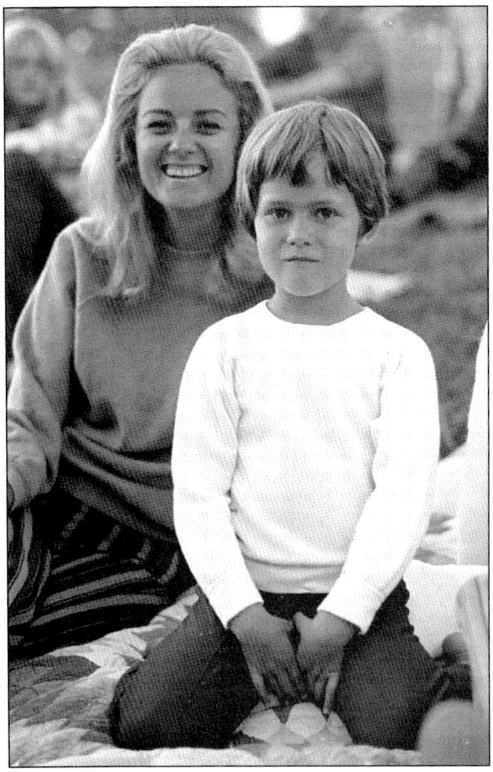

WILMA JENE BOND AND JULIE. Together with her daughter Julie, Wilma Jene Bond enjoyed performances by both Long John Baldry and Buddy Miles on July 20, 1971. Chosen by then-chancellor (and later president) John Rendleman to serve as his executive assistant, Bond subsequently enjoyed a long and distinguished career at SIUE, also working with presidents Andrew Kochman, Ralph Ruffner, Kenneth "Buzz" Shaw, Earl Lazerson, and Nancy Belck. Bond played a substantial role in helping to initiate and sustain the festival.

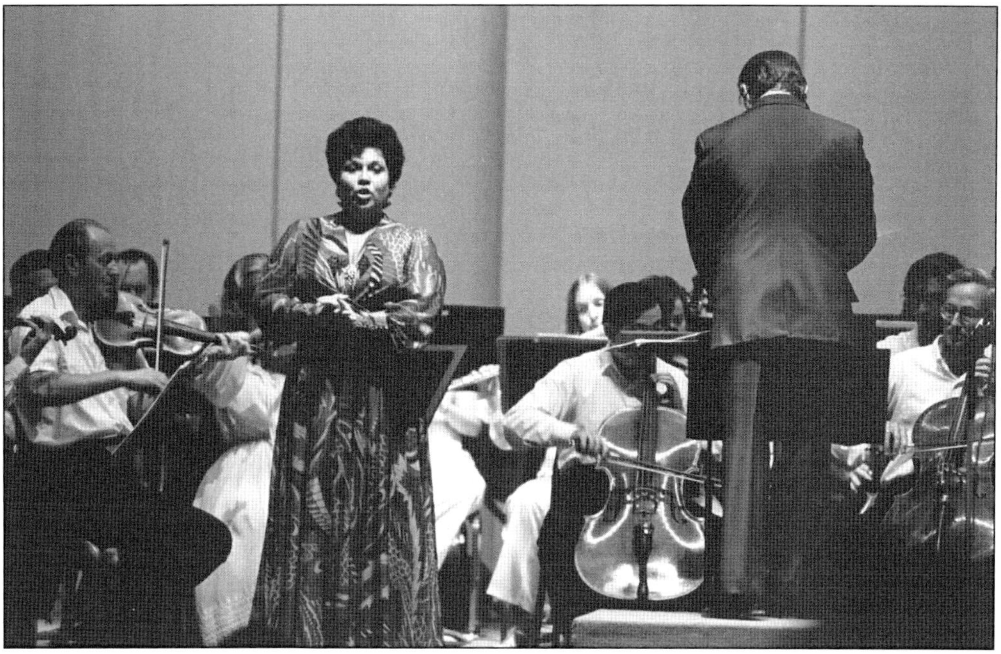

MARILYN HORNE. Opera fans from throughout the region flocked to the festival on July 24, 1971. They gathered to hear soprano Marilyn Horne sing a series of arias during a concert by the St. Louis Symphony Orchestra under the direction of Walter Susskind. The concert concluded with a presentation of the *William Tell Overture* by Rossini.

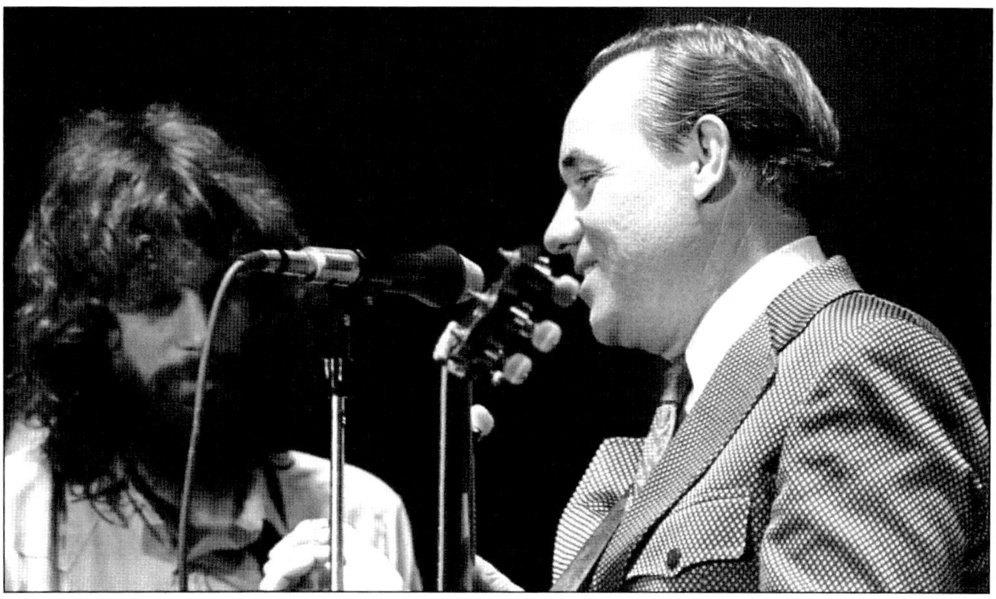

EARL SCRUGGS AND JOHN HARTFORD. The Earl Scruggs Revue (Earl, Randy, Steve, and Gary Scruggs; Lea Jane Berinati; and Jody Maphis) opened the July 27, 1971, bluegrass concert, followed by John Hartford. Earl Scruggs played many of his favorite numbers, including "Foggy Mountain Chimes" and "Little Maggie." Norman Blake, Vassar Clements, Tut Taylor, and Randy Scruggs worked with Hartford, who closed his encores with his own famous composition "Gentle on My Mind." The finale featured Hartford and Scruggs performing together.

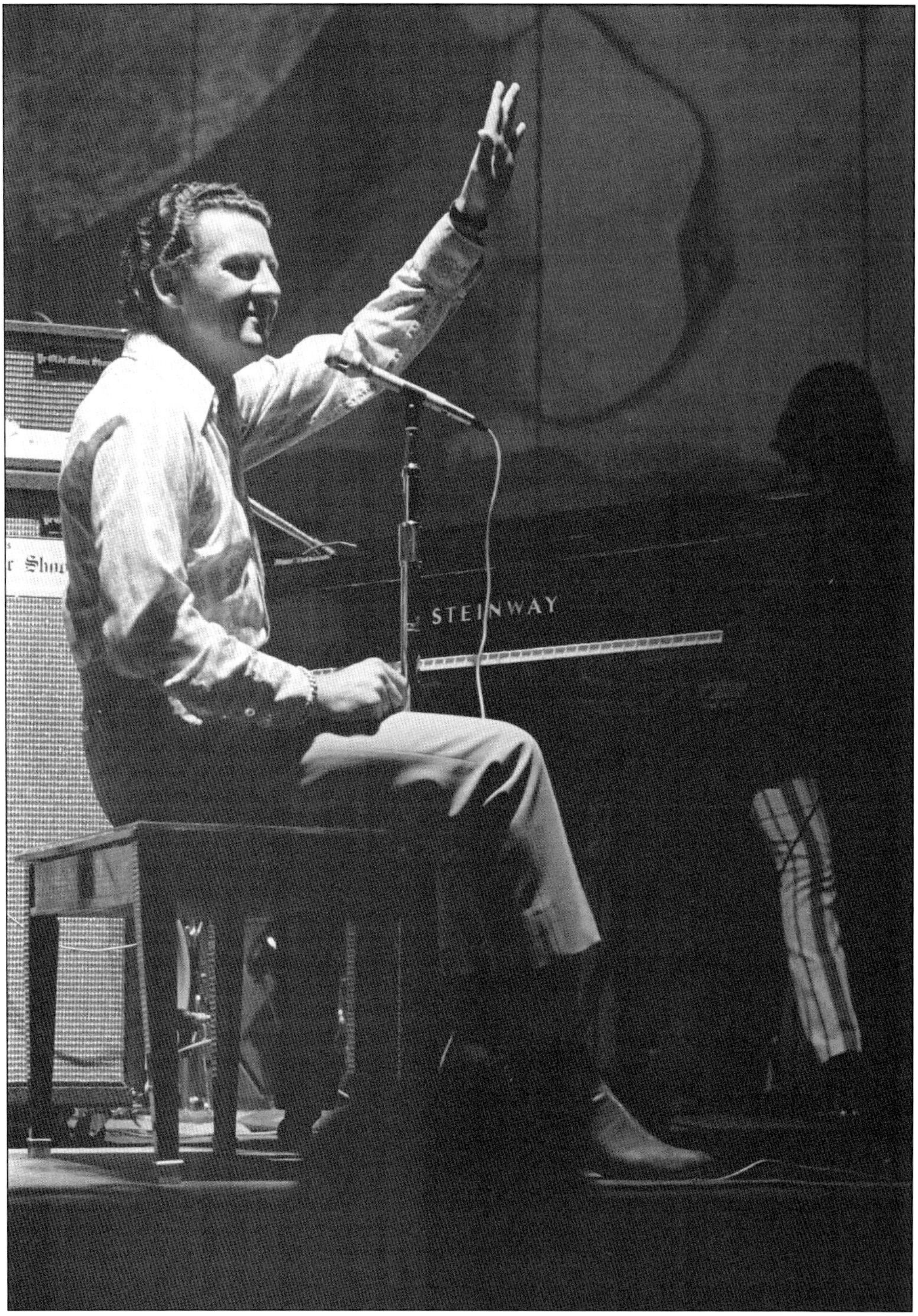

JERRY LEE LEWIS. Billy Peak and The Sound Company opened a "rock and roll revival" in the rain on the night of July 29, 1971. They also backed individual performances by four rock pioneers: Gary "U. S." Bonds, Jerry Lee Lewis, Bo Diddley, and Chuck Berry. Lewis included both "Great Balls of Fire" and "Whole Lotta Shakin' Goin' On" in his animated set.

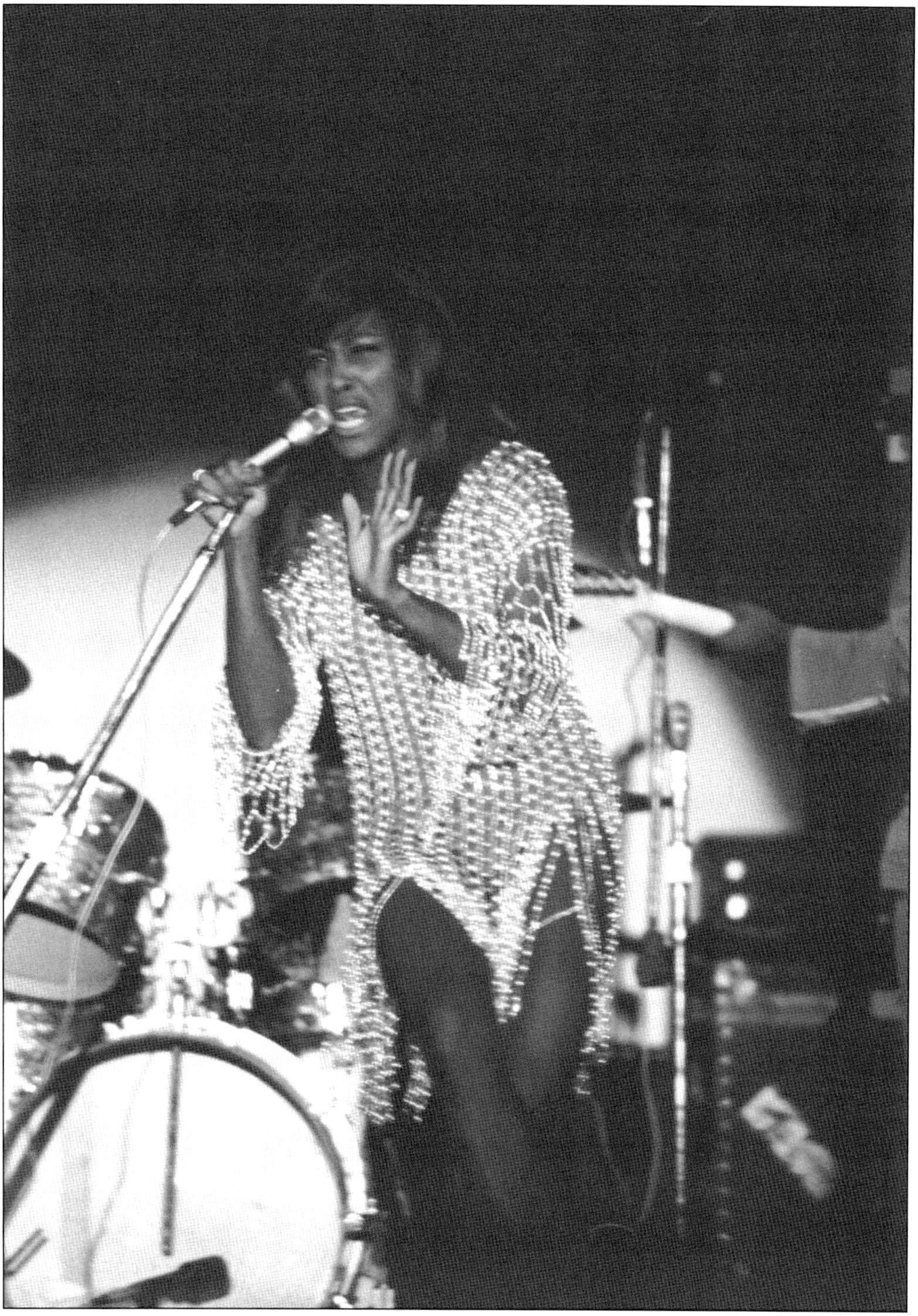

TINA TURNER. On an unusually cool summer evening, July 30, 1971, Ike and Tina Turner, the Kings of Rhythm, and the Ikettes brought their energetic show to the festival. Wilderness Road, a Chicago group, opened the festivities for Ike and Tina. They played for 90 minutes for an audience huddling in coats or under blankets because the featured act did not arrive on time.

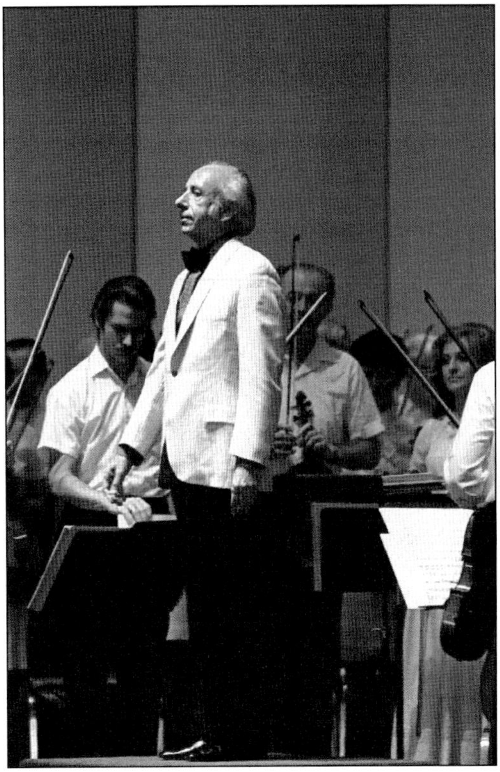

MORTON GOULD. On August 1, 1971, guest conductor Morton Gould led the St. Louis Symphony Orchestra in a performance featuring his compositions *American Salute*, *Latin American Symphonette*, and *Pavanne*. Gould returned to the festival on August 7, 1971, and conducted works by Bizet, Tchaikovsky, and Ravel, as well as another of his own creations, *Soundings*.

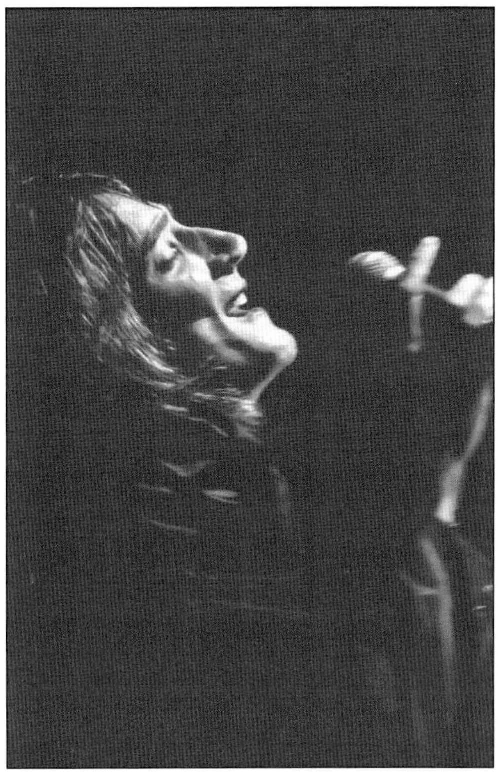

ROD STEWART. Matthews Southern Comfort (featuring Ian Matthews and Carl Barnwell) opened the festivities on August 4, 1971. Matthews and his colleagues expressed great admiration for the MRF facility to everyone on the staff. The membership of the lead act included Rod Stewart with Ian McLagan, Ronnie Lane, and Ron Wood as Faces. The concert drew a paid crowd of 9,539 persons.

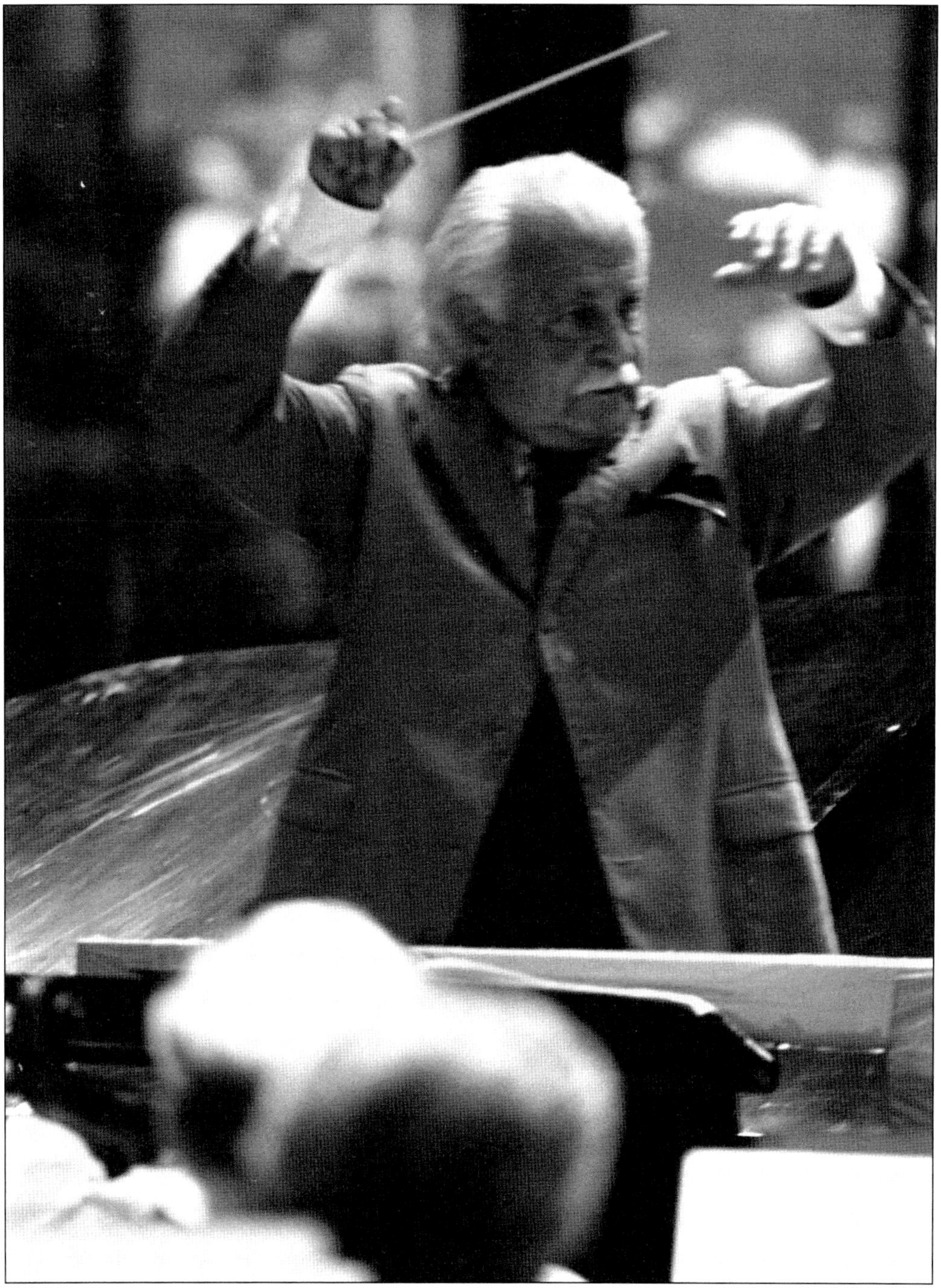

ARTHUR FIEDLER. The long-time conductor of the Boston Pops, Arthur Fiedler, served as guest conductor of the St. Louis Symphony Orchestra on August 8, 1971. Pianist Ruth Slenczynska, an SIUE faculty member, appeared for the second time as a festival soloist and played Liszt's Piano Concerto no. 1. The program included Sousa's "Stars and Stripes Forever" as well as three rousing encore numbers: "St. Louis Blues," "Look What They've Done to My Song," and "Look Sharp, Be Sharp." Fiedler later returned for a second festival visit on August 6, 1972.

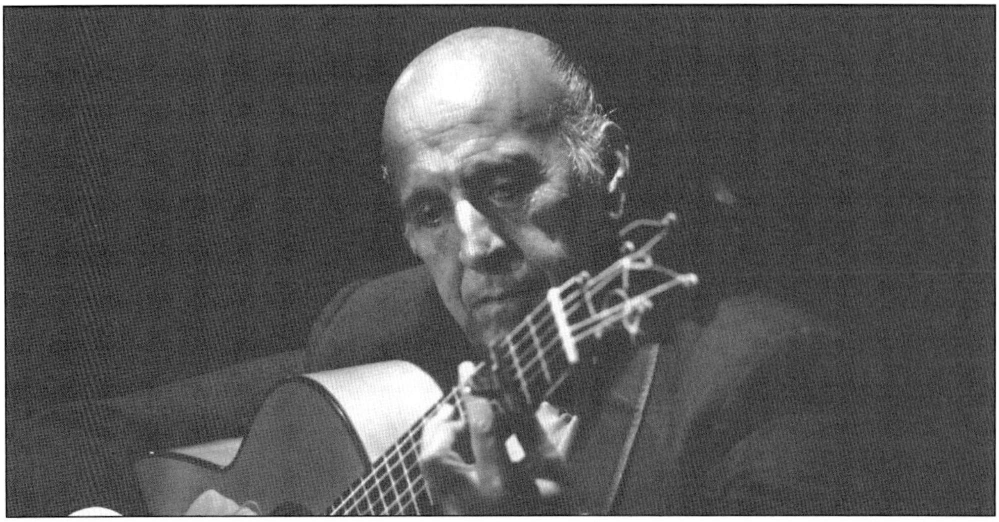

CARLOS MONTOYA. Carlos Montoya came to the festival on August 12, 1971. He played seated by himself on the darkened stage and illuminated by just a single spotlight. Working without accompaniment and before a quietly reverential audience, the master of the Flamenco guitar performed two sections consisting of six pieces, and a third section of five numbers, followed by two encores.

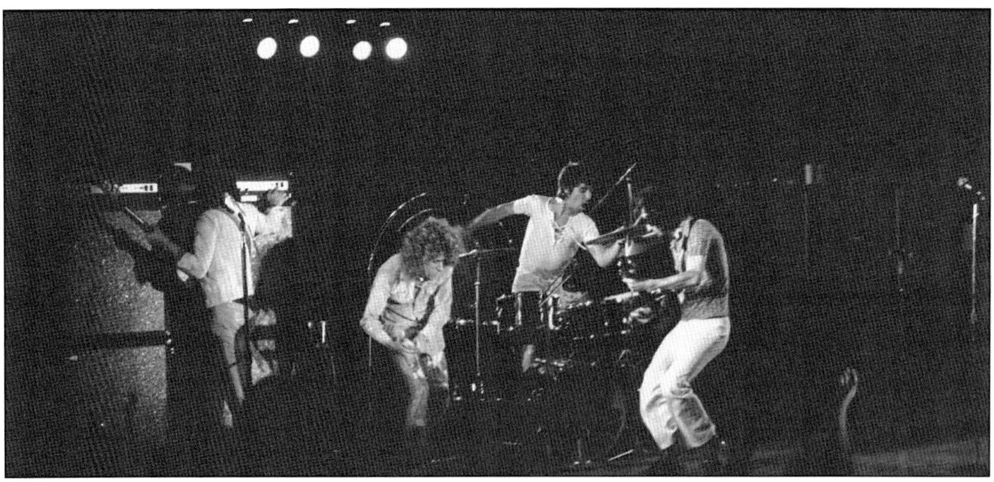

THE WHO. Peter Townshend (guitar), Roger Daltry (vocals), Keith Moon (drums), and John Entwistle (bass) performed before, by far, the largest crowd ever to attend the festival on August 16, 1971. The final concert of the third MRF season proved to be an artistic and financial success without equal in the life of the festival. The attendance far exceeded any other outdoor music event in the St. Louis area, including the Beatles. For their encore, The Who played "Magic Bus."

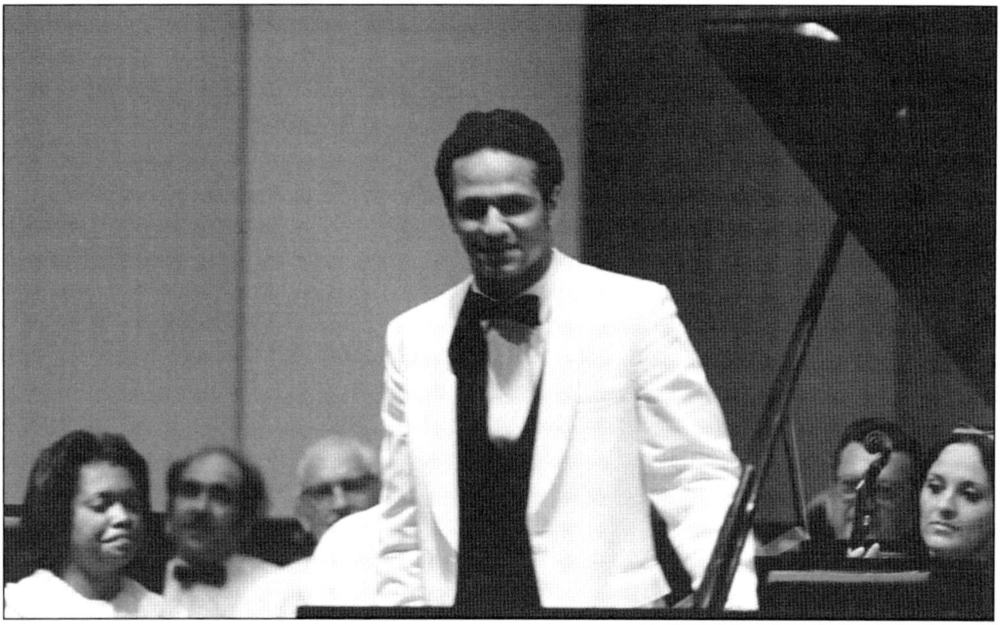

ANDRE WATTS. At the opening concert of the 1972 season, pianist Andre Watts appeared as a soloist with the St. Louis Symphony Orchestra under the baton of Walter Susskind. During the July 8, 1972, program, Watts performed Chopin's Piano Concerto no. 2. The rest of the program included works by Smetana, Tchaikovsky, and Stravinsky. Watts had appeared twice previously at the festival, on July 2 and 4, 1970.

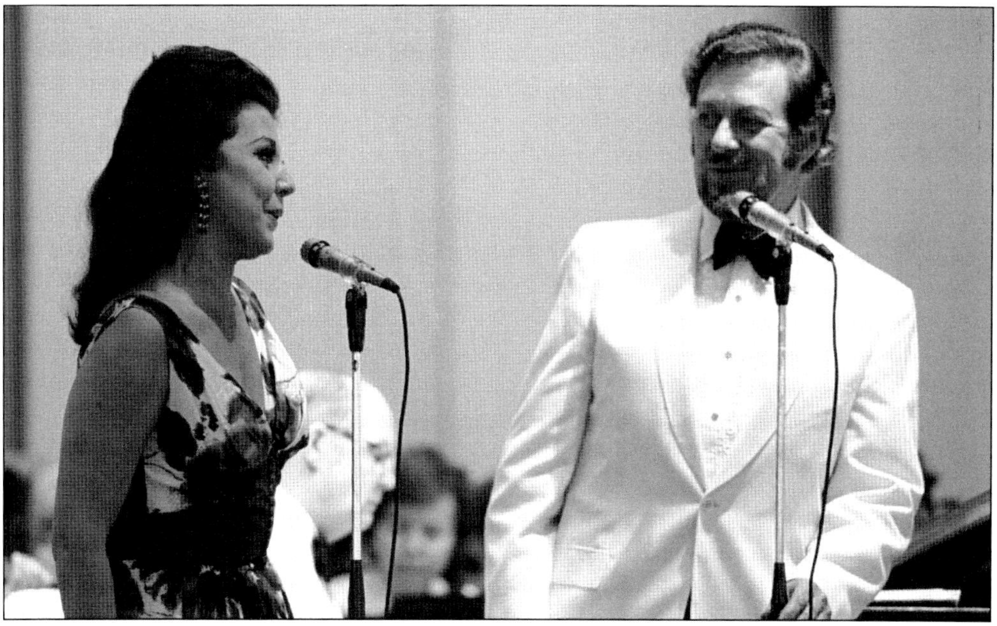

EARL WRIGHTSON AND LOIS HUNT. Baritone Earl Wrightson and soprano Lois Hunt appeared together for the second time at the festival on July 16, 1972. Margaret Harris, music director of *Hair*, conducted the St. Louis Symphony Orchestra in a program that contained selections from various Broadway musicals including *Camelot*, *Paint Your Wagon*, *Show Boat*, and *Kiss Me Kate*. Wrightson and Hunt concluded by singing "Wunderbar."

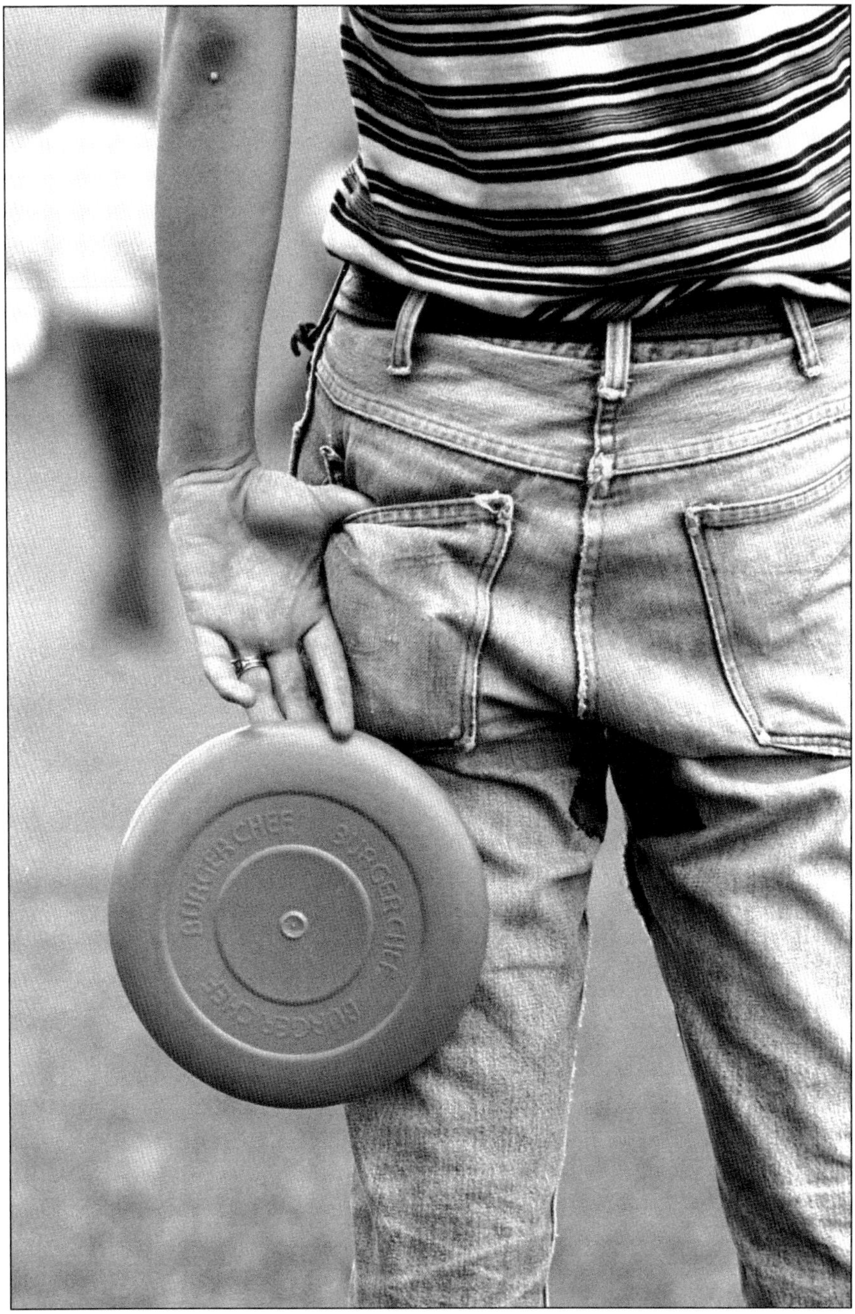

Me and My Frisbee. One popular way of whiling away the time until the concert started involved playing catch with a Frisbee. The pastime originated in New England, where students in the late 19th century learned to toss the empty pie tins that originally held the baked products of the Frisbie Baking Company of Bridgeport, Connecticut. In 1948, Walter Frederick Morrison of Los Angeles invented a plastic version and sold his invention to the Wham-O Company who created the Frisbee name. The concertgoer in this image found himself waiting for Chet Nichols to open up a Brewer and Shipley concert on July 18, 1972. Mark Naftalin, Billy Mundi, and Billy Baracini backed up headliners Mike Brewer and Tom Shipley.

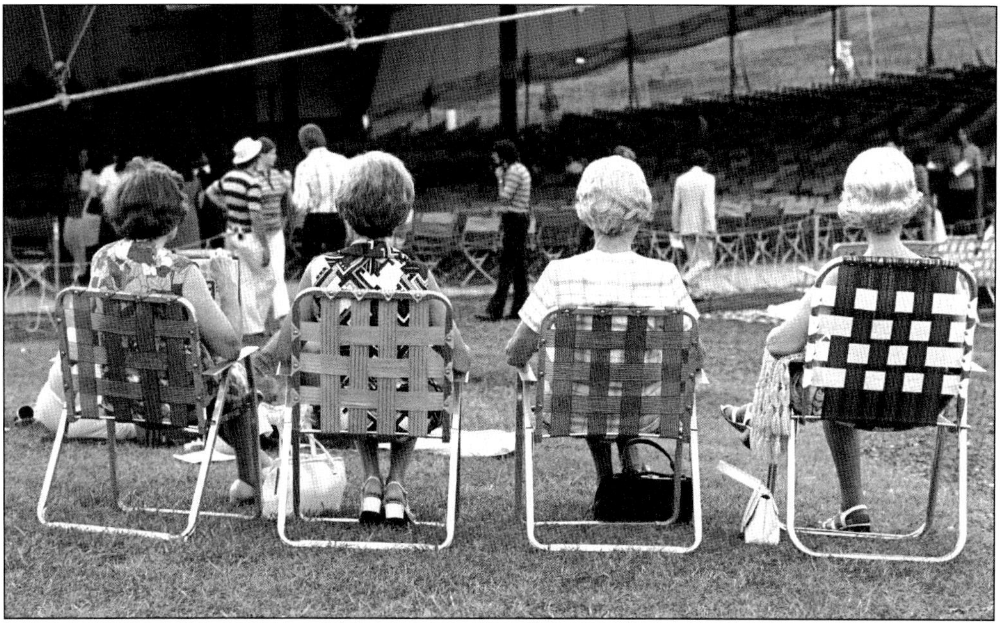

LAWN CHAIR LADIES. While students often preferred to bring blankets to the festival and spread them out on the lawn, symphony audiences frequently brought along their own lawn chairs. In this photograph, taken on July 22, 1972, several lawn chair ladies had taken up residence outside the tent in time to enjoy a St. Louis Symphony Orchestra program conducted by Walter Susskind. Violin soloist Teiko Maehashi performed the Sibelius Violin Concerto.

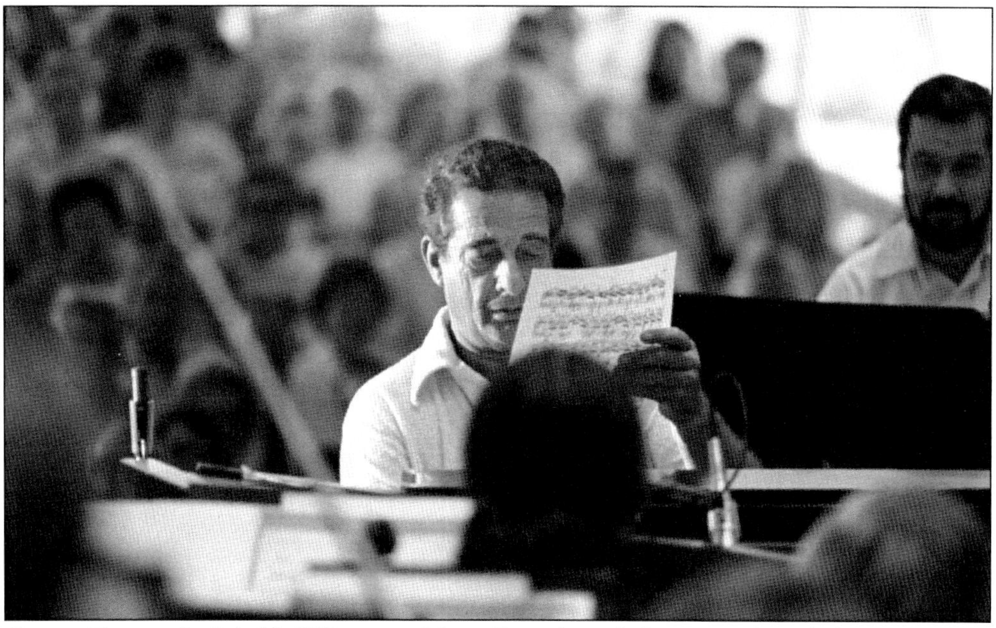

VICTOR BORGE. On July 23, 1972, pianist Victor Borge brought his unique brand of musical humor to the festival. Borge shared the conducting duties with Leonard Slatkin and also performed Gershwin's Concerto in F as a soloist with the St. Louis Symphony Orchestra. Soprano Marilyn Mulvey sang arias from three operas. Borge's appearance brought 3,885 paid customers to the festival, the tenth-largest audience to attend a symphony event.

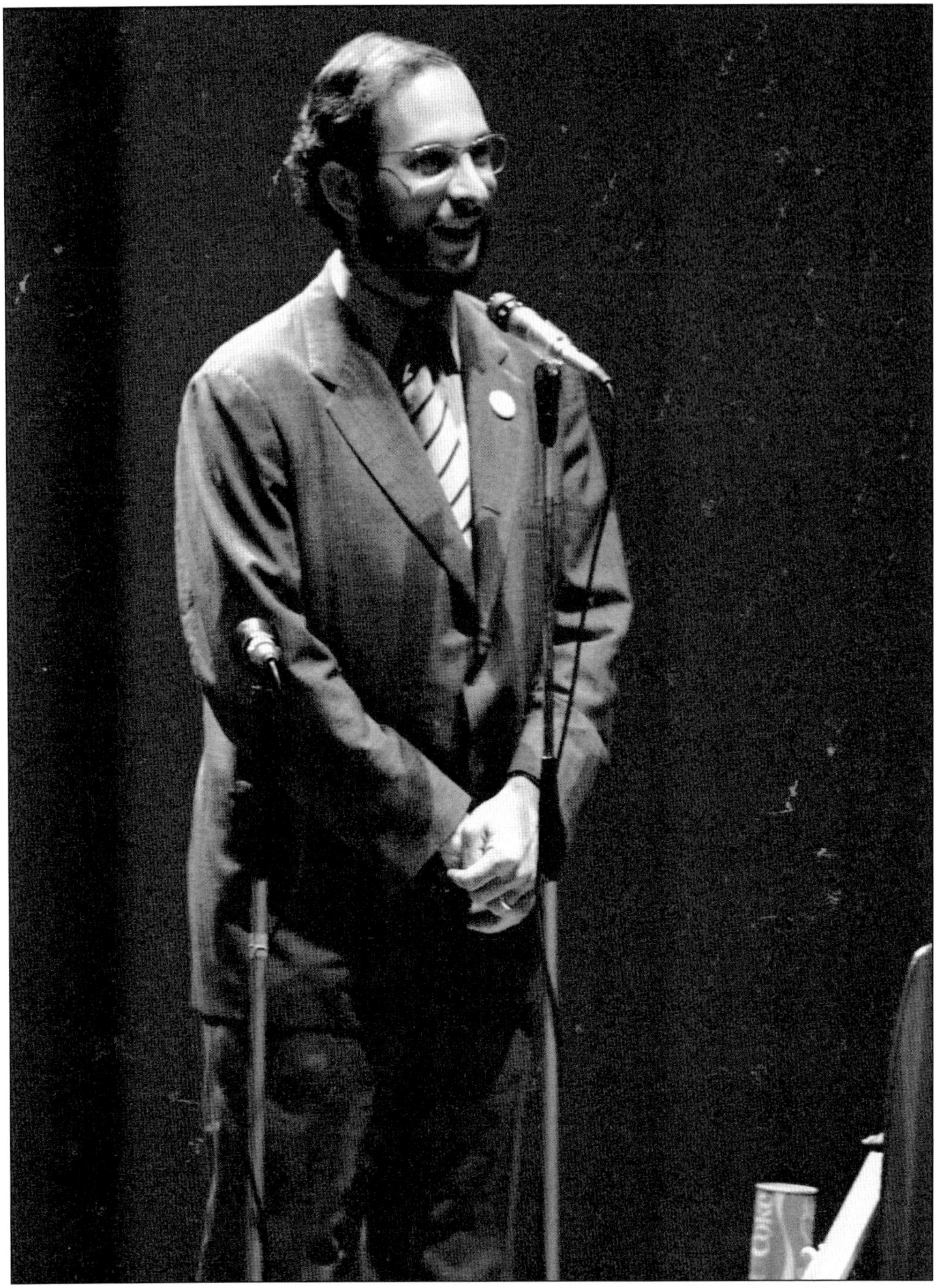

PETER PASTREICH. As the executive responsible for managing the business affairs of the St. Louis Symphony Orchestra, Peter Pastreich played an essential role in the negotiations that established the festival partnership, in the planning for the series, and in the selection of performers during the first six seasons (1969–1974). Later in his career, Pastreich achieved tremendous success as the chief administrator and fund-raiser for the San Francisco Symphony. He subsequently received an honorary doctorate from SIUE on May 6, 2006.

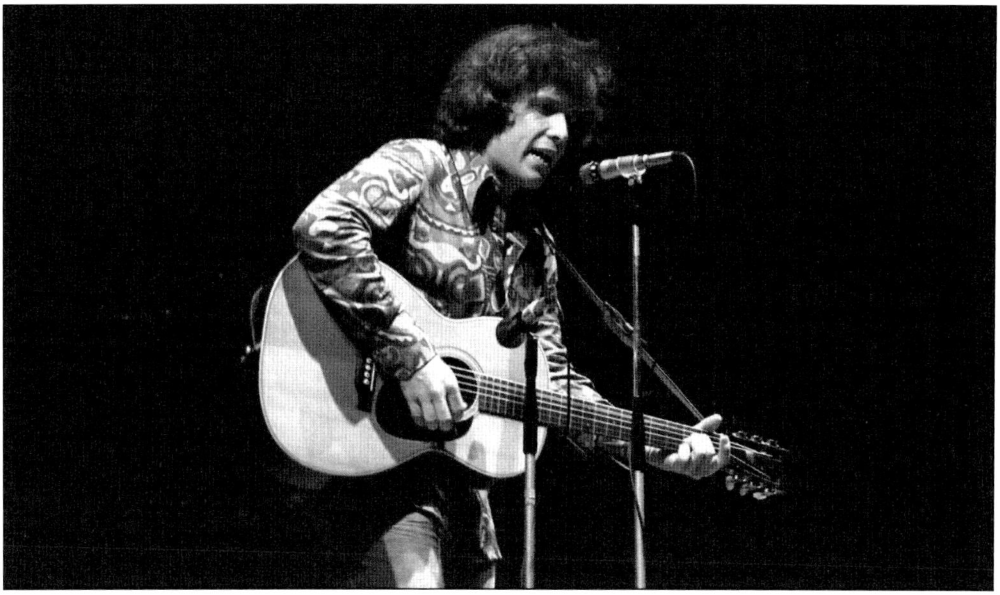

DON MCLEAN. Although Don McLean did not appear to enjoy performing his greatest commercial hit, "American Pie," on July 25, 1972, he did seem to take pleasure in singing another song entirely appropriate to an outdoor evening concert, the unforgettable "Vincent (Starry, Starry Night)." Eventually McLean gave three encores to three standing ovations. Carol Hall, a songwriter who had written for Barbra Streisand, Kris Kristofferson, and Neil Diamond, opened for McLean.

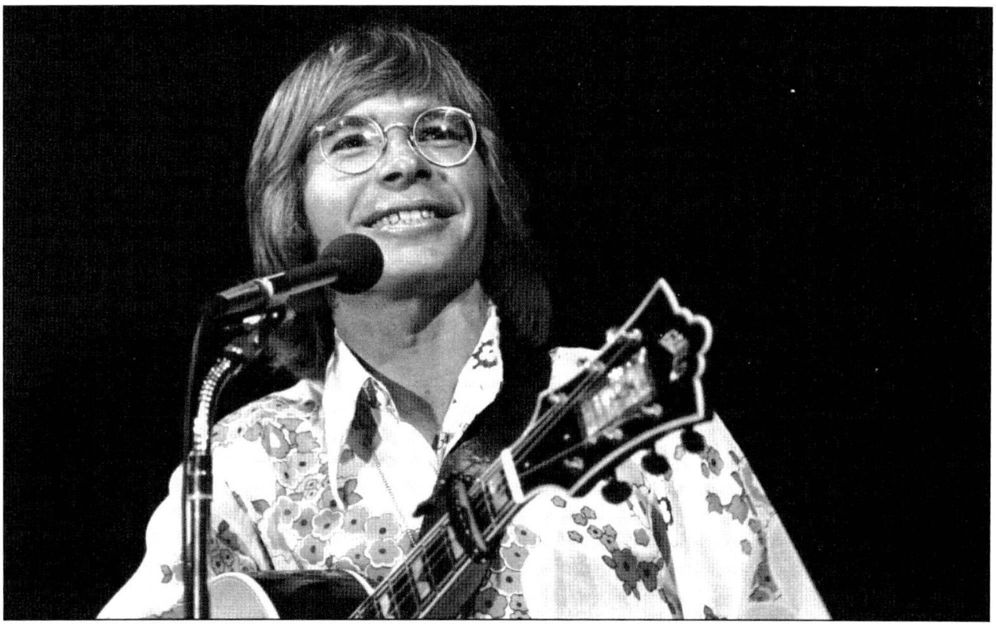

JOHN DENVER. In preparation for his appearance on August 1, 1972, John Denver played a round of golf with SIUE president John Rendleman. Denver sang with accompaniment by Dick Kniss (bass) and Mike Taylor (guitar). His concert included some recent songs such as "Rocky Mountain High" and "Goodbye, Again" and he concluded the second set of his show with a performance of "Take Me Home, Country Roads."

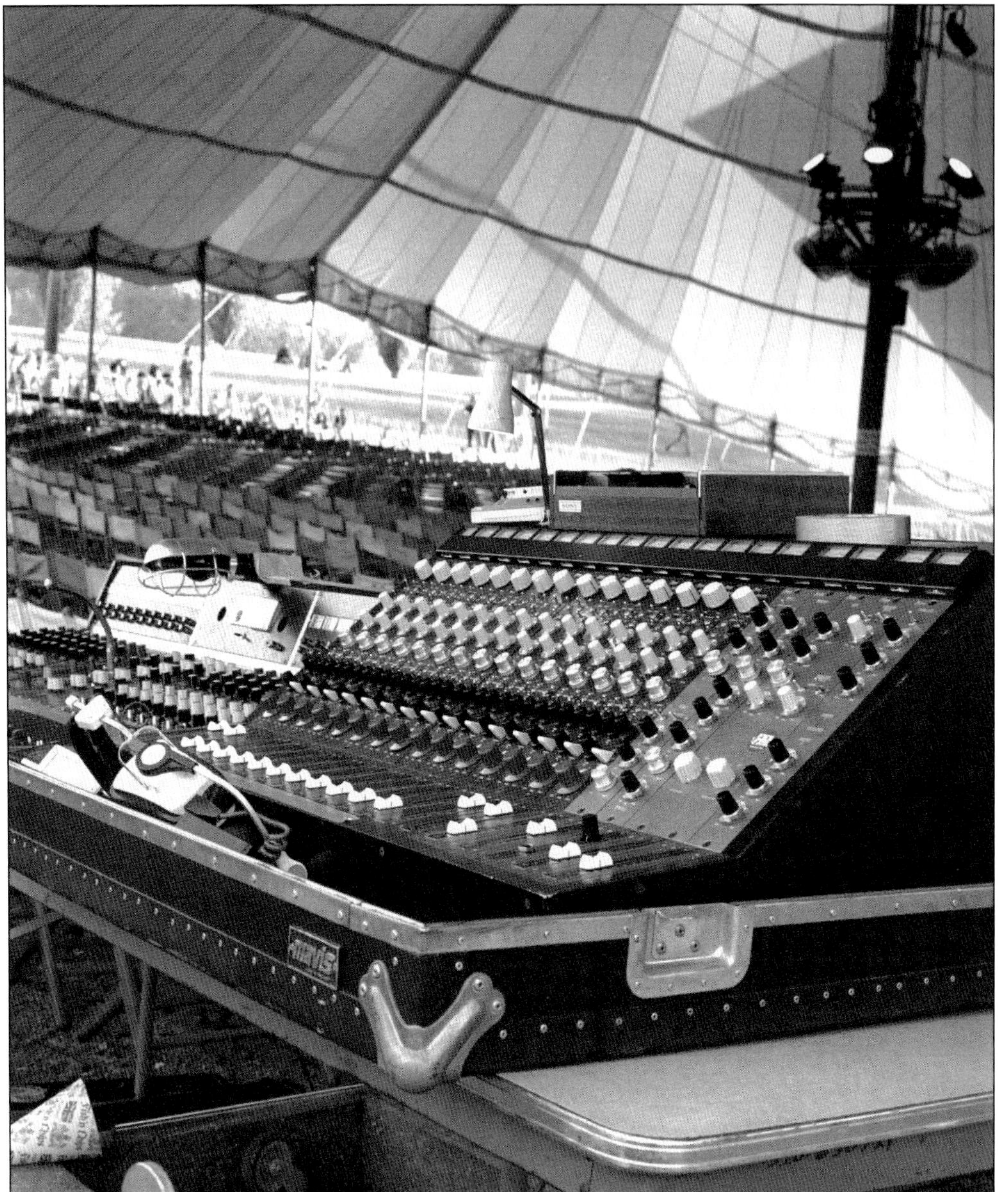

Bob Heil. A resident of the region, from Marissa, Bob Heil provided live sound production for many of the most notable bands of the late 1960s and the 1970s. His association with the giants of the popular music industry began with a 1970 telephone call from Jerry Garcia requesting assistance for a show at the Fox Theatre in St. Louis. This photograph, taken August 9, 1972, portrays some Heil equipment on the stage of the MRF. The Rock and Roll Hall of Fame in Cleveland, Ohio, opened a display of Bob Heil memorabilia (including a mixing board used under the tent) with a dedication party on June 7, 2006.

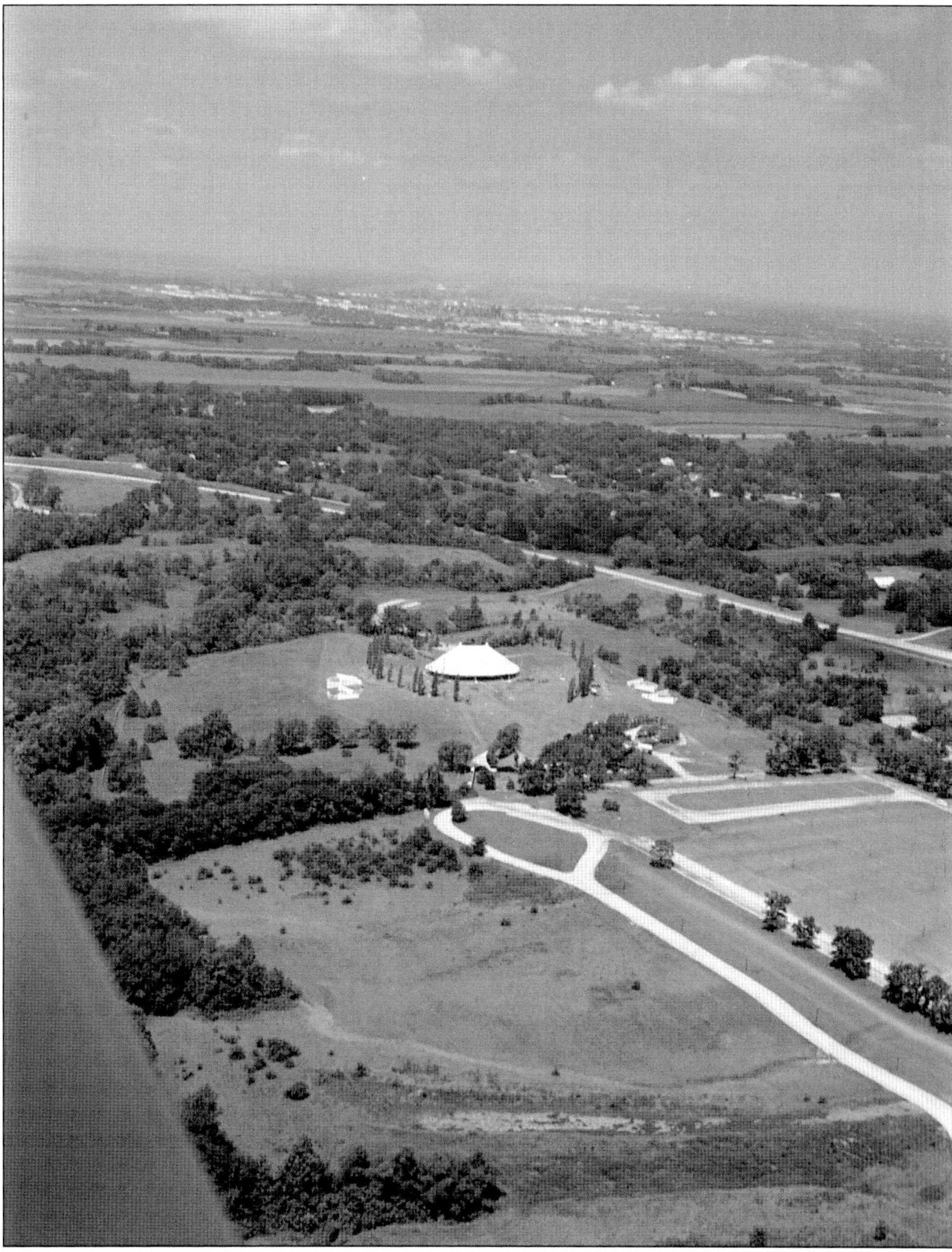

THE FRONT DOOR. During a periodic photographic reconnaissance flight over the university, the photographer snapped this shot of the northern portion of the campus. Looking from the southeast to the northwest, this image illustrates the roads and parking space available in front of the festival site.

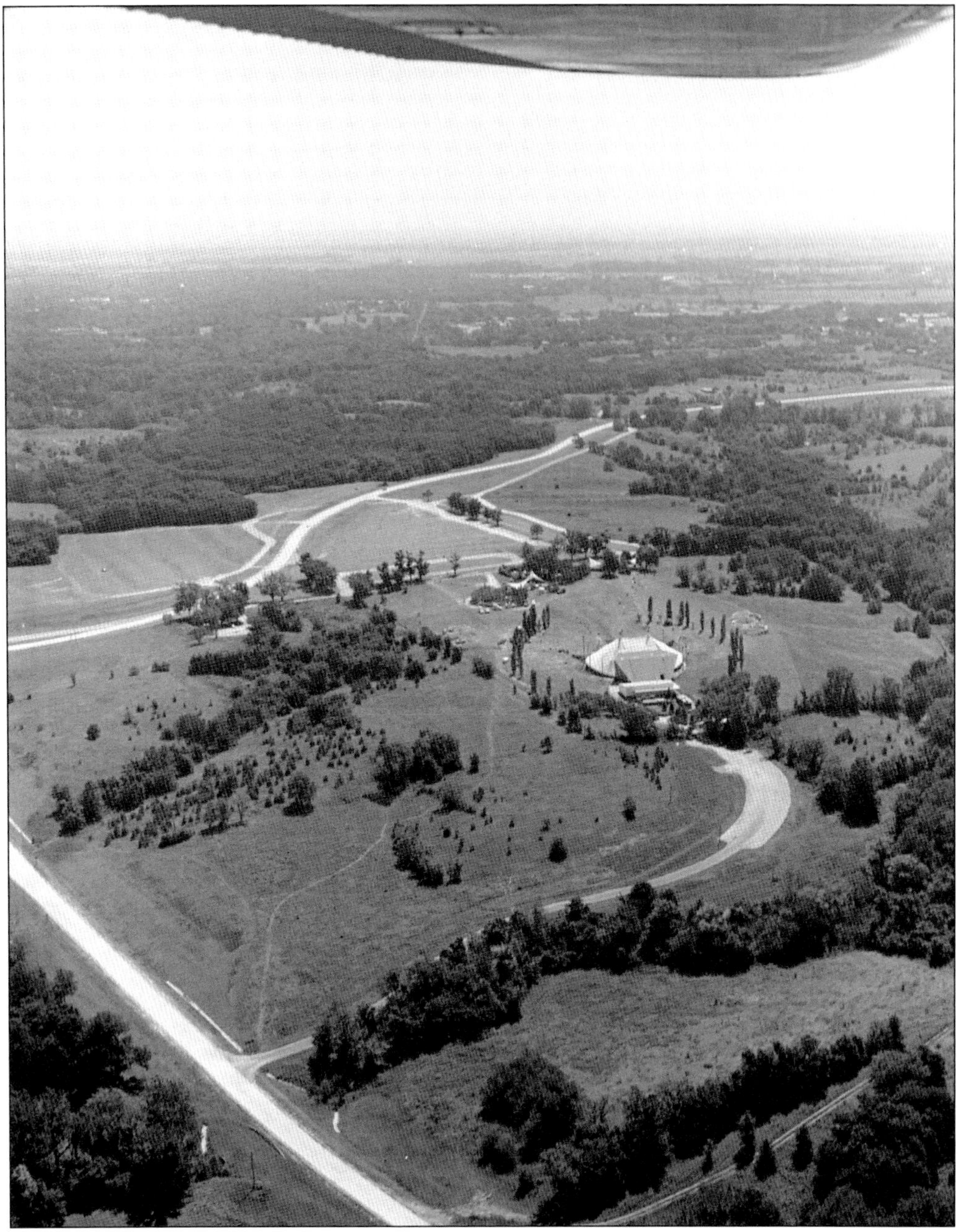

The Back Door. This photograph shows a view of the MRF site looking from northwest to southeast. The rear access road used for bringing band and orchestra equipment to the stage area is clearly visible in this shot.

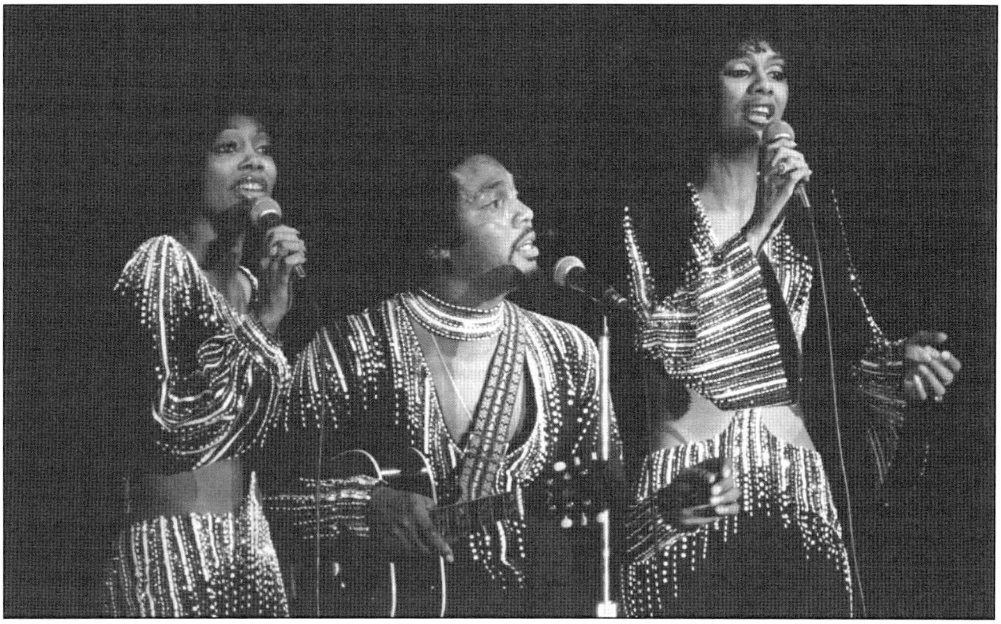

THE FIFTH DIMENSION. Bill Withers, best known for "Lean on Me," appeared August 11, 1972, as the opening act for the Fifth Dimension. Marilyn McCoo, Florence LaRue, Billy Davis Jr., Lamont McLemore, and Ron Townsend performed their hits such as "Aquarius, Let the Sunshine In," and "Wedding Bell Blues." During their finale, while they sang "Higher," the artists invited members of the audience onstage to dance with them.

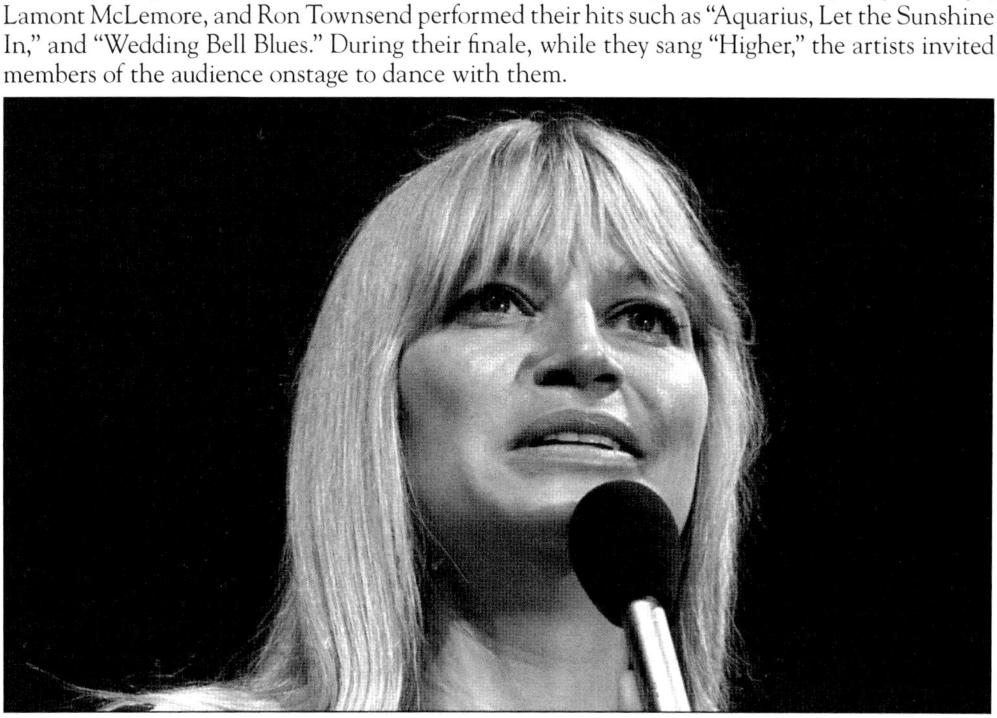

MARY TRAVERS. Following the breakup of Peter, Paul, and Mary in 1970, Mary Travers continued to perform as a single act. Her appearance at the festival on August 15, 1972, backed by three guitars and a piano, delighted the audience. Visibly shaken by the warmth of the crowd's reception, Travers performed three encores: "Leavin' on a Jet Plane," "Blowin' in the Wind," and "The First Time Ever I Saw Your Face."

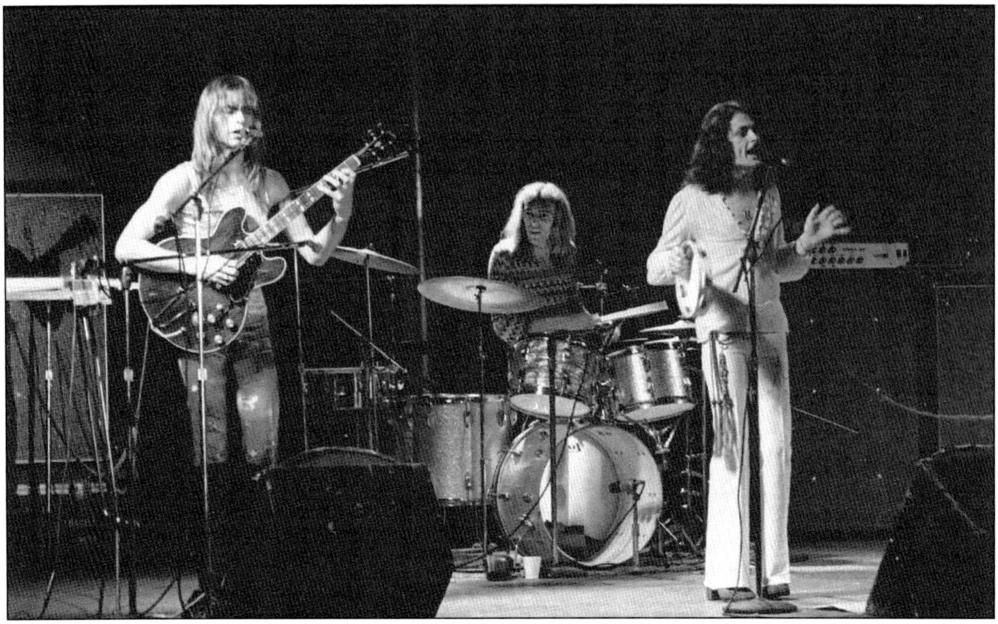

YES. Their visit on August 21, 1972, marked the first of three festival concerts performed by Yes (vocalist Jon Anderson, keyboard player Rick Wakeman, guitarist Steve Howe, bassist Chris Squire, and drummer Alan White). Yes later returned twice, on July 9, 1975, and August 11, 1976. As the opening act, Jackson Browne (supported by David Lindley) made his first of three appearances under the tent.

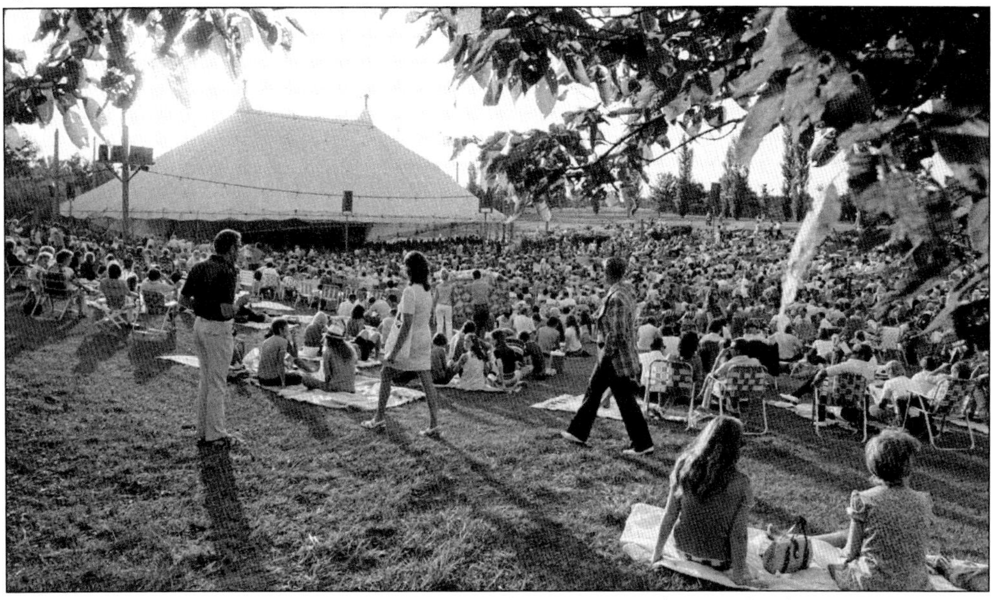

DOC SEVERINSEN. Familiar to all through his role on NBC's *The Tonight Show*, trumpeter Doc Severinsen ranked as one of the most popular artists to perform with the St. Louis Symphony Orchestra at the festival. His appearances with the symphony on July 25, 1971; July 9, 1972; and July 15, 1973 (when he played Floyd Werle's Concerto no. 2 For Trumpet and Orchestra), drew the third-, fifth-, and sixth-largest paid audiences among all symphony concerts. Severinsen also returned with his own supporting cast on July 6, 1974.

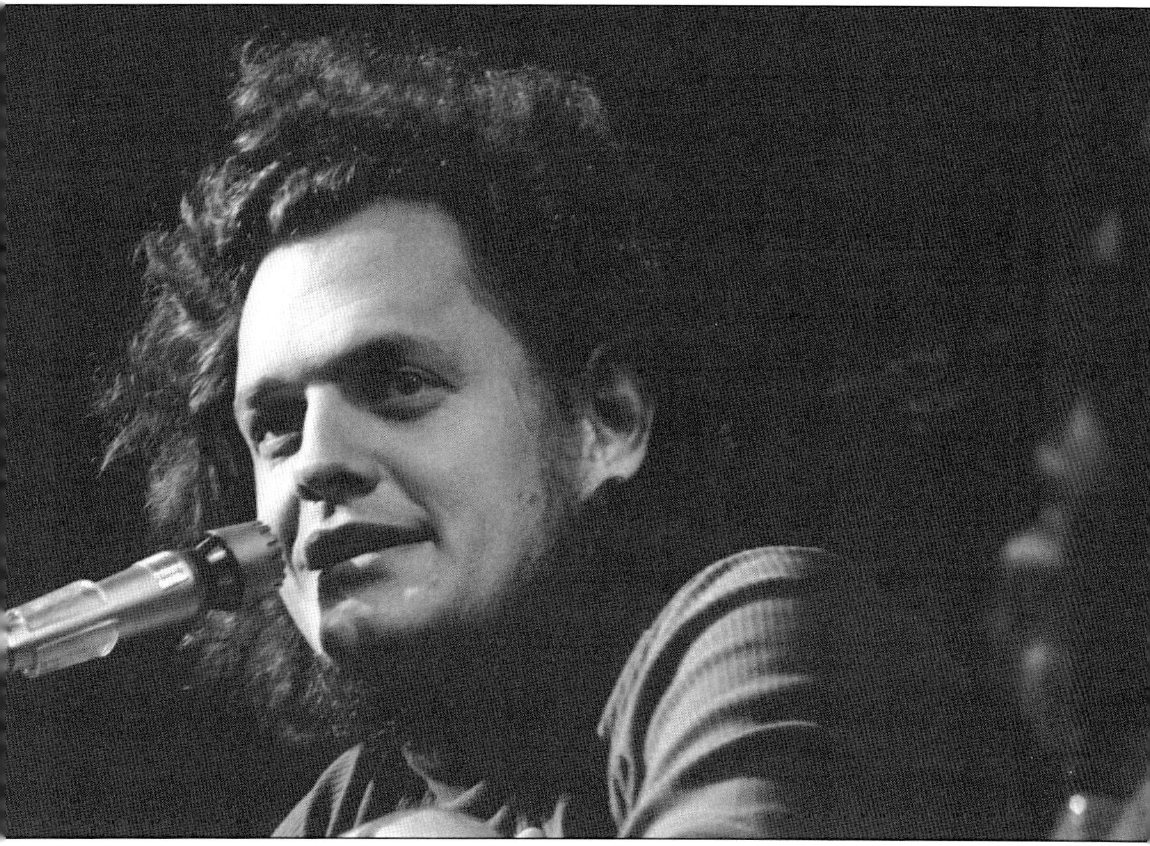

HARRY CHAPIN. Without question, Harry Chapin and Judy Collins must be regarded as the two popular performers most representative of the artistic excellence consistently demonstrated at the MRF. Each singer performed five times and each entertained their audiences with memorable performances that have withstood the test of time. On July 17, 1973, Chapin made his first appearance at the festival, accompanied by Ron Palmer (guitar), Mike Masters (cello), and John Wallace (bass). As the opening act, guitarist Leo Kottke also made his initial festival appearance.

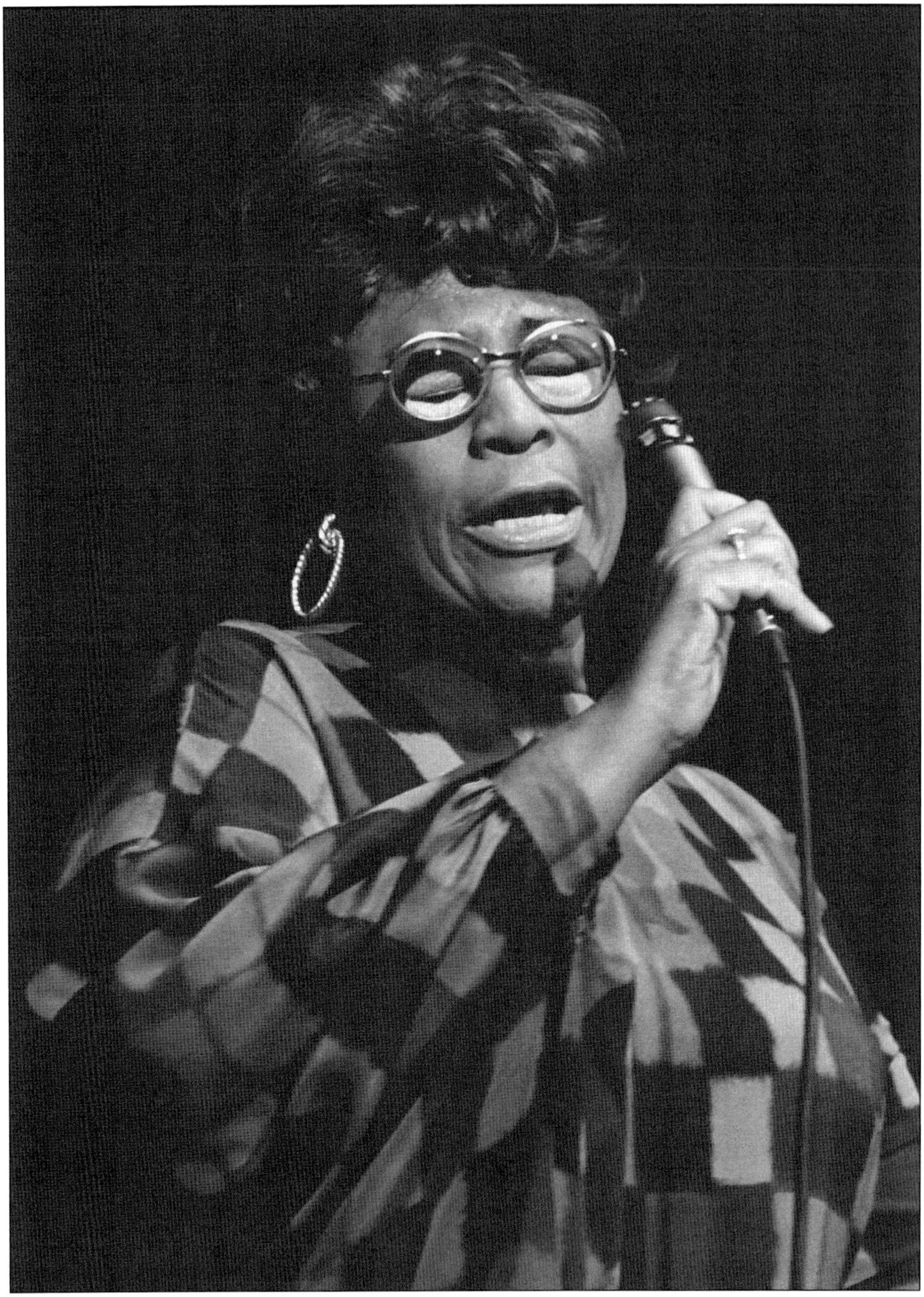

ELLA FITZGERALD. The artists supporting Ella Fitzgerald in her only appearance under the tent on July 20, 1973, included Tommy Flanagan (piano), Joe Pass (guitar), Freddy Watts (drums), and Keter Betts (bass). Fitzgerald performed "You've Got a Friend" and "St. Louis Blues" as her encores. Members of a youth dance troupe instructed by Katherine Dunham also took part in the Fitzgerald concert.

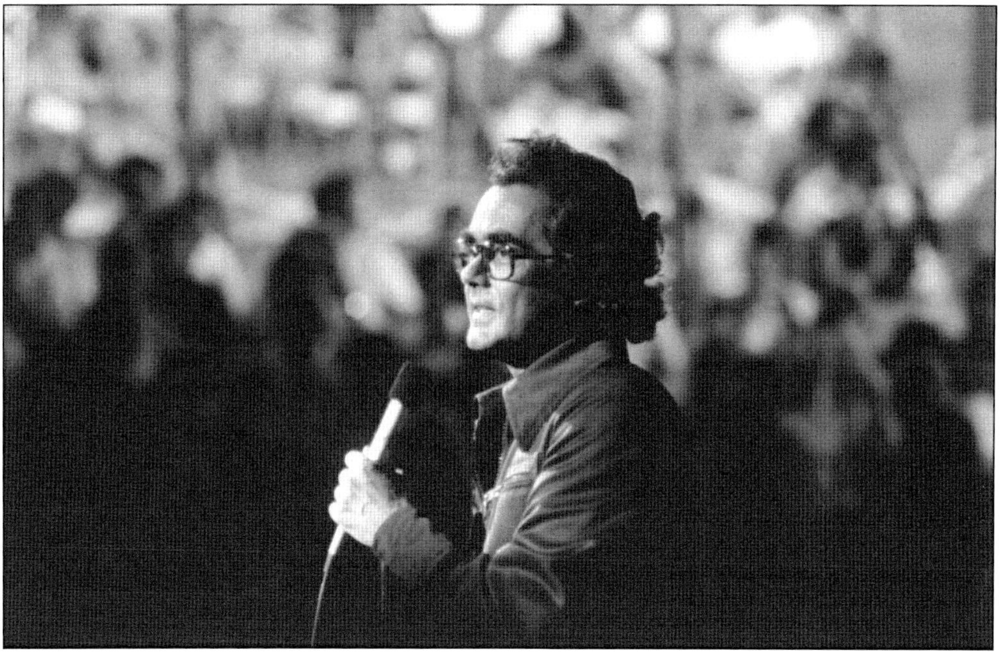

MICHEL LEGRAND. Both American vocalist Johnny Mathis and French singer/composer Michel Legrand appeared with the St. Louis Symphony Orchestra on July 22, 1973. Mathis performed the curtain raiser and then yielded to Legrand, who moved between the conductor's platform and the piano, performing works such as "Brian's Song," "Summer of '42," and "Windmills of Your Mind."

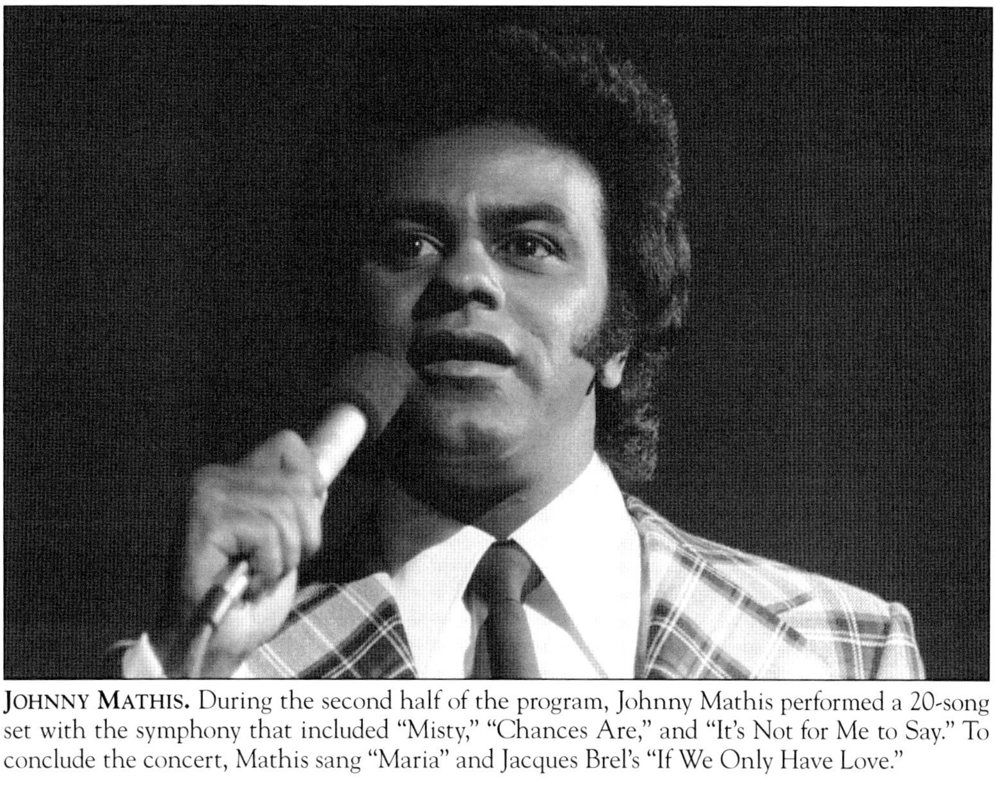

JOHNNY MATHIS. During the second half of the program, Johnny Mathis performed a 20-song set with the symphony that included "Misty," "Chances Are," and "It's Not for Me to Say." To conclude the concert, Mathis sang "Maria" and Jacques Brel's "If We Only Have Love."

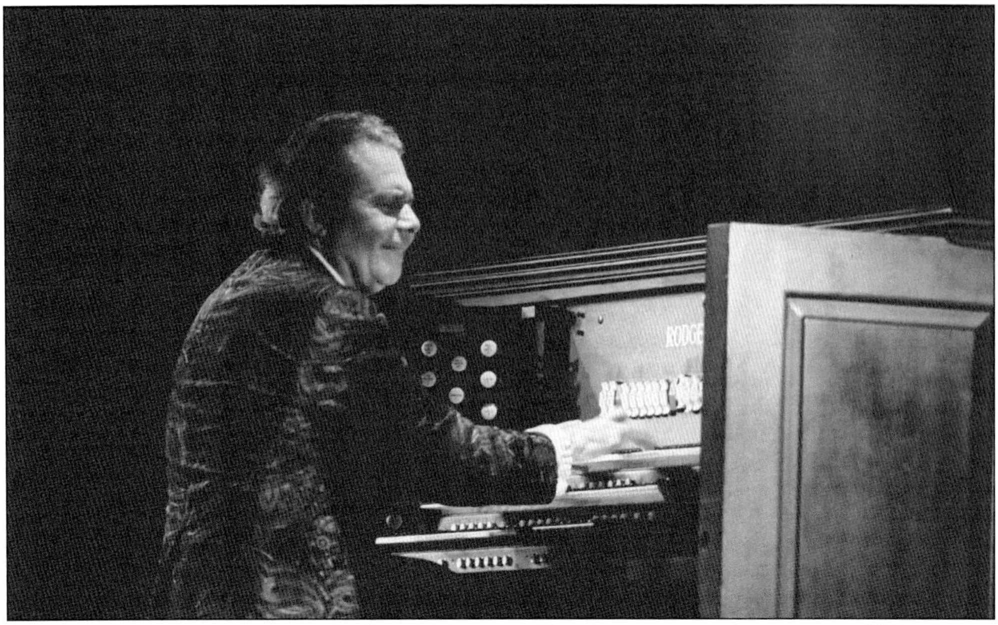

VIRGIL FOX. Perhaps the most brilliant organist of his century, Virgil Fox created his "Heavy Organ" tour to educate people about the genius of Johann Sebastian Bach. Before playing each piece, Fox would explain everything possible about it so as to prepare his audience. Revelation Lights provided a light show of projected images to accompany the music. On July 24, 1973, Fox presented a passionate performance lasting two and a half hours.

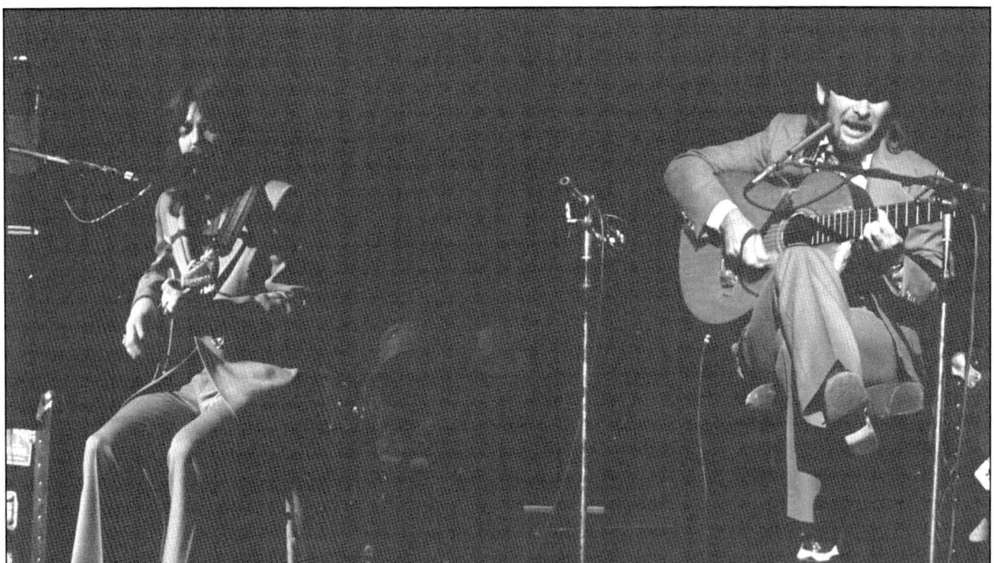

JIM SEALS AND DASH CROFTS. In spite of a thunderstorm, Seals and Crofts made their first of two visits to the festival on July 25, 1973, with support from Jeff Porcaro (drums), Bob Lichtig (bass and flute), David Paich (piano), and Roger Johnson (guitar). Jim Seals played the guitar, mandolin, and fiddle; while Dash Crofts worked the drums, mandolin, keyboards, and guitar. The program attracted 20,988 fans, which was the eighth-largest paid attendance during the festival. Seals and Crofts returned once more on August 24, 1974.

FERRANTE AND TEICHER. Twin pianists Arthur Ferrante and Louis Teicher achieved extensive fame through their concert and television appearances and record sales. They appeared at the festival on the stormy evening of July 27, 1973. An unscripted highlight of the concert took place when a driverless motorized cart rolled down the lawn and crashed into the cart used by Skip Manley. Ferrante and Teicher had trained and also taught at the Julliard School of Music in New York City.

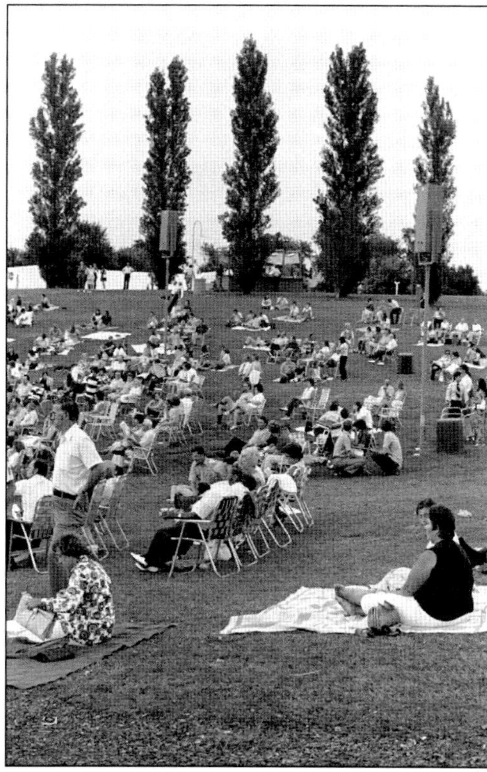

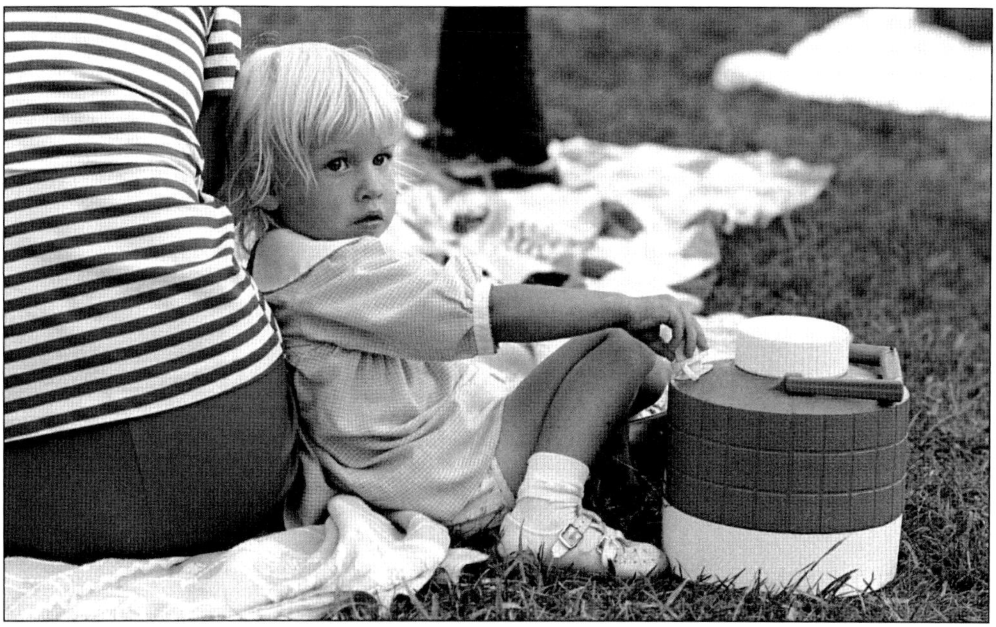

BOBBY GOLDSBORO. Songwriter/singer Bobby Goldsboro made his only festival appearance on August 3, 1973, backed by an assortment of horns, strings, piano, bass, and drums. Unusual among MRF performers, Goldsboro conducted a question-and-answer session with the crowd during his show. His list of songs included "Watching Scotty Grow" and Carole King's "Been to Canaan."

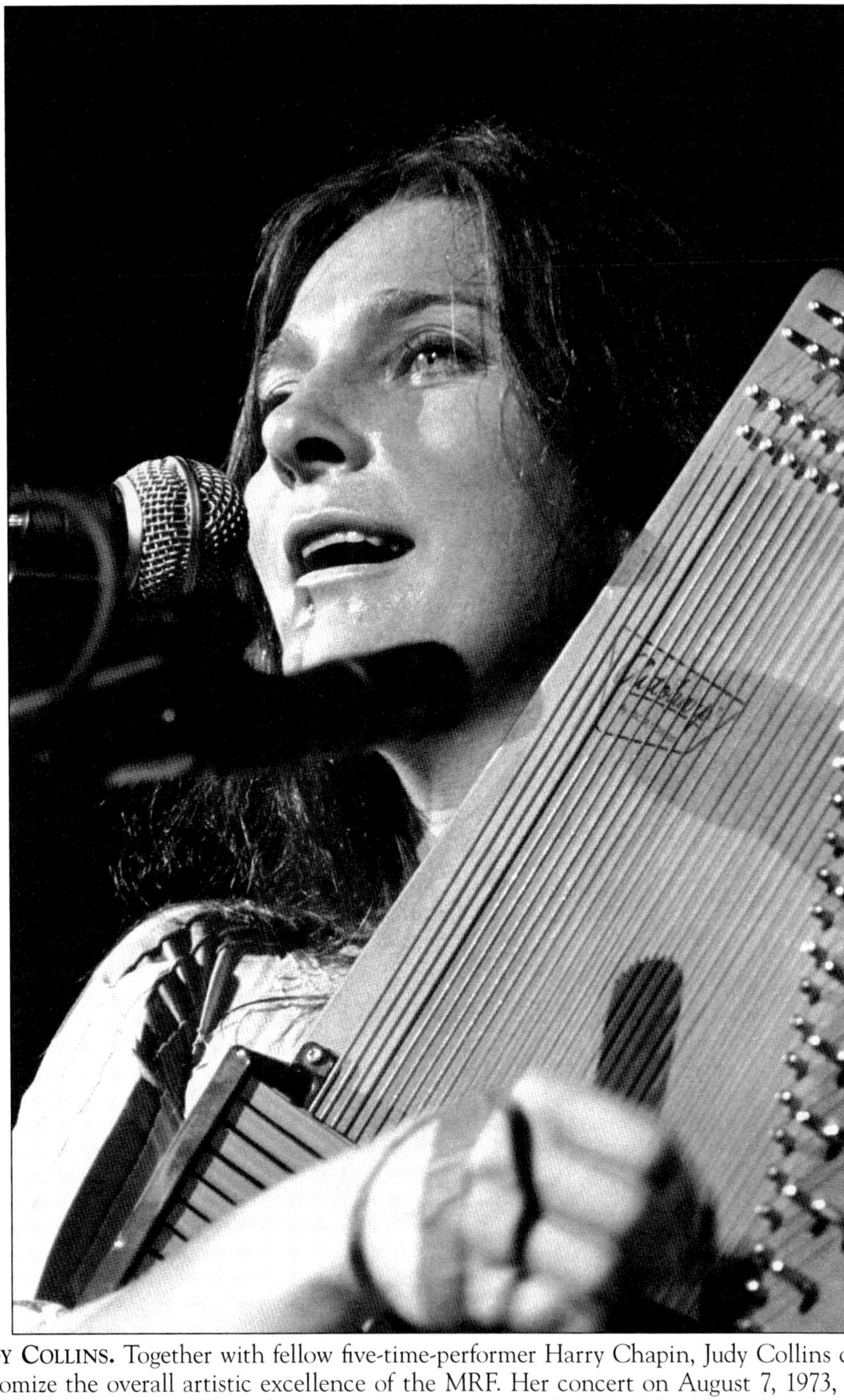

JUDY COLLINS. Together with fellow five-time-performer Harry Chapin, Judy Collins came to epitomize the overall artistic excellence of the MRF. Her concert on August 7, 1973, marked her third of five visits. The others took place on August 5, 1970; July 15, 1971; July 22, 1975; and August 3, 1976. In 1973, despite suffering from a severe case of sunburn, Collins played two sets lasting approximately two hours in all with accompaniment by Steve Mandel (guitar) and Donny Brooks (harmonica).

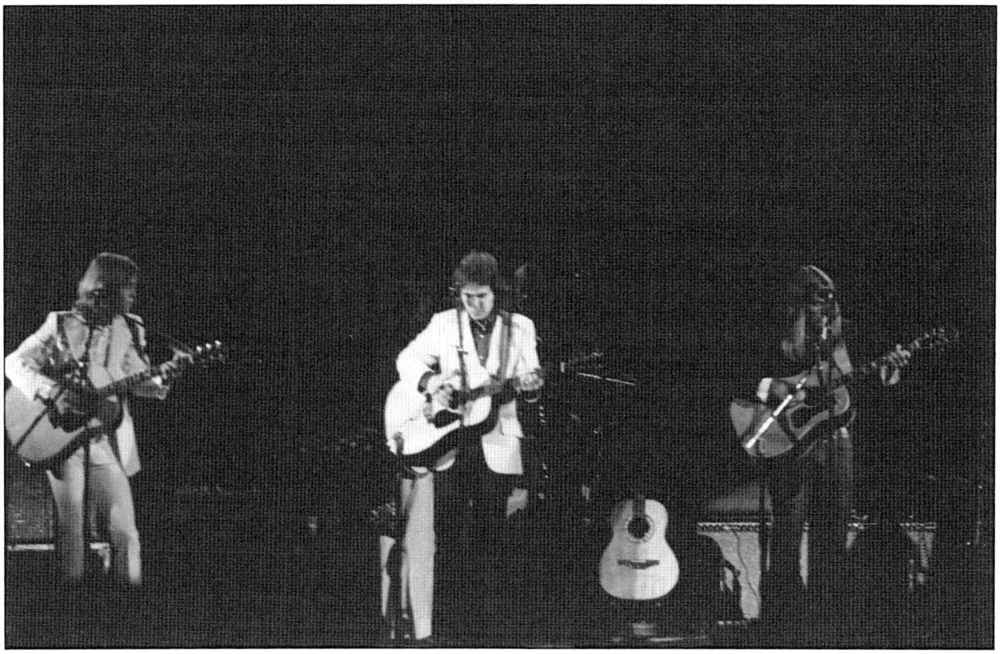

AMERICA. On a stage decorated with dozens of potted plants, Dewey Bunnell, Dan Peek, and Gerry Beckley made their first of four appearances at the festival on August 8, 1973. America subsequently visited the festival again on August 10, 1975; June 22, 1978; and June 16, 1979. Opening act Jackson Browne (backed by David Lindley) performed at the MRF for the second time.

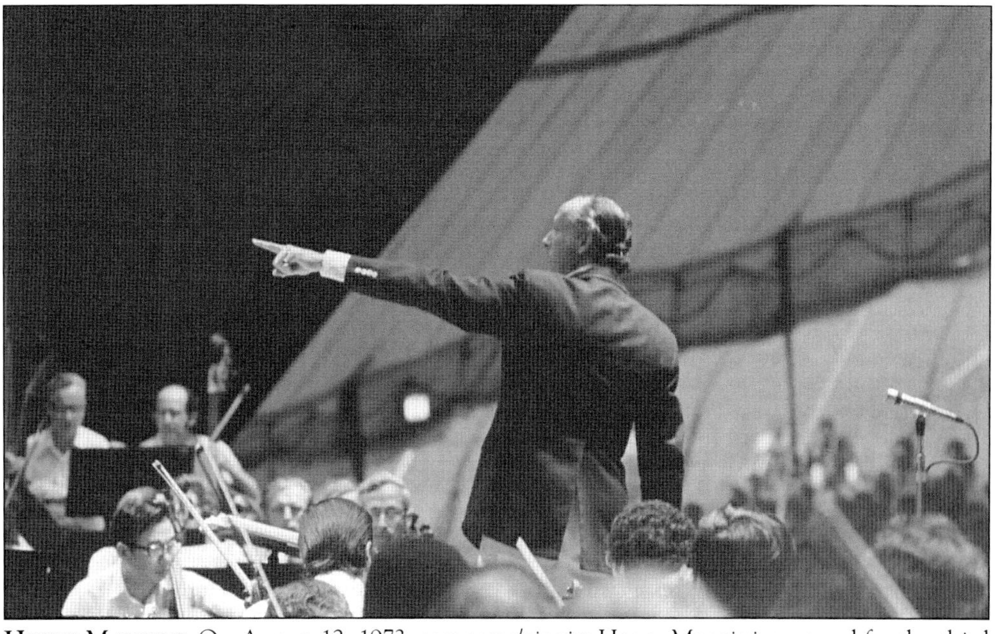

HENRY MANCINI. On August 12, 1973, composer/pianist Henry Mancini appeared for the third of five times at the festival and conducted the St. Louis Symphony Orchestra. Mancini's earlier appearances with the symphony, on July 12, 1970, and July 18, 1971, resulted in the two largest paid crowds ever to attend symphony concerts under the tent. He also performed on July 13, 1975, and August 14, 1977.

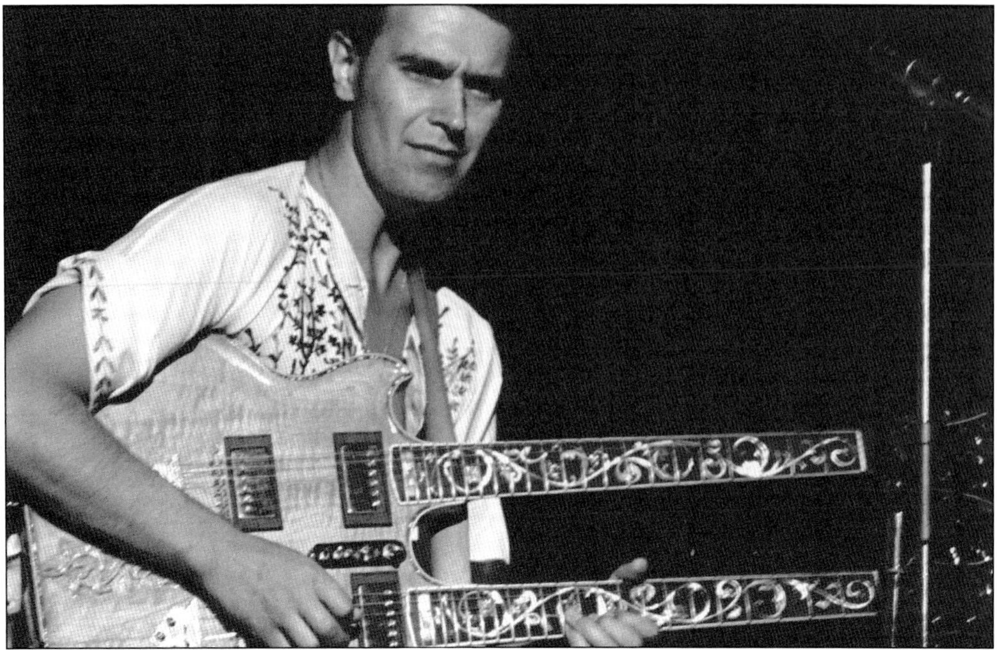

JOHN MCLAUGHLIN. Between 1971 and 1973, jazz guitarist John McLaughlin led the Mahavishnu Orchestra, an early fusion group. In his August 14, 1973, visit to the festival, McLaughlin played his signature double-necked guitar and received support from Jerry Goodman (violin), Jan Hammer (synthesizer), Rick Laird (bass), and Billy Cobham (drums). Section appeared as the opening act for McLaughlin.

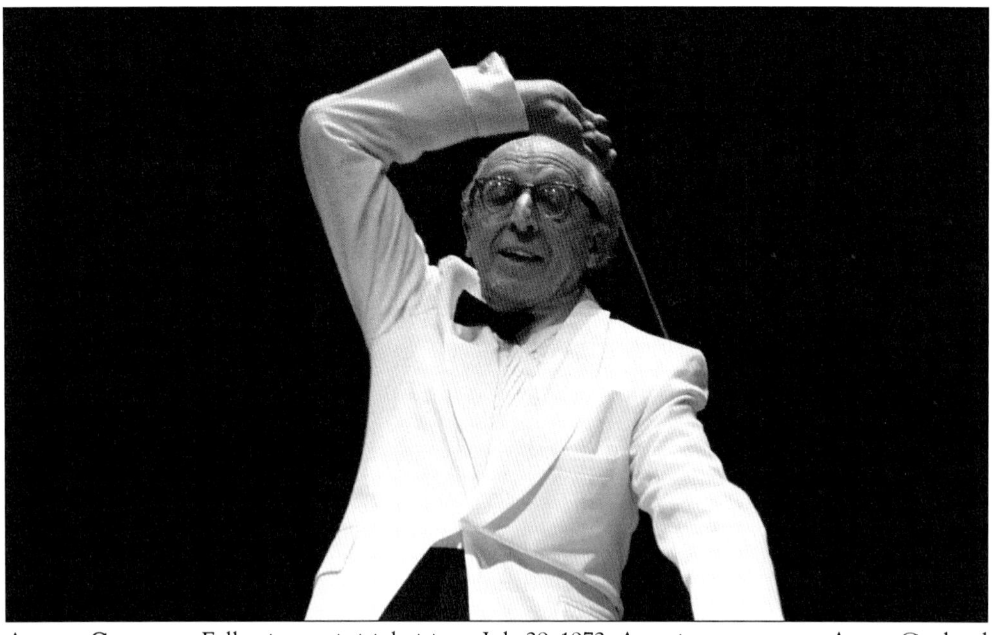

AARON COPLAND. Following an initial visit on July 29, 1972, American composer Aaron Copland returned to conduct the St. Louis Symphony Orchestra a second time on August 18, 1973. Clarinetist George Silfries played Copland's Concerto for Clarinet and Strings. The program on August 18 also included another Copland work, Four Dance Episodes from the Rodeo Ballet.

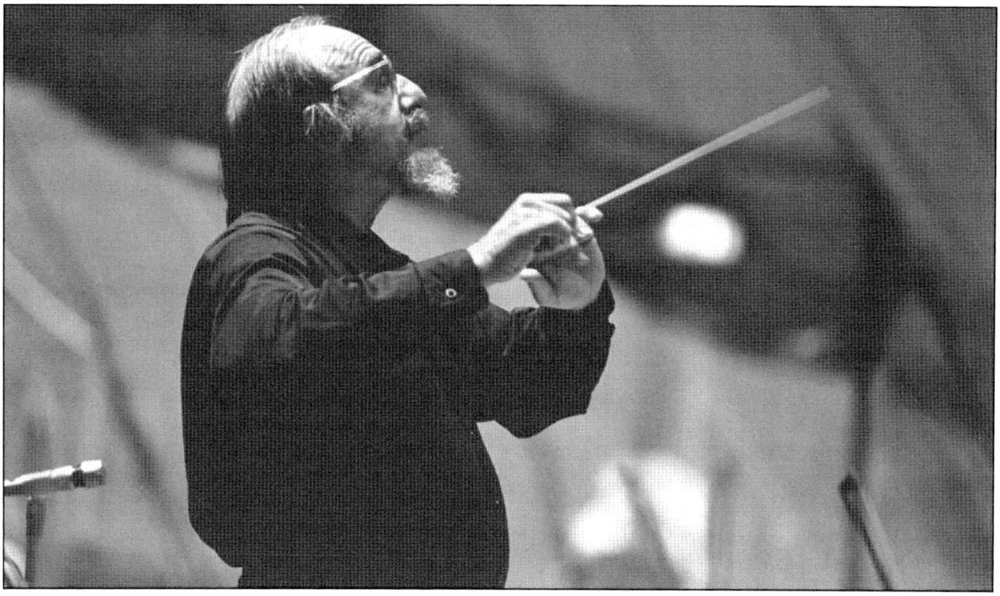

MITCH MILLER. The widely-recognized host of a popular 1960s television show, *Sing Along with Mitch*, Mitch Miller appeared at the festival to conduct the St. Louis Symphony Orchestra for a second time on August 19, 1973. Violinist Mark Kaplan played Vieuxtemp's Concerto no. 4. As expected, the evening concluded with an audience sing-along to old favorites such as "Shine On Harvest Moon," "Four-Leaf Clover," and "Good Night, Ladies." Miller's earlier collaboration with the symphony had taken place the previous year on July 30, 1972.

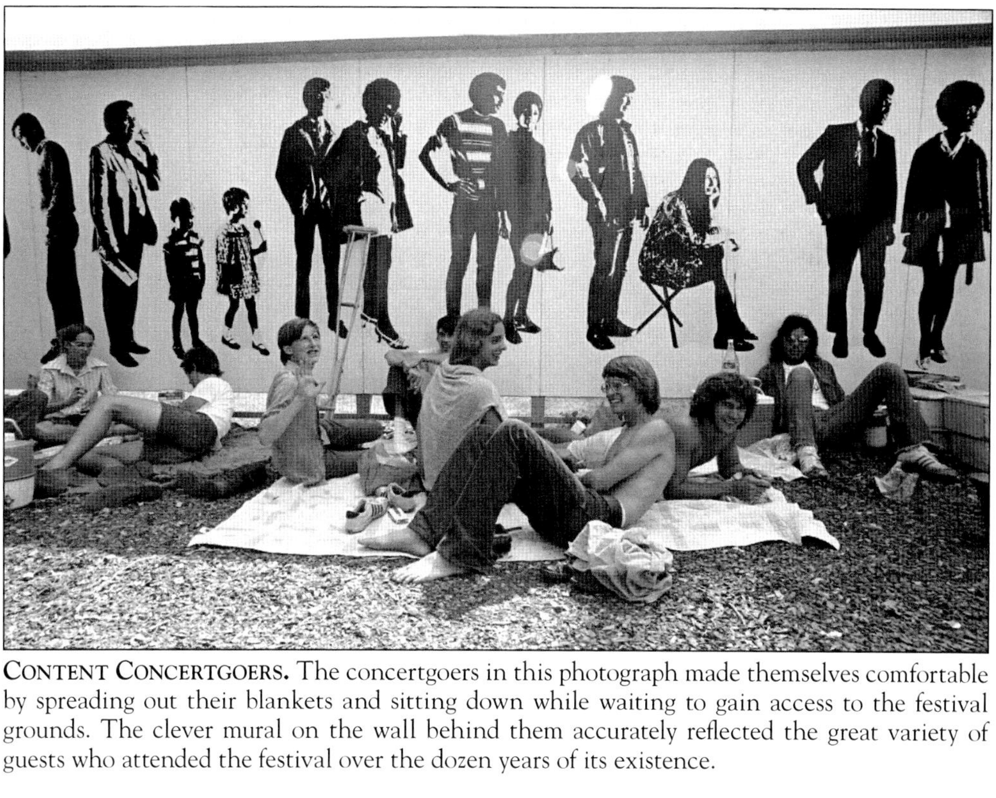

CONTENT CONCERTGOERS. The concertgoers in this photograph made themselves comfortable by spreading out their blankets and sitting down while waiting to gain access to the festival grounds. The clever mural on the wall behind them accurately reflected the great variety of guests who attended the festival over the dozen years of its existence.

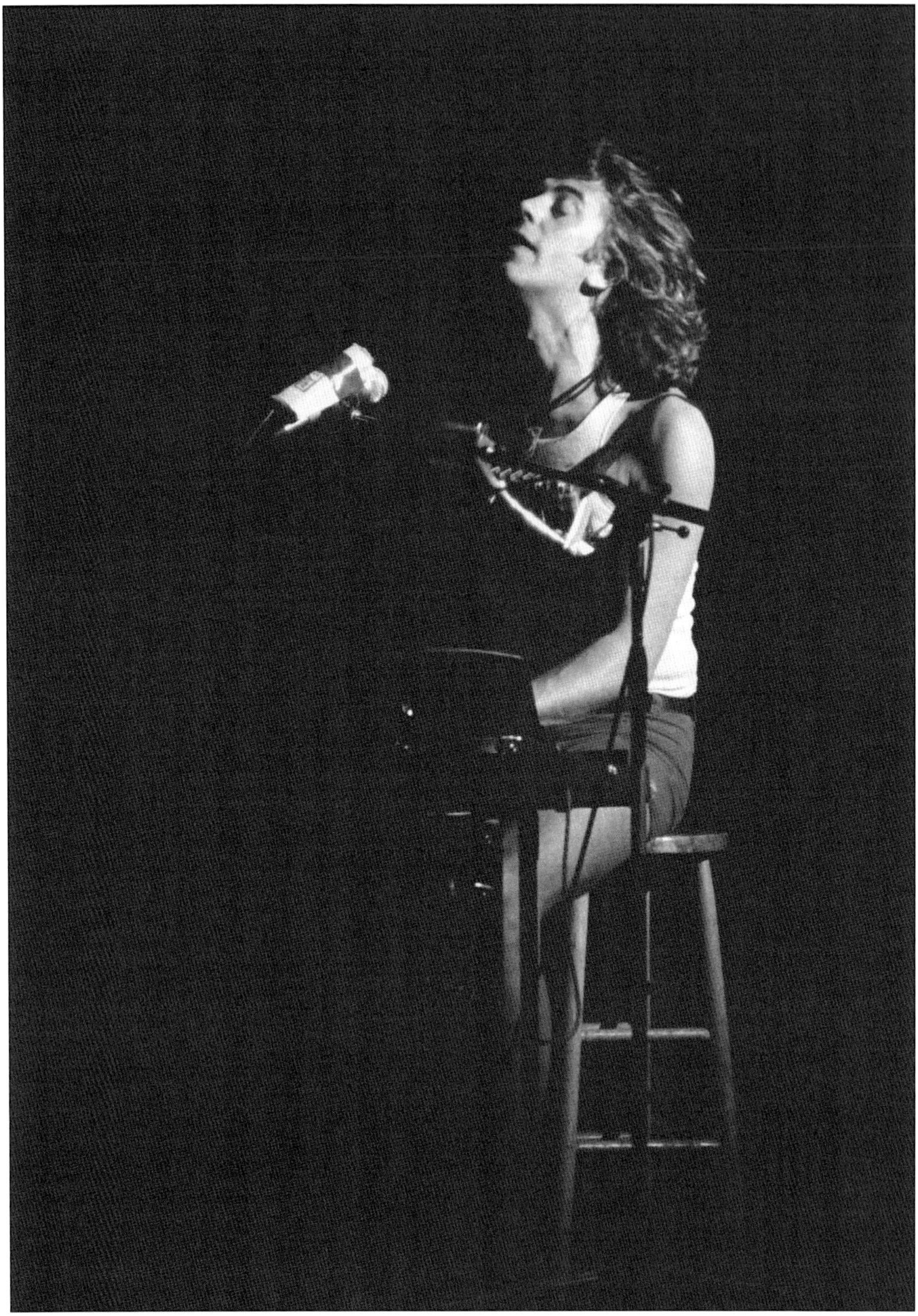

John Mayall. Blues artist John Mayall appeared only once at the festival, on August 21, 1973, as the featured act preceded by Bonnie Bramlett. Sugarcane Harris, Red Holloway, and Keef Hartley performed with Mayall. The low point of the evening arrived when the crowd booed off the stage, prior to the second act, an unfunny comedian auditioning with Mayall.

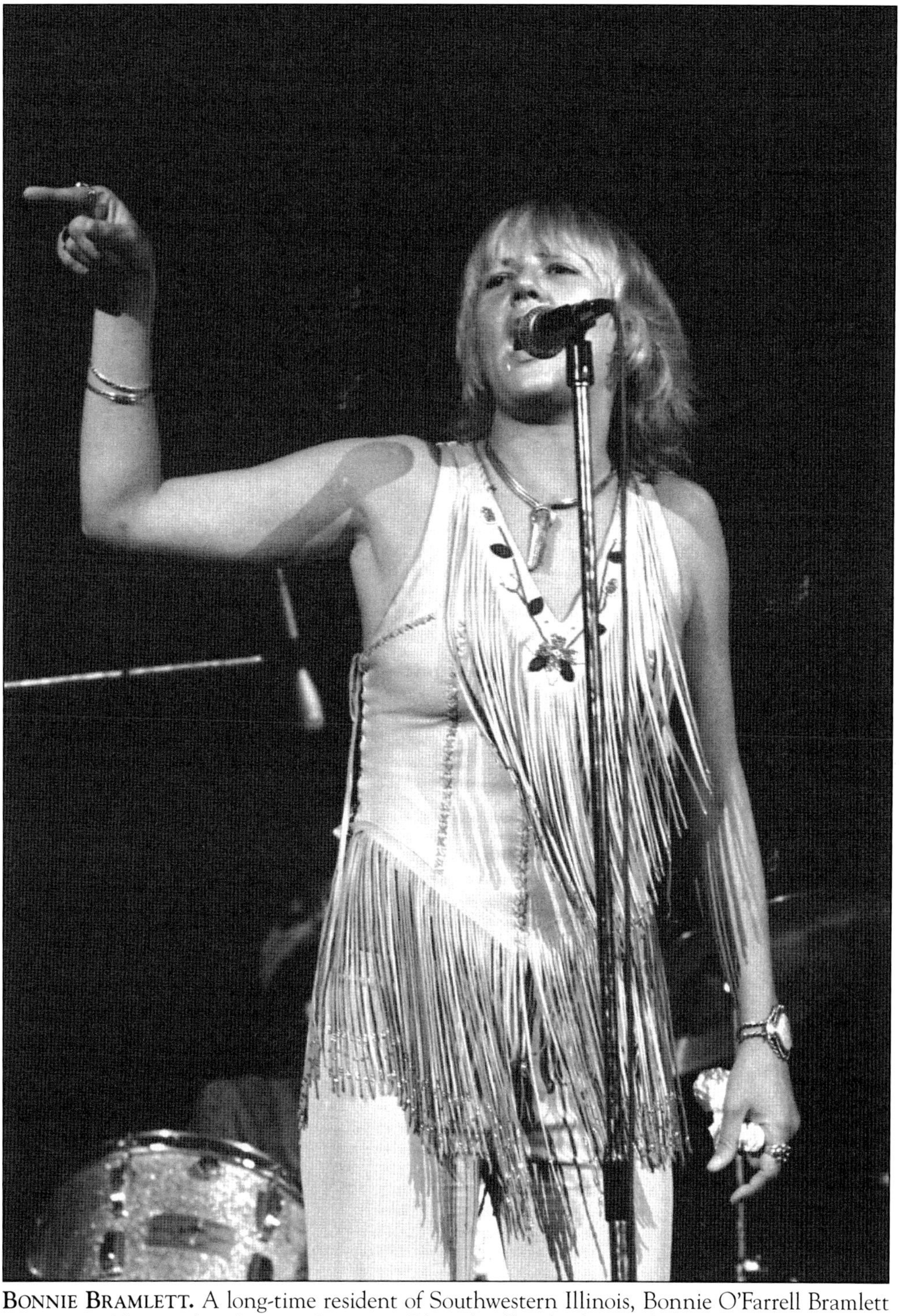

Bonnie Bramlett. A long-time resident of Southwestern Illinois, Bonnie O'Farrell Bramlett grew up in Alton and in Granite City, near Edwardsville. She first performed at the festival with her husband, Delaney Bramlett, as Bonnie and Delaney, on July 25, 1970. Bonnie later came back a third time, on June 29, 1979, together with Greg Allman.

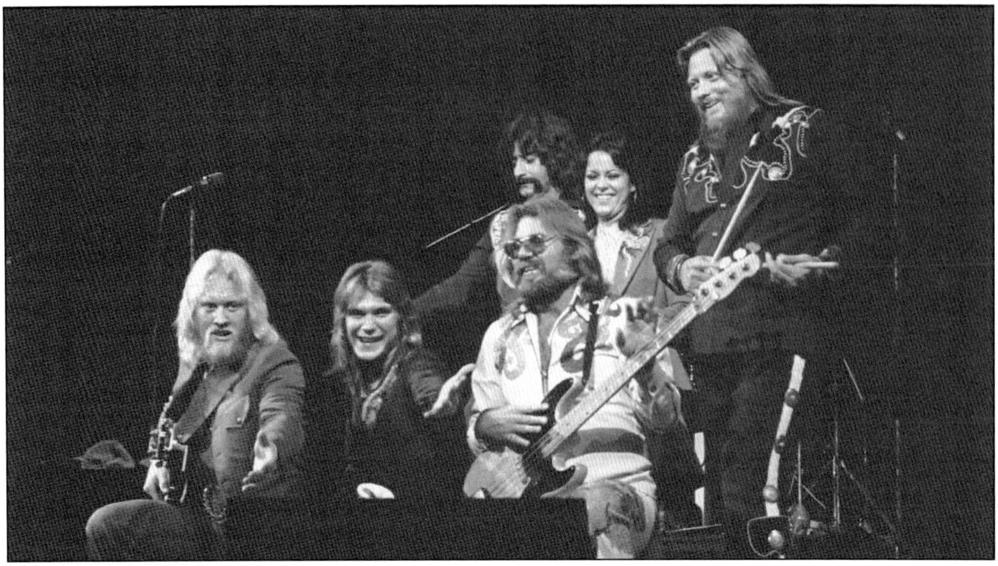

KENNY ROGERS. The first and only festival appearance by Kenny Rogers came on August 24, 1973. Kenny Rogers and the First Edition included Terry Williams (guitar), Gene Lorenzo (keyboard), and Mickey Jones (drums). Opening act John Stewart had sung with the Kingston Trio between 1961 and 1967, when his composition "Daydream Believer" became a major hit for the Monkees. Rogers and his associates displayed an attitude of humility somewhat unusual among performers by arriving in a rented station wagon and willingly signing autographs before and after the show.

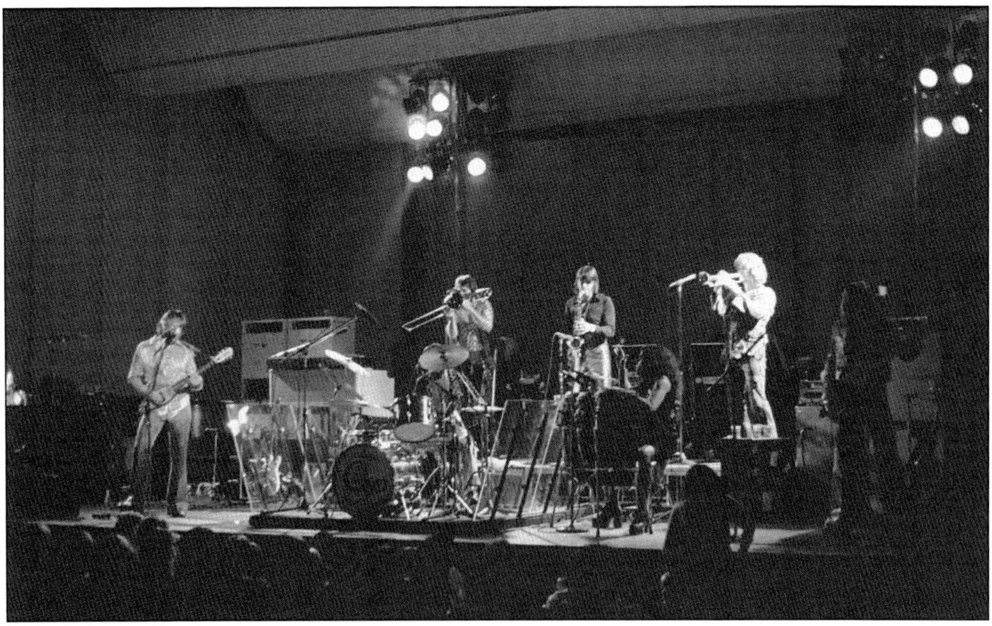

CHICAGO. More fans paid to attend Chicago concerts at the festival than concerts by any other act. Their performance on the hot and humid evening of August 25, 1973, opened by the Pointer Sisters, sold 28,377 tickets. This marked the largest attendance since The Who concert and would eventually rank as the number three night overall in terms of ticket sales. Chicago also appeared on July 15, 1970; August 21, 1974; and August 22, 1978.

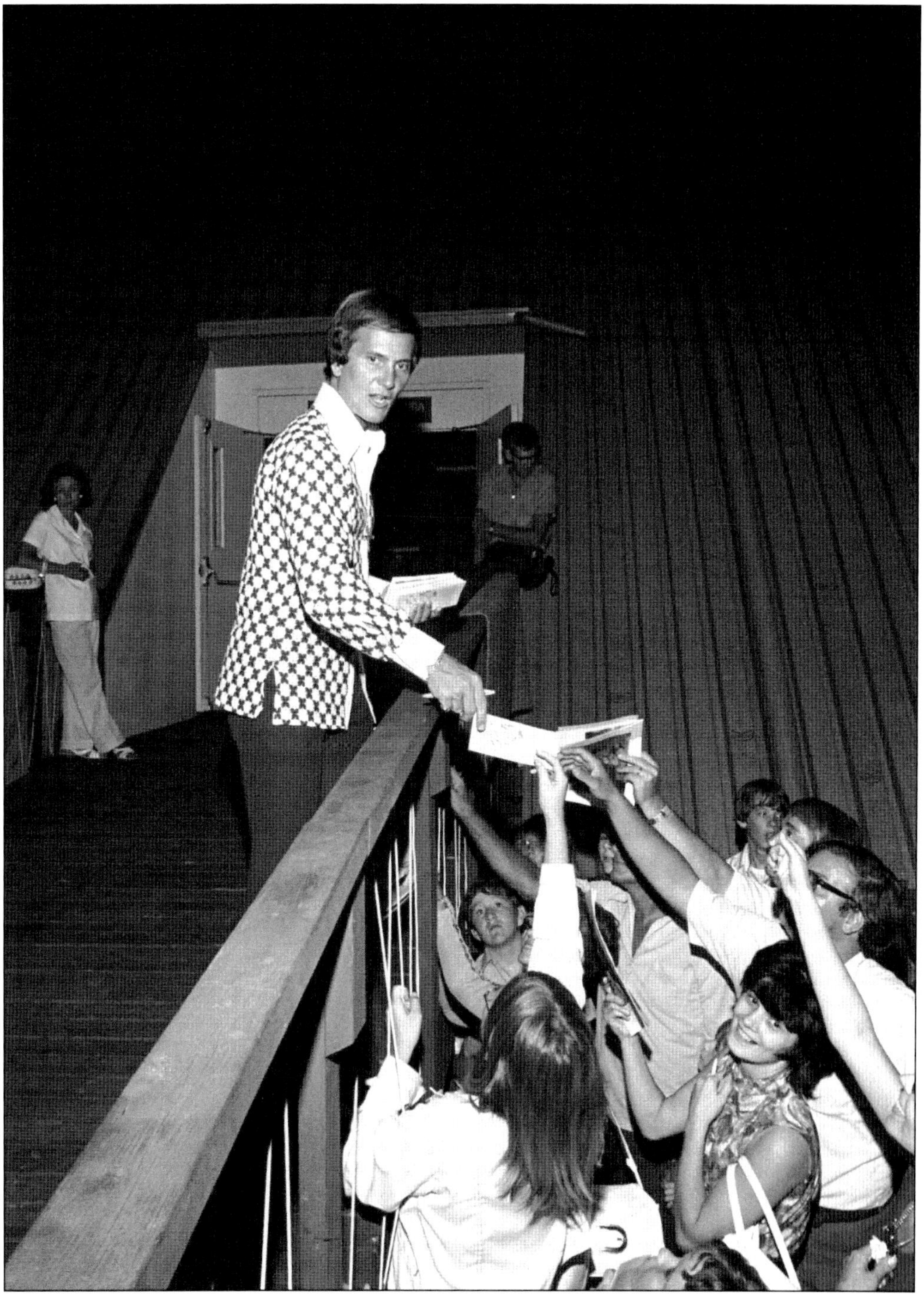

PAT BOONE. Between his dressing room and the stage, vocalist and one-time teen heartthrob Pat Boone took time to sign autographs for fans gathered behind the tent. Boone, who at this stage of his career often traveled and sang with his family, performed at the festival on August 26, 1973. The former teen idol, who had perhaps sold more records in the 1950s than anyone besides Elvis Presley, had married the daughter of country music singer Red Foley.

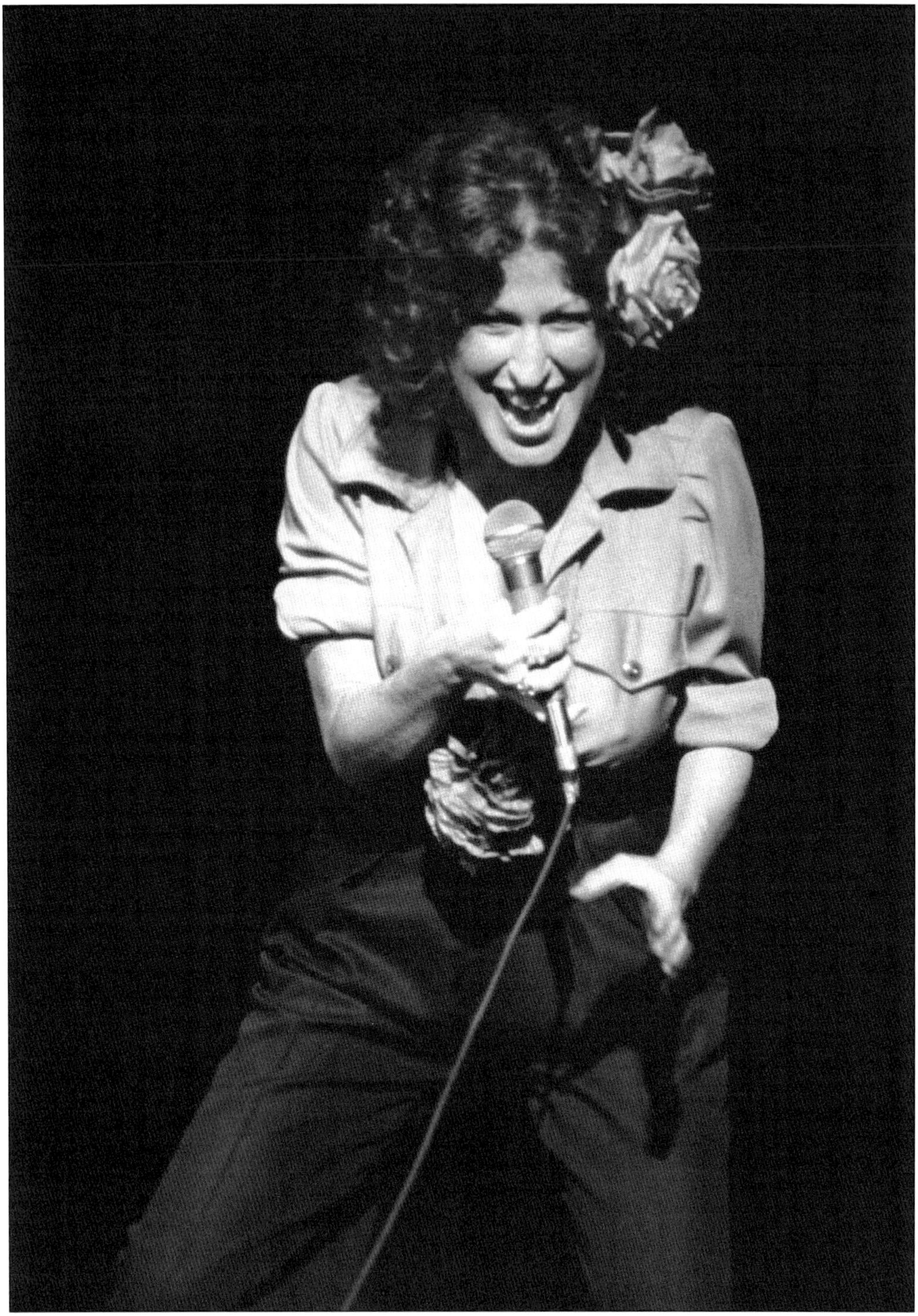

Bette Midler. The unique Bette Midler, the Divine Miss M, brought her freewheeling act to the festival for the first and only time on August 28, 1973. To the delight of a paid crowd of 4,144 persons, Midler punctuated her performance with caustic commentary directed at Richard Nixon and his administration's involvement in the notorious Watergate burglary.

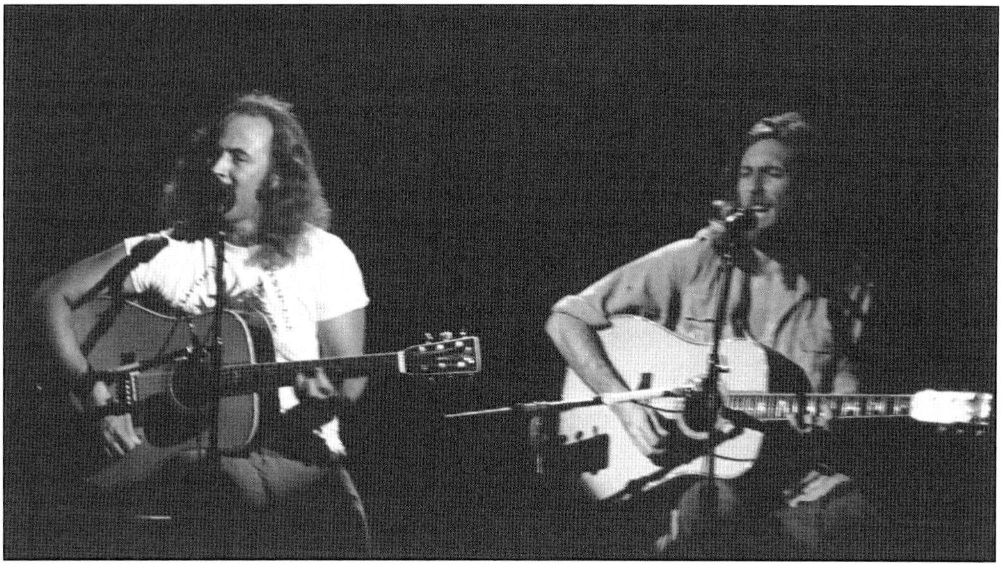

DAVID CROSBY AND GRAHAM NASH. Lightning, thunder, rain, and strong winds temporarily interrupted John David Souther's opening act on August 29, 1973. Throughout the evening, the bad weather forced workers repeatedly to lower and raise the weather shield around the outside of the tent. Feature act David Crosby and Graham Nash followed Souther to the stage in the first of their two festival appearances. The second came three years later, on August 18, 1976. Their former Crosby, Stills, Nash, and Young associate Stephen Stills performed three times at the festival.

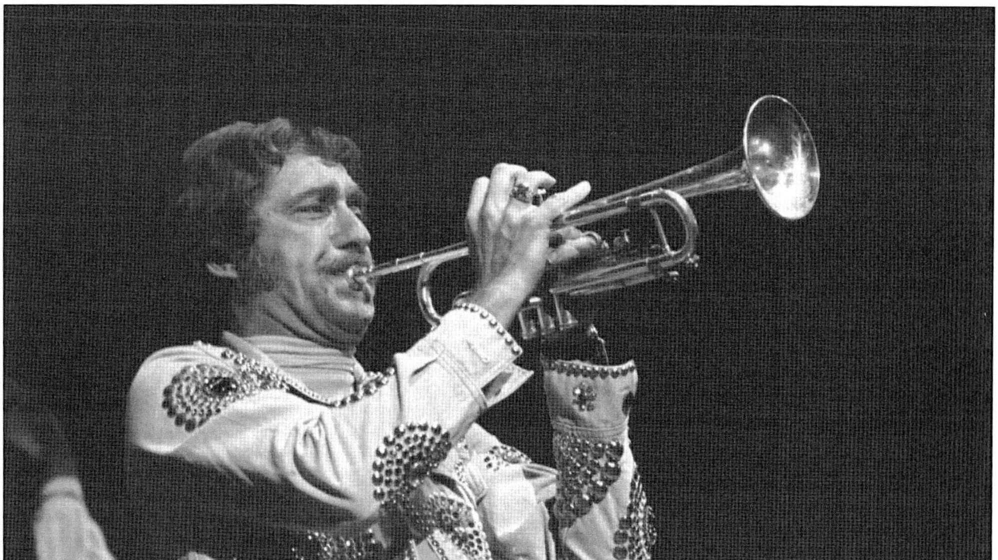

TRUMPET CALL. Doc Severinsen returned to the MRF for the fourth time on July 6, 1974. Severinsen had previously performed as a soloist with the St. Louis Symphony, but on this occasion he headlined a popular music concert featuring a backup band that he called the Now Generation Brass (mostly members of *The Tonight Show* orchestra) and an eight-member singing group Today's Children. Since the concert happened to coincide with Severinsen's birthday, his friend Leonard Slatkin surprised the trumpeter with a birthday cake.

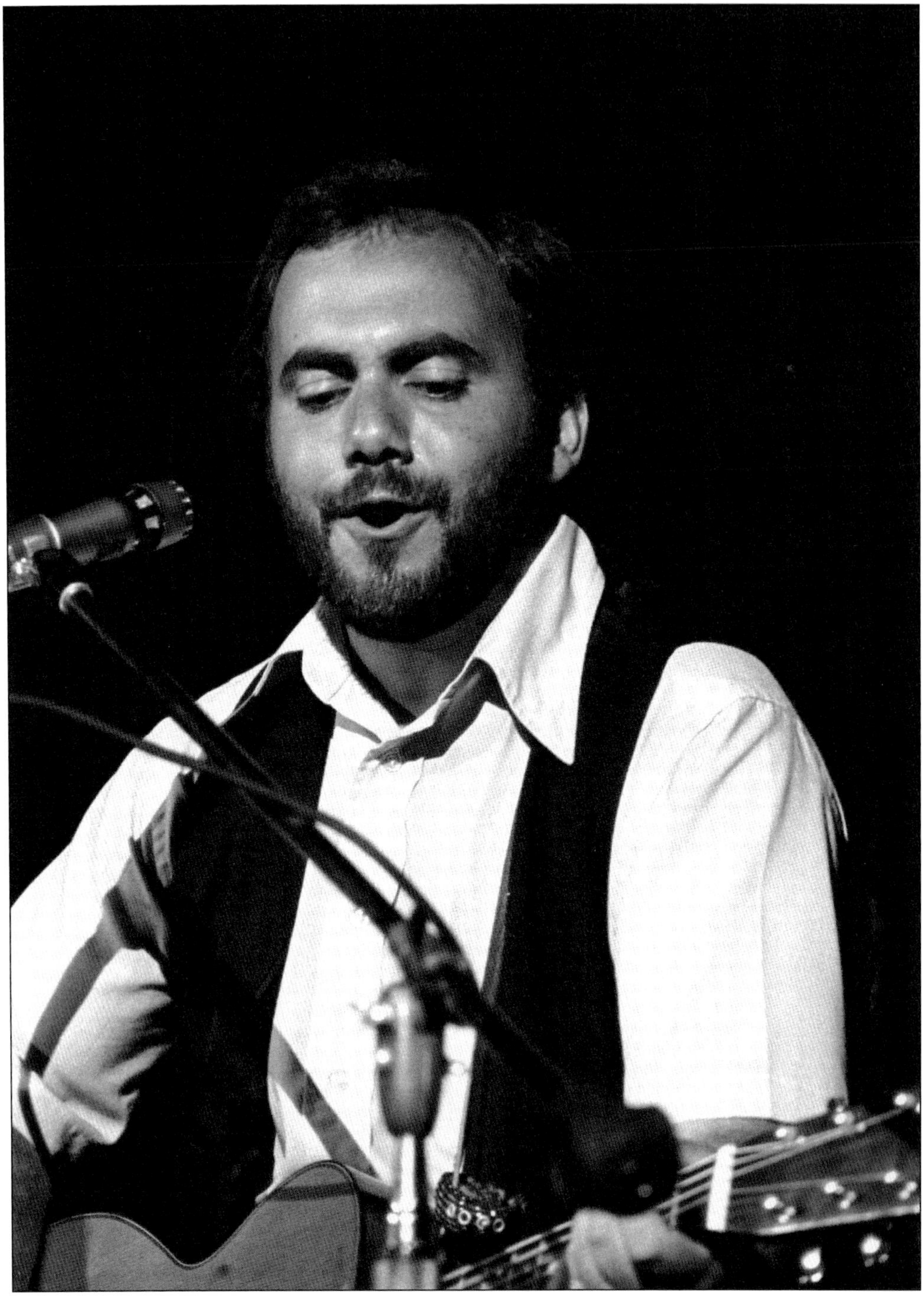

STEVE GOODMAN. Three guitarists shared the program on July 9, 1974: Megan McDonough, Steve Goodman, and Leo Kottke. Goodman, a Chicagoan and an active composer, performed one of his creations especially appropriate to the Mississippi River Festival—"City of New Orleans." Goodman's "You Never Even Called Me by My Name" became a country hit in 1975 for David Allen Coe.

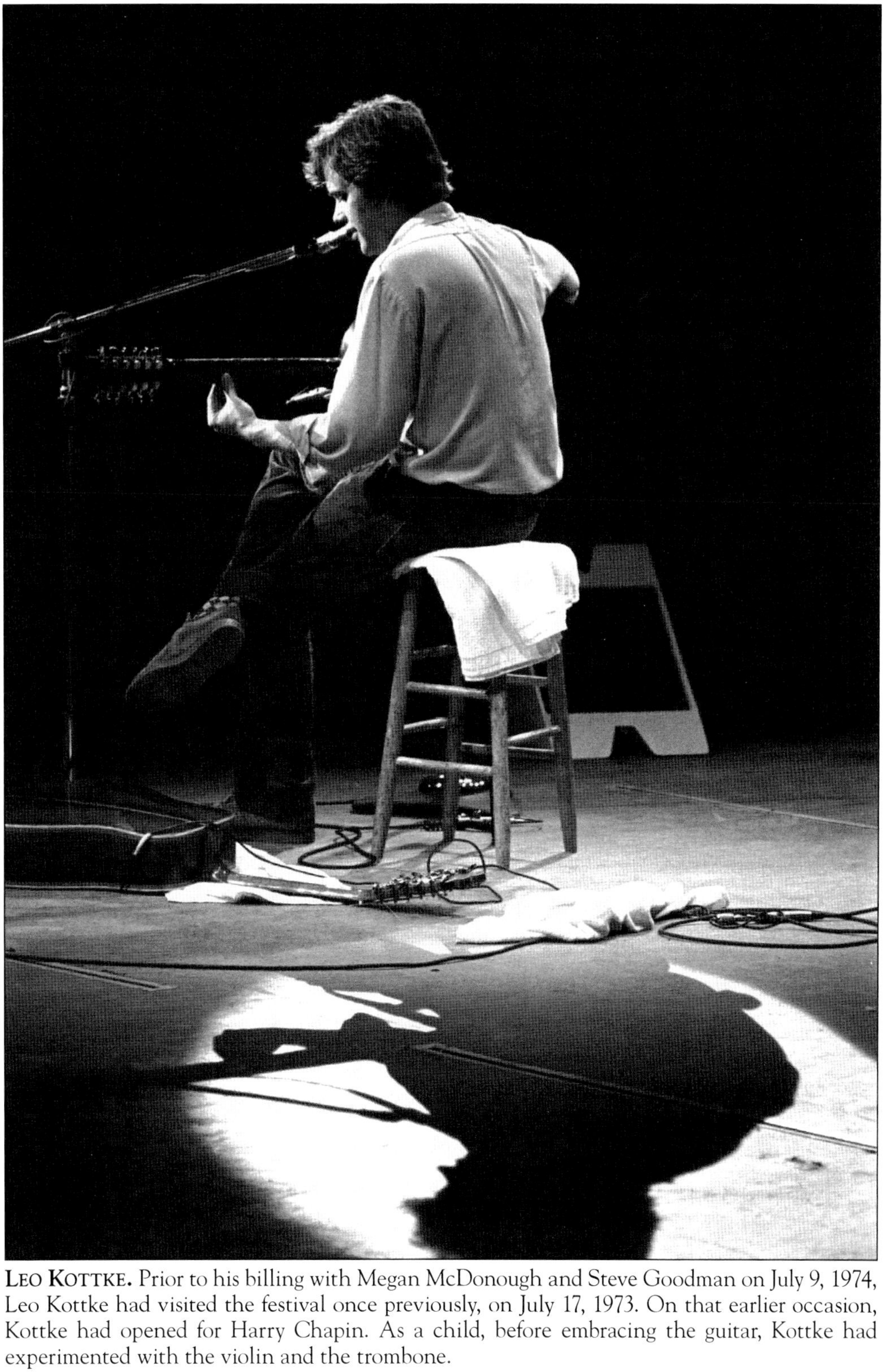

LEO KOTTKE. Prior to his billing with Megan McDonough and Steve Goodman on July 9, 1974, Leo Kottke had visited the festival once previously, on July 17, 1973. On that earlier occasion, Kottke had opened for Harry Chapin. As a child, before embracing the guitar, Kottke had experimented with the violin and the trombone.

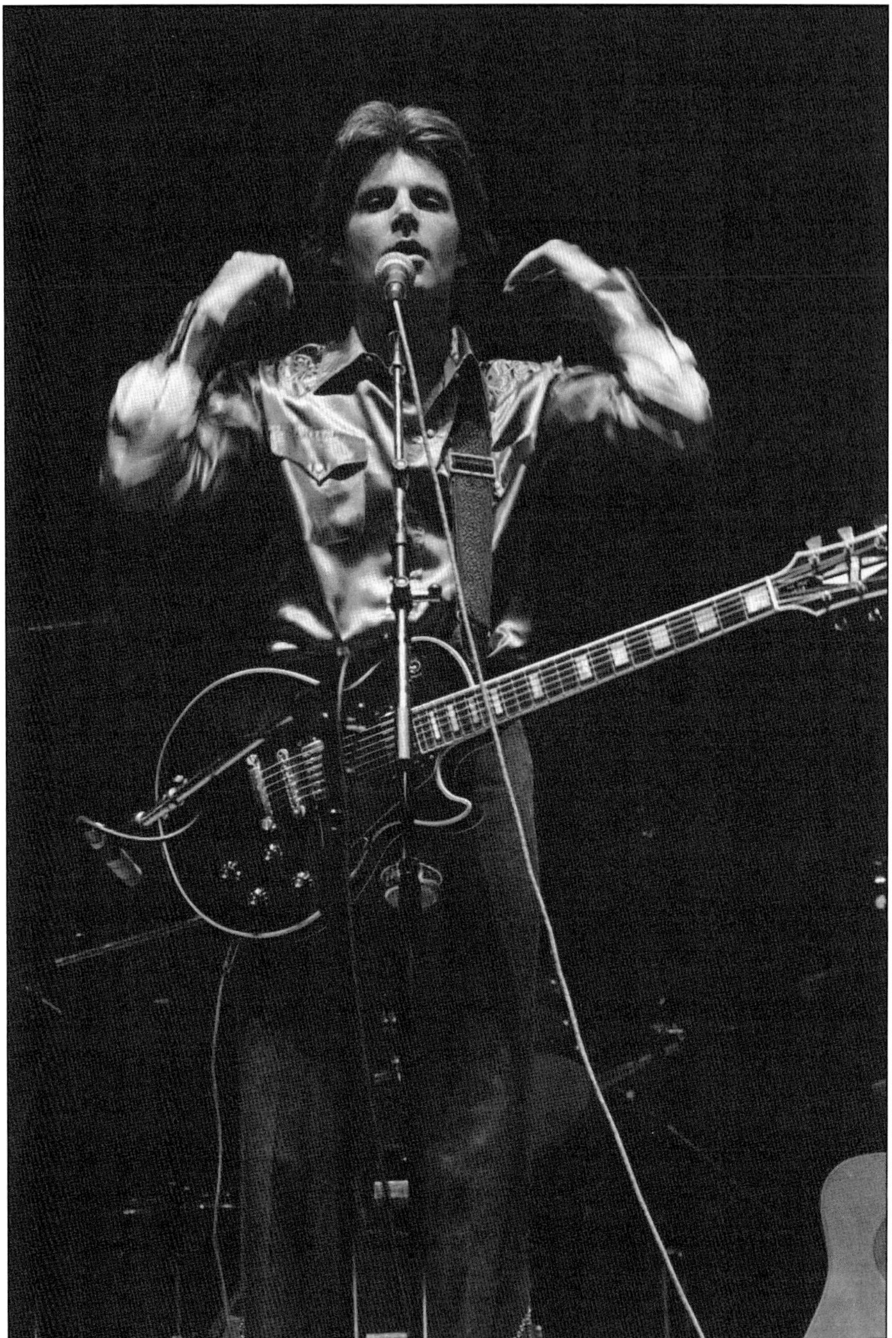

RICK NELSON. A performer who had grown up before the eyes of the nation on television, and achieved tremendous commercial success as a young singer, Rick Nelson faced a difficult challenge as he attempted to mature as an artist. When he came to the festival on July 12, 1974 with his Stone Canyon Band, Nelson sang the song that he had written to capture the essence of his personal struggle, "Garden Party." A power failure that forced the use of an emergency generator led to speaker problems that plagued his show.

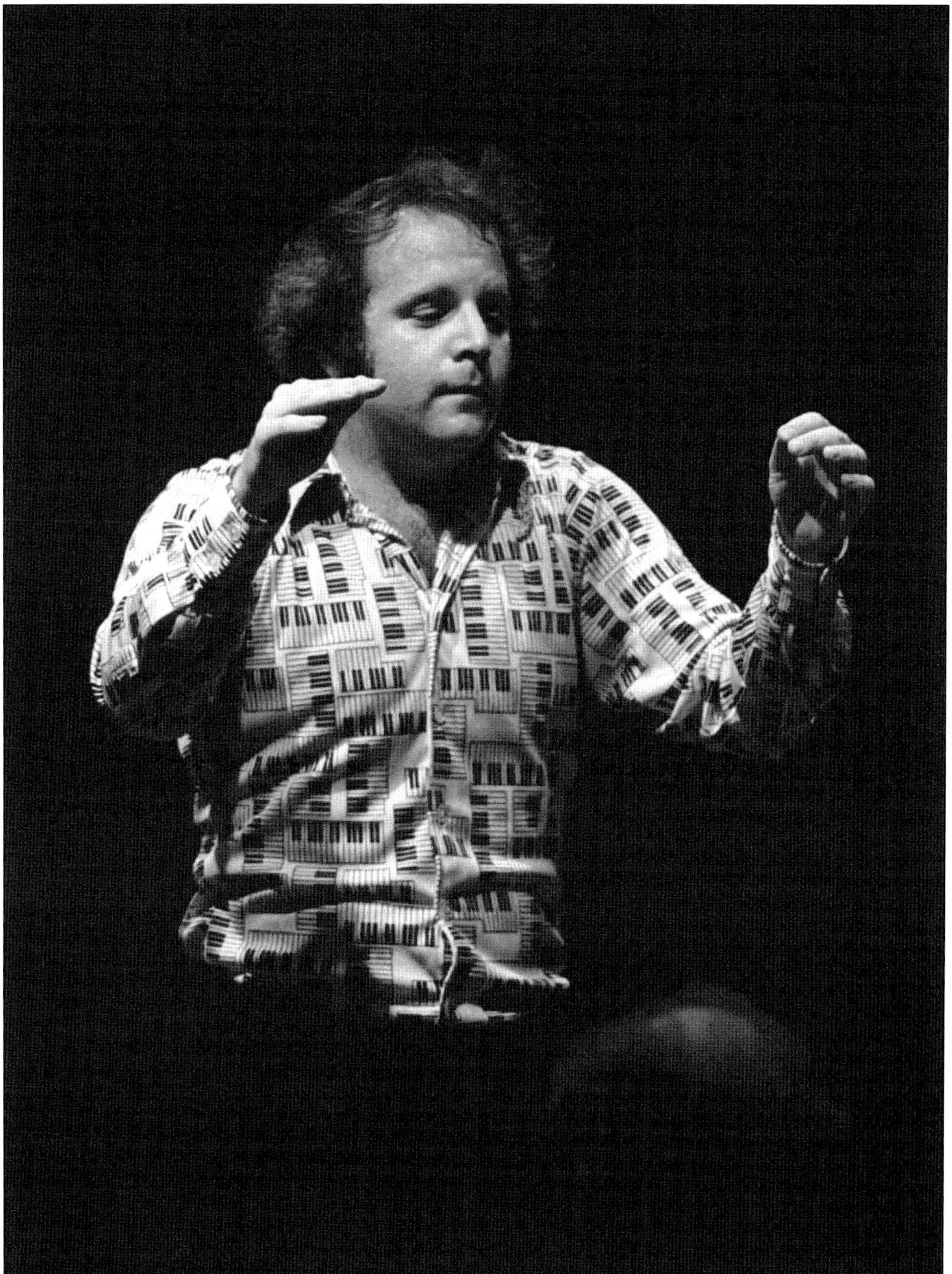

LEONARD SLATKIN. The July 13, 1974, concert by the St. Louis Symphony initiated the orchestra's sixth summer season in Edwardsville. A celebration featuring sky divers, magicians, and animals from the St. Louis Zoo preceded the concert. It began with the "Star-Spangled Banner" and the "Marseillaise" and ended with fireworks. Pianist Arthur Gold and Robert Fizdale appeared with the orchestra as soloists. Leonard Slatkin joined the St. Louis Symphony Orchestra as assistant conductor in 1968.

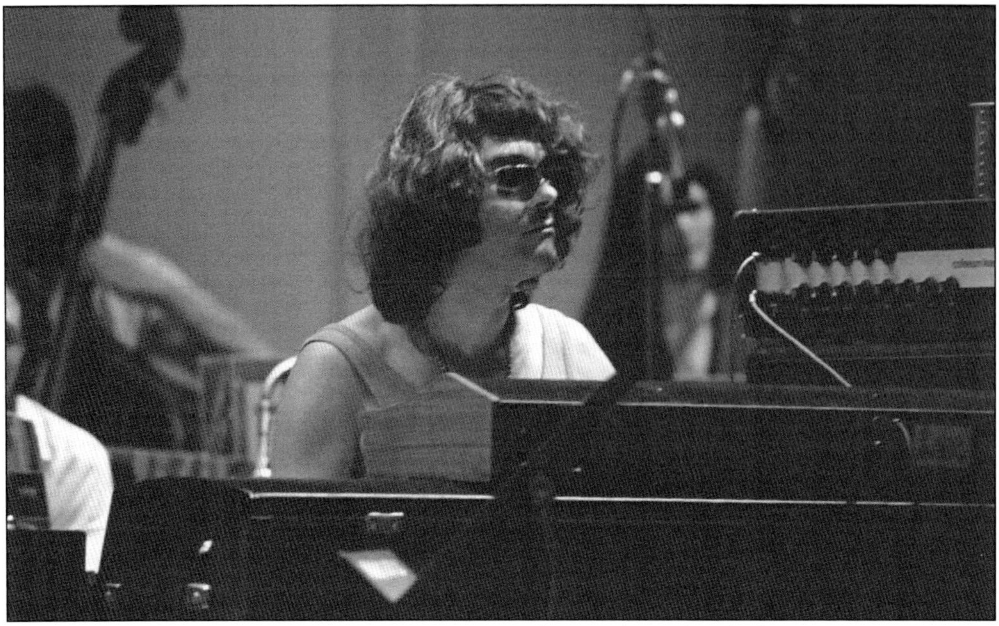

EUMIR DEODATO. The Brazilian native Eumir Deodato performed with the St. Louis Symphony Orchestra and, under the direction of conductor Leonard Slatkin, for the festival concert on July 14, 1974. In the second half of the evening, Deodato played his own arrangement of "Also Sprach Zarathurstra" prepared for the motion picture *2001: A Space Odyssey*. His performance survives in an album titled *Artistry* released by MCA records in 1974.

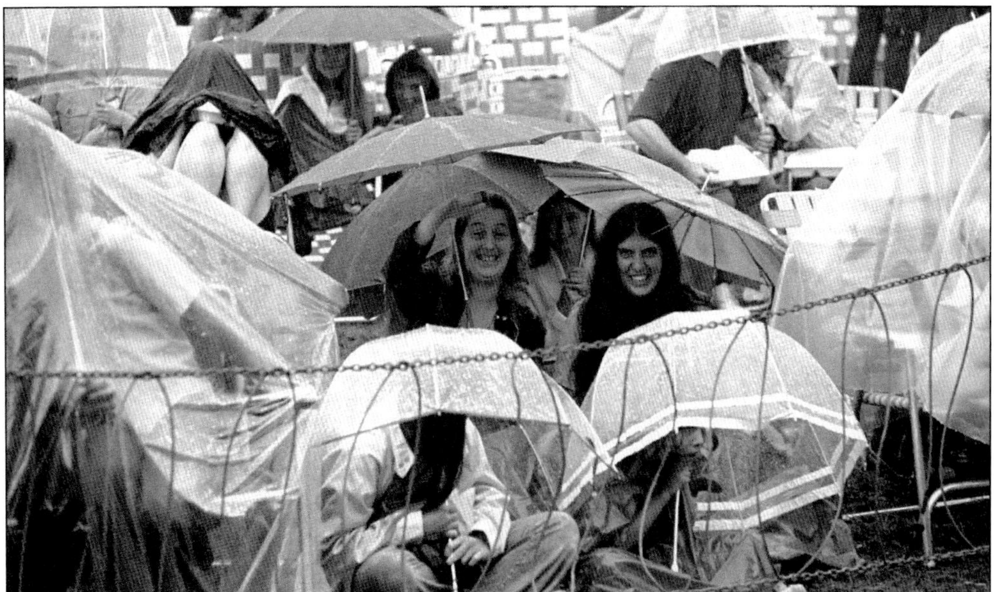

RAIN. Heavy rain fell when Mac Davis made his first of three visits to the festival on August 2, 1974. Davis concluded his performance by singing "I Believe in Magic." As on all such inclement weather occasions, the lawn crowd covered itself with a variety of materials but could do little to cope with the flow of water down the slope during serious downpours. Anne Murray served as the opening act for Davis, accompanied by Dianne Brooks and Laurel War.

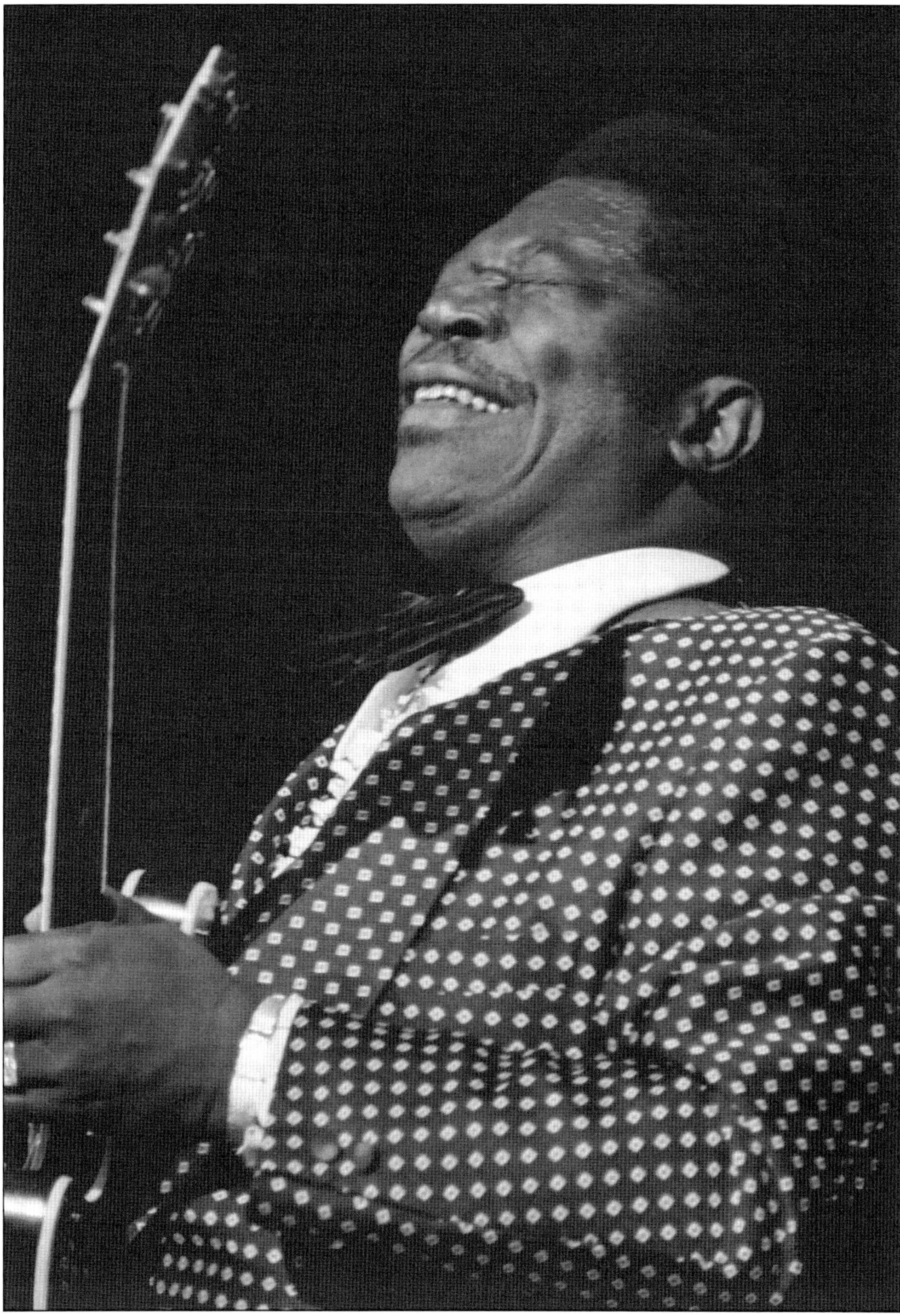

B. B. KING. Blues great B. B. King and his nine-man, tuxedo-clad band graced the festival stage for a second time on July 16, 1974. King's earlier visit to the tent had occurred on August 8, 1972. Fellow blues legend Muddy Waters appeared for the first time as the opening act for King. A seven-piece combo that included two guitars backed Waters.

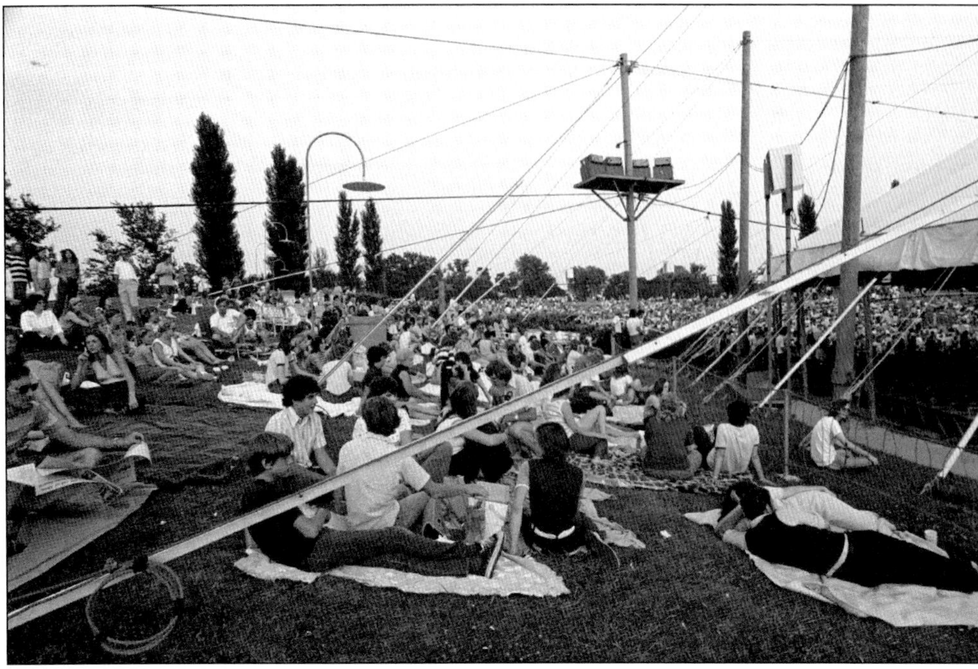

DOWN FRONT. This photograph shows early-arriving members of the lawn crowd seated on their blankets in advantageous positions along the front edge of the MRF tent. In this view it is possible to see the elements of the cable and rope system that sustain the great tent.

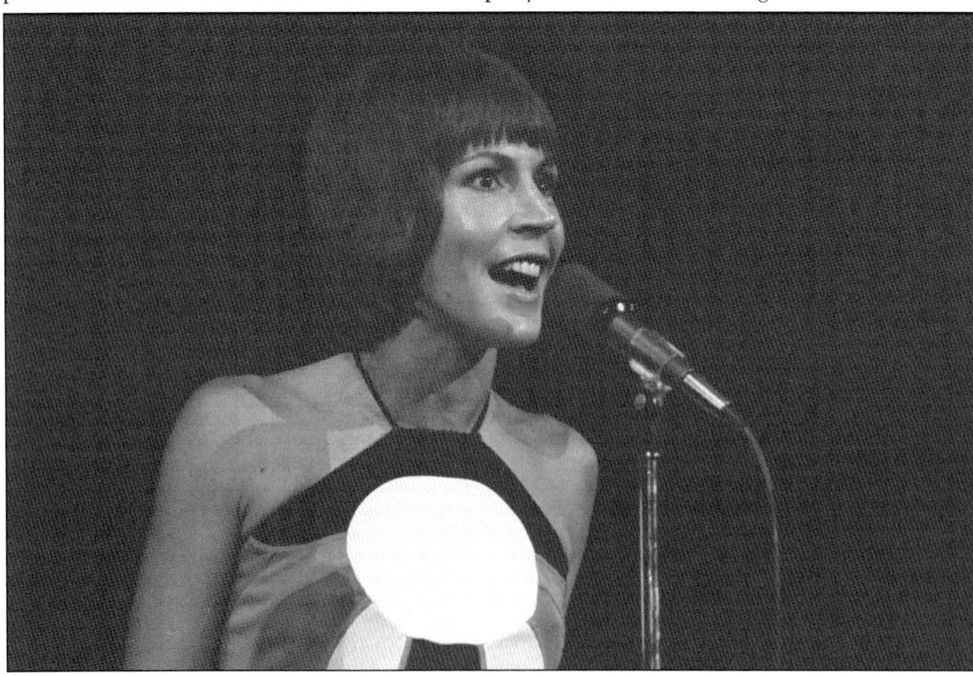

HELEN REDDY. Vocalist Helen Reddy headlined the July 19, 1974, festival program in her only visit to the festival. Reddy performed several of her hits including "Delta Dawn" and the song that had been adopted as a hymn by the movement for equal rights for women, "I Am Woman." Singer/humorist Jim Stafford began the event and greatly pleased the audience in his first festival stint.

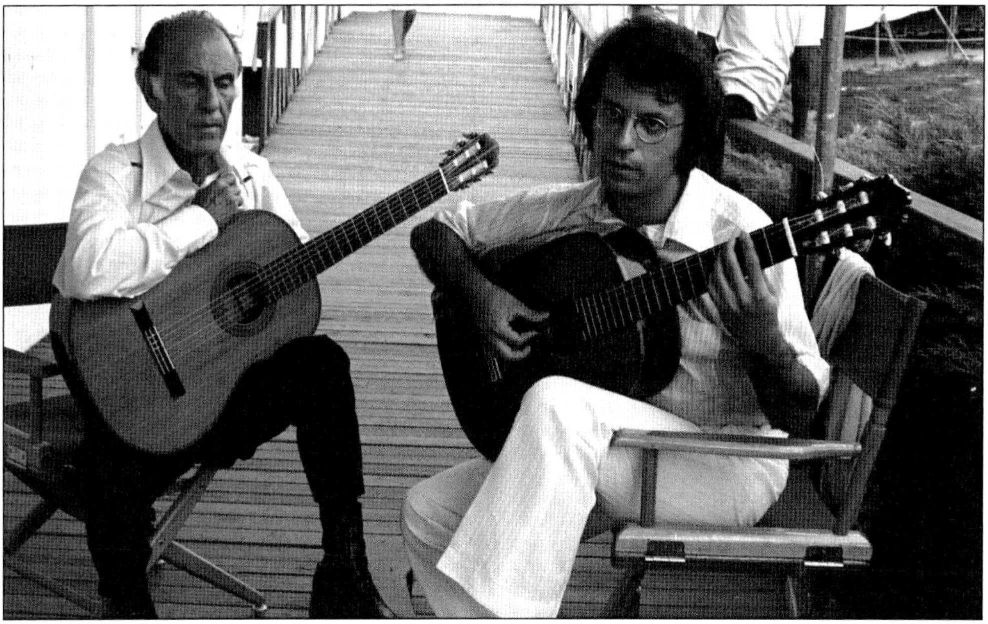

CELEDONIO ROMERO AND SONS. Known as the royal family of the guitar, Celedonio Romero (left) and his sons Celin, Pepe, and Angel appeared with the St. Louis Symphony Orchestra on July 27, 1974. Henry Lewis, music director of the New Jersey Symphony Orchestra, served as guest conductor. The program included the Concierto Andaluz by Joaquin Rodrigo. Angel Romero had performed previously with the symphony on July 17, 1971.

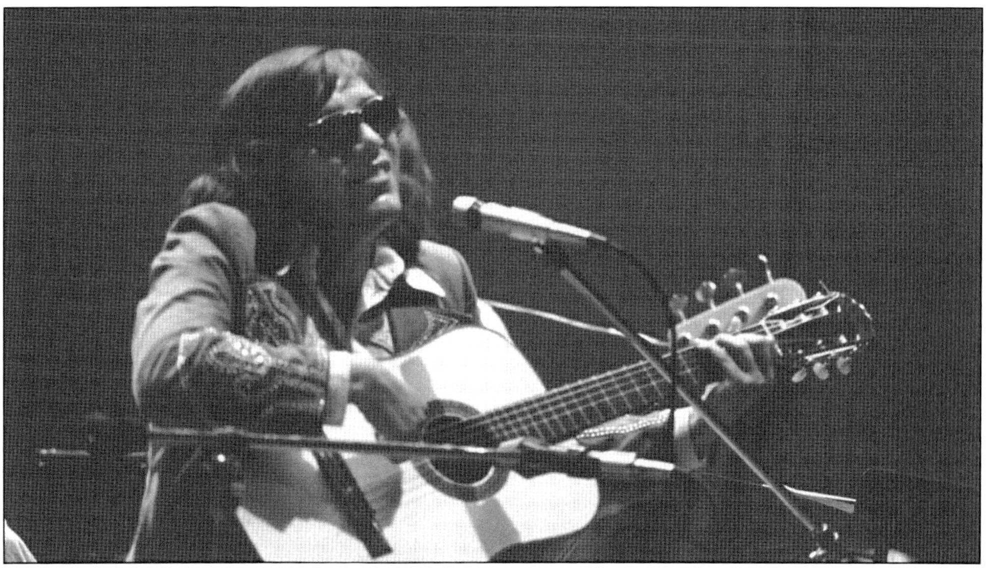

JOSE FELICIANO. Gerhardt Zimmerman conducted the St. Louis Symphony Orchestra on July 28, 1974, when singer/guitarist Jose Feliciano made his second appearance at the festival. Feliciano appeared on the second portion of the program. He encountered problems with his guitar microphone, broke a string, and also experienced some confusion with the orchestra regarding the order of his selections. Toward the end of his show, he introduced a new song intended as the theme for an upcoming television program, "Chico and the Man." Feliciano had visited once before as a single act on August 17, 1973.

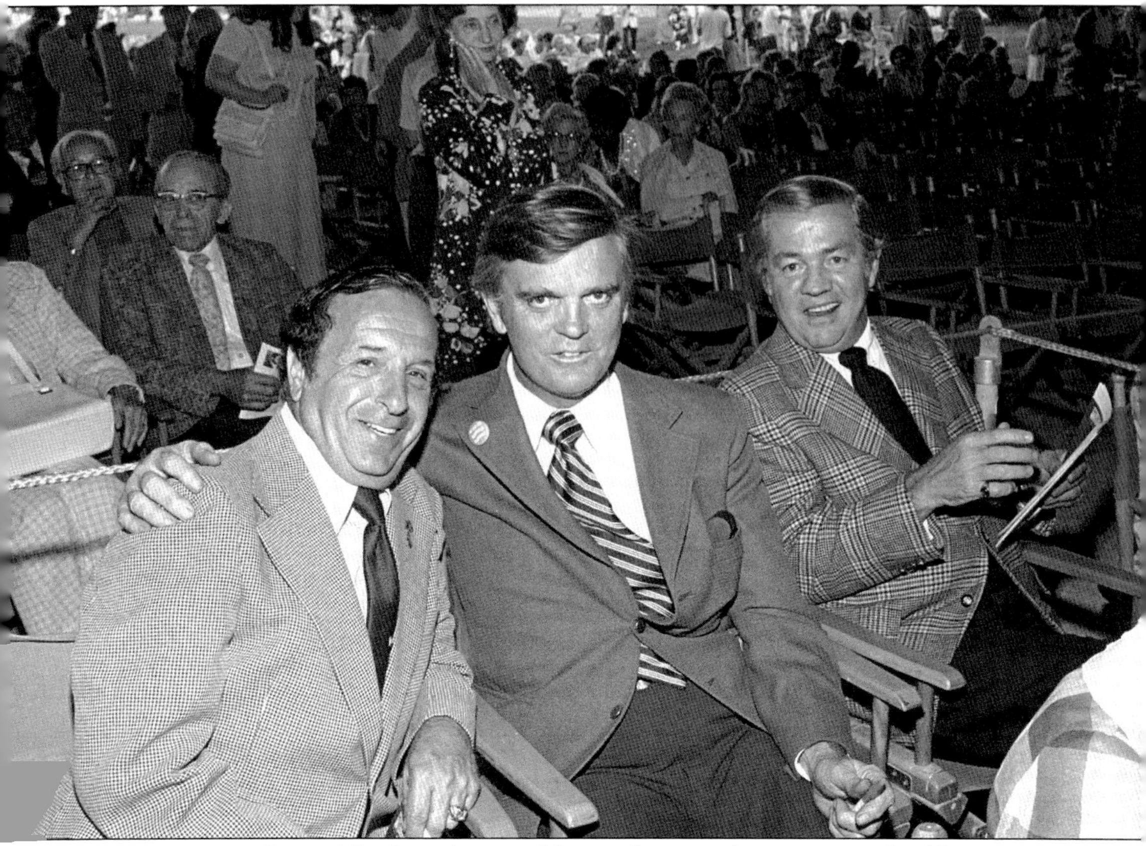

LEGISLATORS NIGHT. The festival received financial support from private and public entities over the years. To inform and thank elected officials about the nature and quality of the entertainment being presented to the community, festival officials invited many guests, including legislators from Illinois and Missouri, to attend special concerts. This photograph portrays SIUE president John Rendleman (right), Illinois governor Dan Walker (center), and Sen. Sam Vadalabene (left) local member of the Illinois state senate on August 4, 1974. Guest conductor Leroy Anderson, one of America's premier instrumental conductors and arrangers, led the St. Louis Symphony Orchestra.

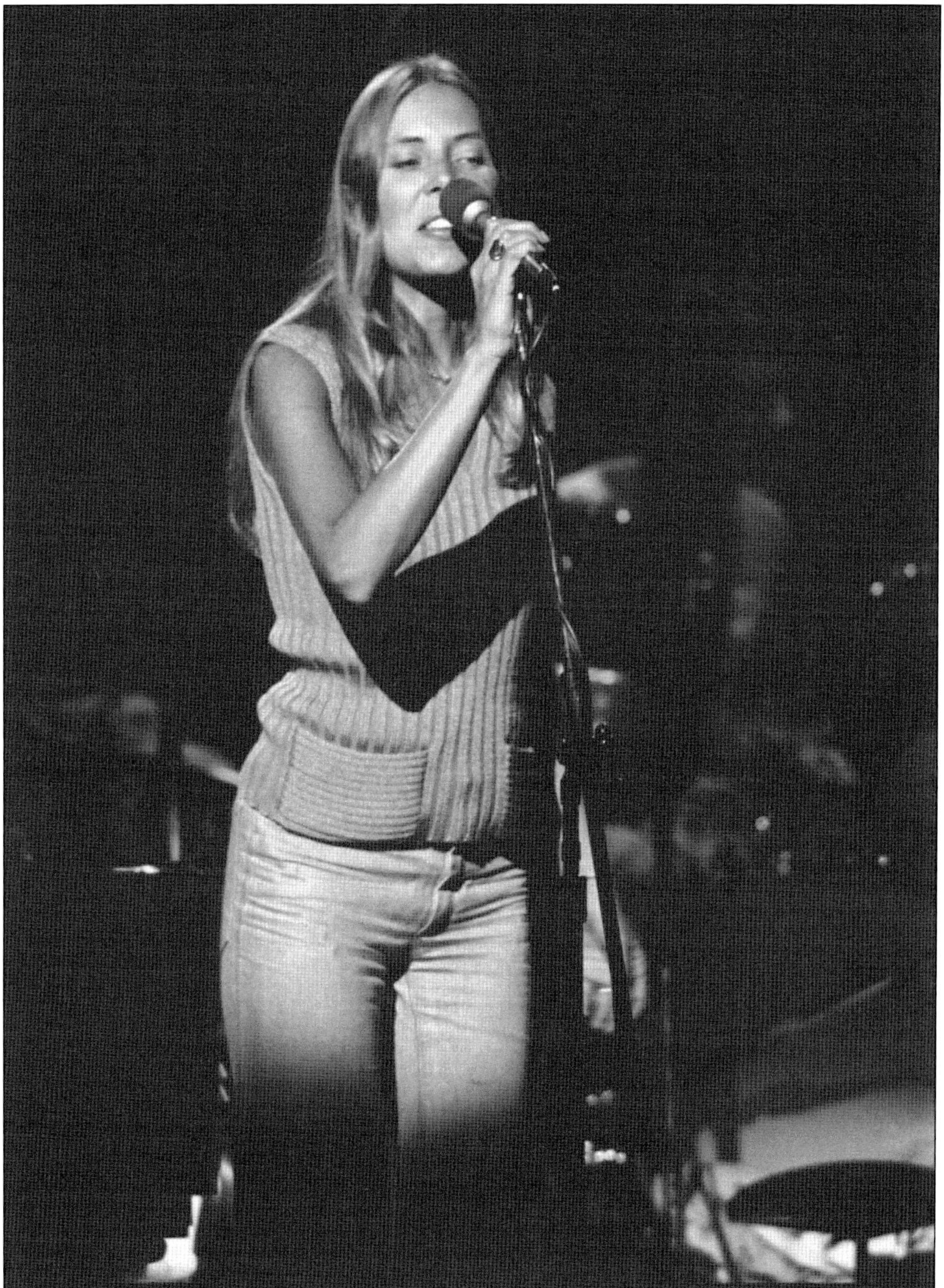

JONI MITCHELL. Due to a power failure and the need to rely on a generator, Joni Mitchell began her August 6, 1974, concert one hour late. Tom Scott and the L. A. Express opened the show and Mitchell joined them during the first set on "Free Man in Paris." Mitchell then appeared throughout the second set following intermission. Tom Scott, Robben Ford, Larry Nash, John Guerin, and Max Bennett made up L. A. Express. Mitchell had first appeared with Arlo Guthrie on July 7, 1969, and later returned on August 9, 1979.

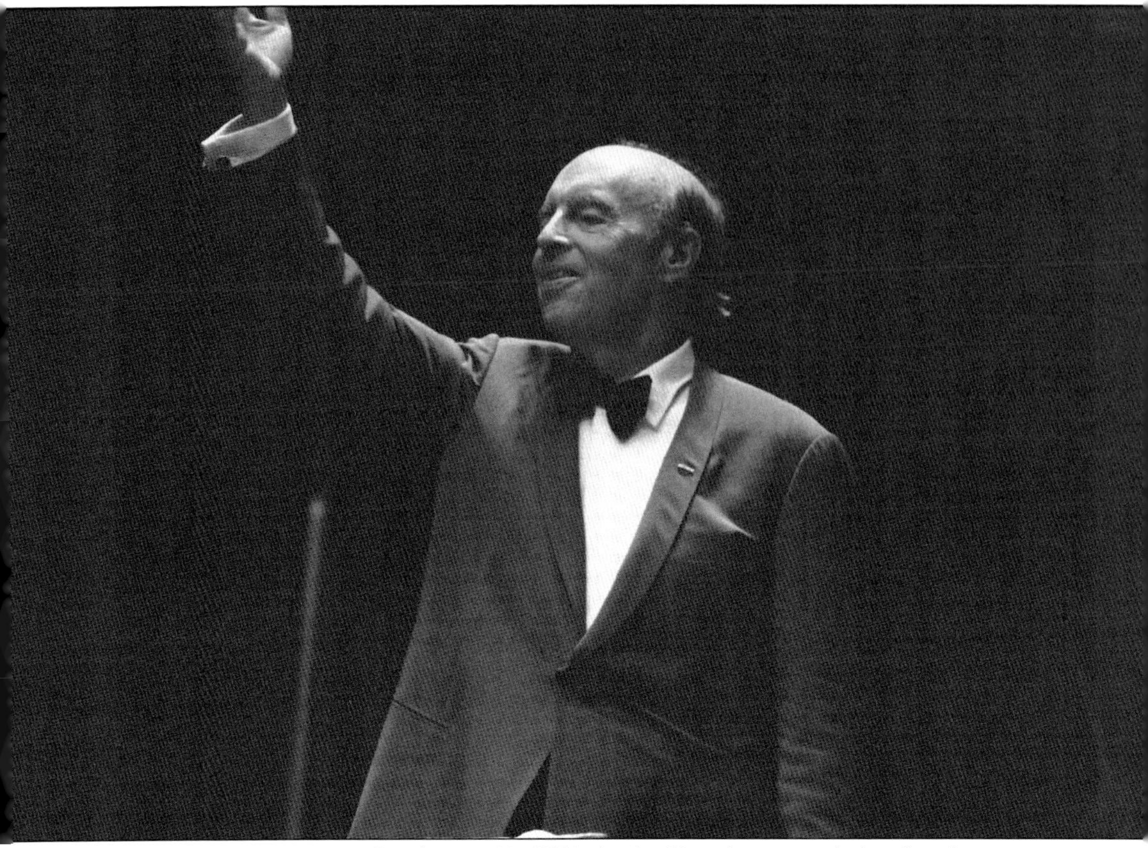

ANDRE KOSTELANETZ. On August 11, 1974, Andre Kostelanetz made his fourth consecutive annual appearance under the tent. He had conducted the St. Louis Symphony Orchestra three times previously, on August 15, 1971; August 13, 1972; and July 29, 1973. Kostelanetz and the symphony performed Debussy's *Claire de Lune* and a short piece by Khachaturian as encores.

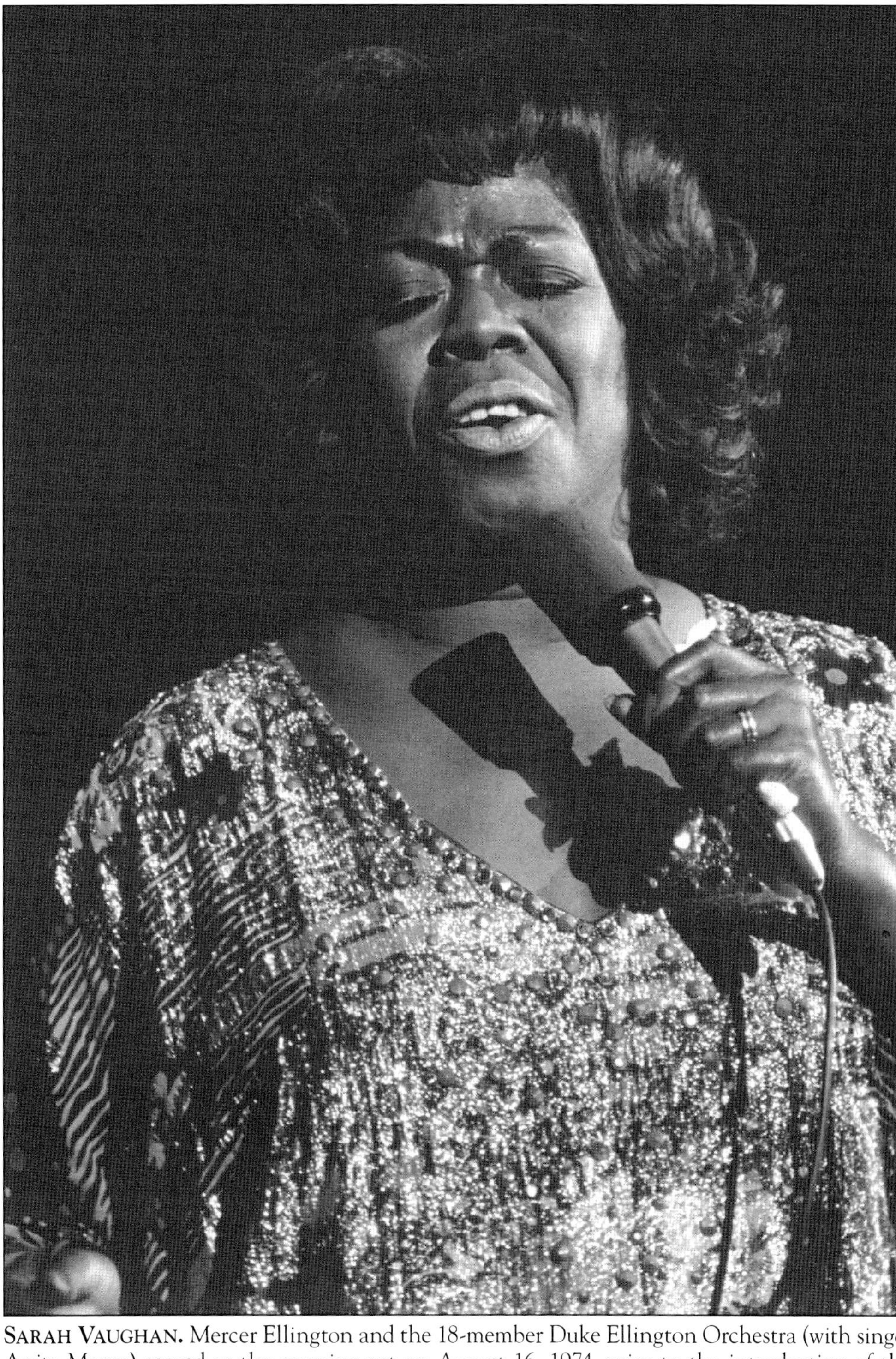

SARAH VAUGHAN. Mercer Ellington and the 18-member Duke Ellington Orchestra (with singer Anita Moore) served as the opening act on August 16, 1974, prior to the introduction of the evening's headliner, Sarah Vaughan. The concert continued for nearly three hours. In tribute to Duke Ellington, Vaughan sang two encores: "Take the A Train" and "Satin Doll."

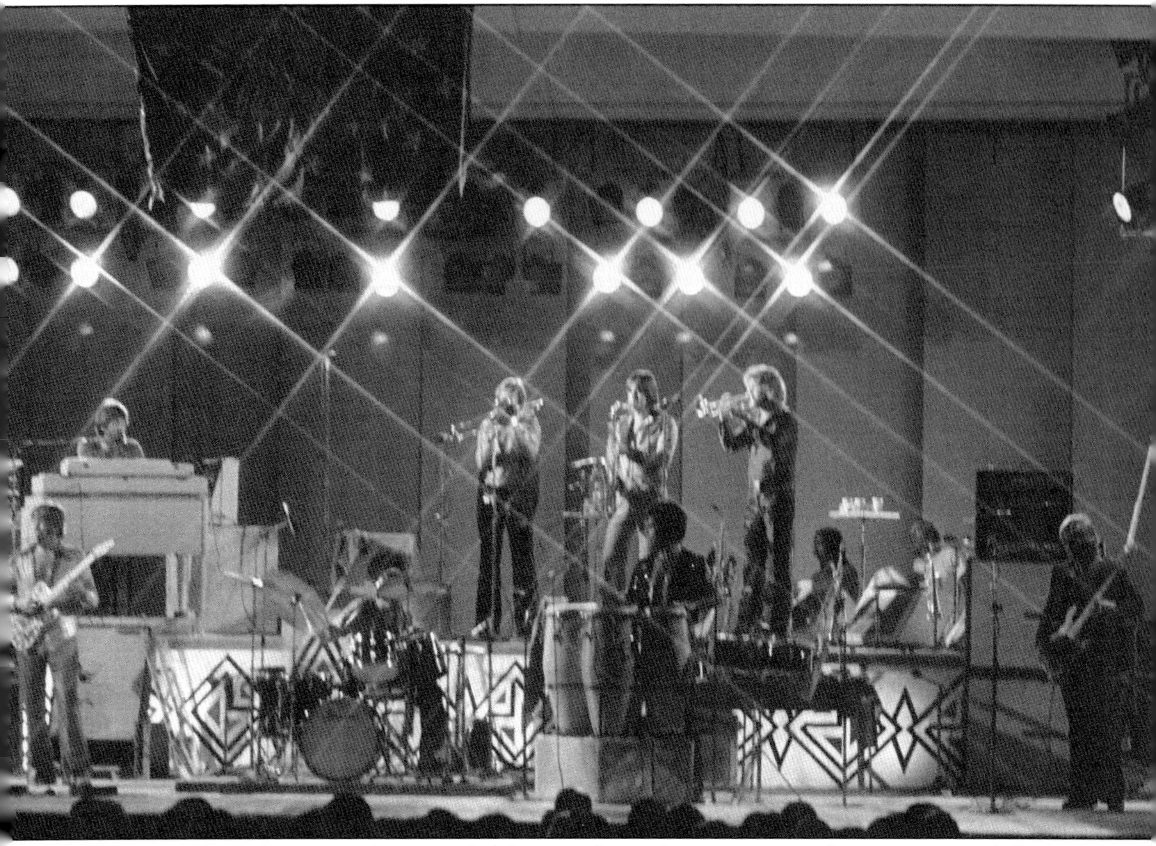

THIRD TIME AROUND. As part of elaborate physical preparations, the crew covered the stage floor with white carpeting prior to the August 21, 1974, concert by Chicago. Robert Lamm, Peter Cetera, Daniel Seraphine, Terry Kath, James Pankow, Lee Loughnane, and Walter Parazaider all performed at this engagement. At the conclusion of the concert, James Pankow told the crowd: "Thank you. See you next year."

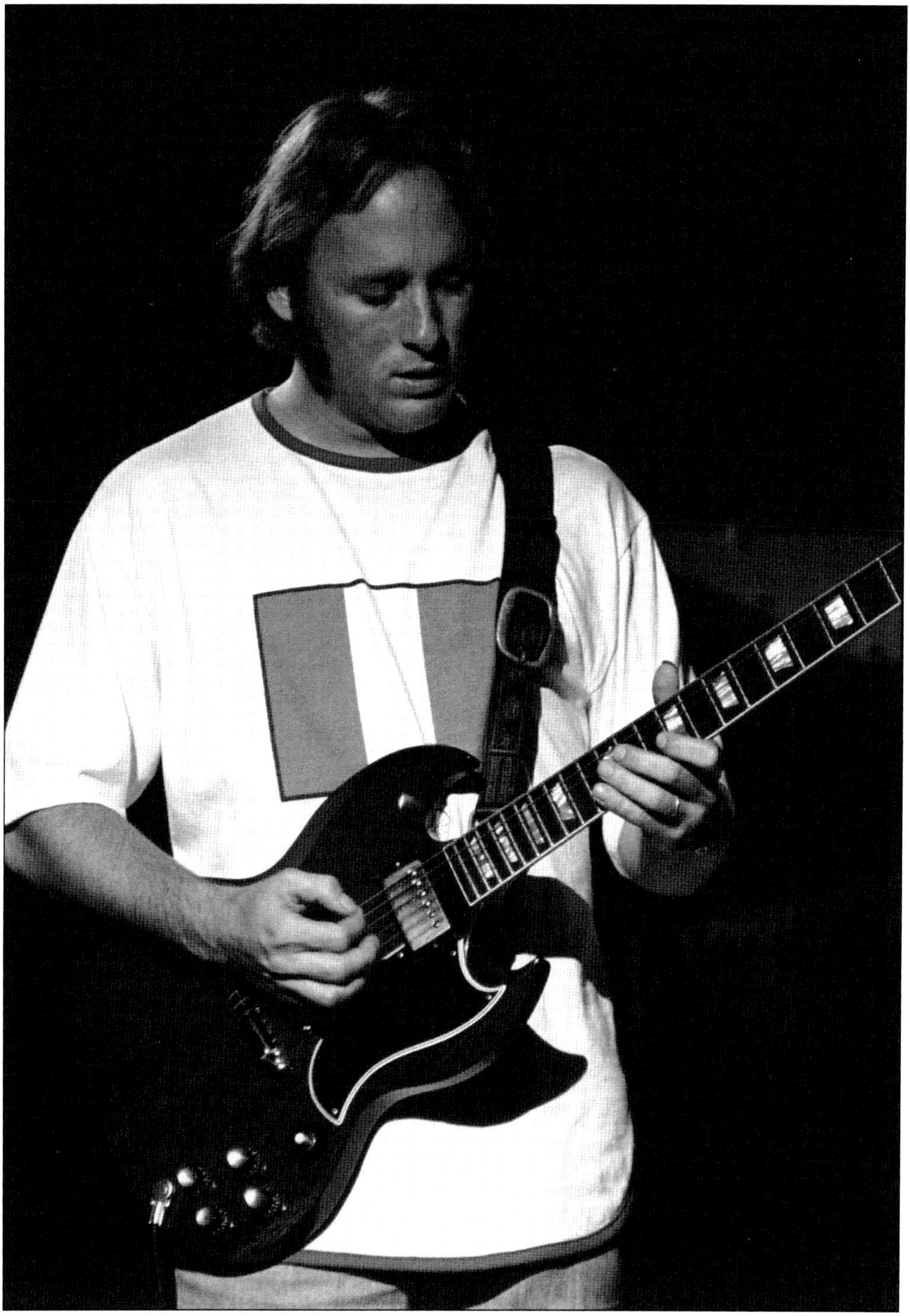

STEPHEN STILLS. The opening concert of the festival's 1975 season (on July 1) featured Stephen Stills, who chose to begin his show by performing "Love the One You're With." Stills had come to Edwardsville once before, on August 1, 1973 (with Joe Walsh as opening act), and subsequently returned once more, on June 19, 1979 (without an opening act).

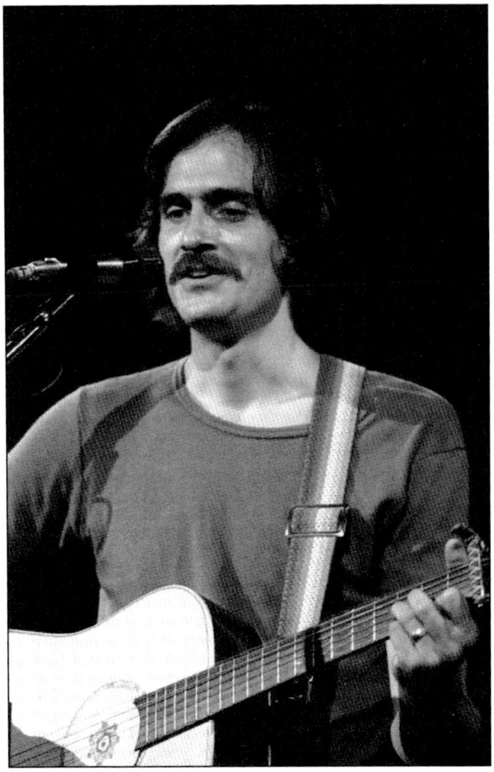

JAMES TAYLOR. In retrospect, it seems slightly surprising that James Taylor did not grace the festival stage prior to the concert of July 3, 1975. On that date, Taylor appeared with sidemen Russ Kunkel, Danny Kortchmar, Clarence McDonald, and Leland Sklar. His ensemble performed two sets covering more than two hours in total. Taylor later returned to the MRF on July 4 and 5, 1979.

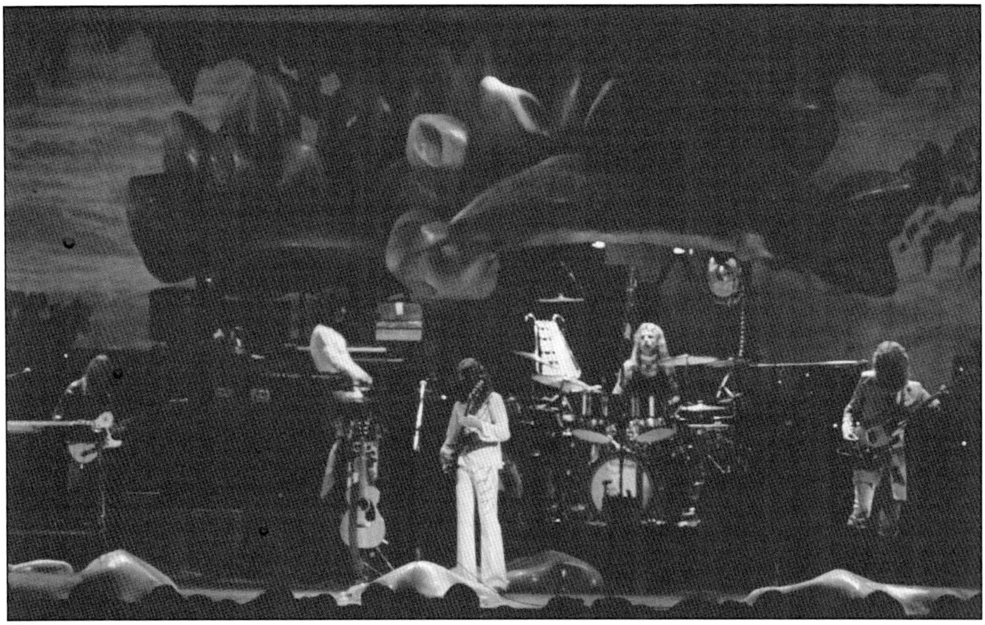

YES, MORE PLEASE. On July 9, 1975, in their second appearance, Yes attracted 25,574 paid customers to the MRF, the fourth-largest audience to attend a concert up until that time. Jon Anderson, Alan White, Patrick Moraz, Steve Howe, and Chris Squire came on stage following an opening act called Ace. Yes performed in front of a huge backdrop and consumed 200 pounds of dry ice for visual effects.

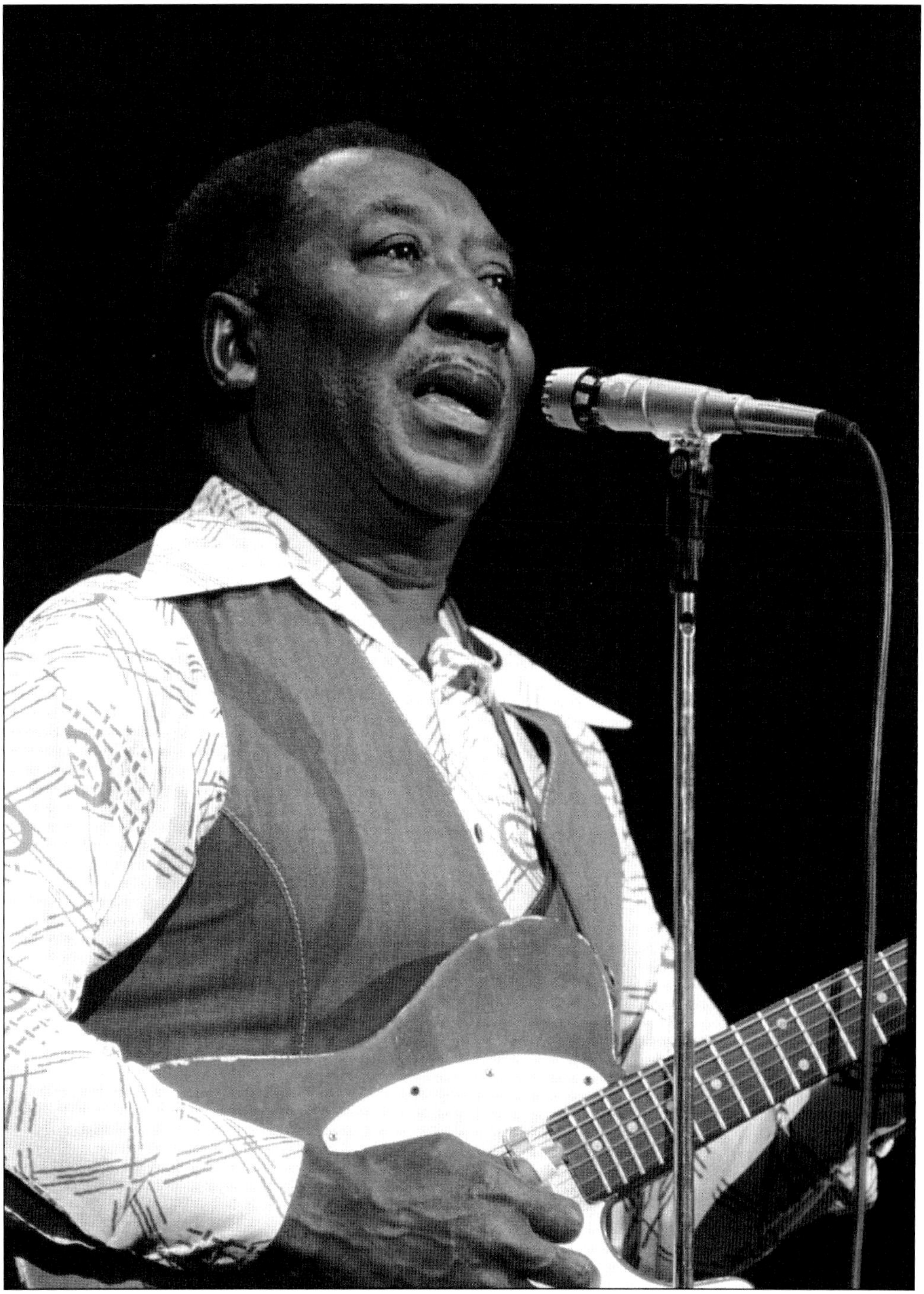

MUDDY WATERS. Blues singer/guitarist Muddy Waters headlined the festival on July 15, 1975, backed by a five-man supporting cast. Luthor Allison performed as the opening act and delivered a tribute to the career of Chuck Berry. Waters had first appeared at the MRF during the previous season, when he opened for B. B. King on July 16, 1974. Born in Mississippi, Waters achieved fame on the Chicago blues scene.

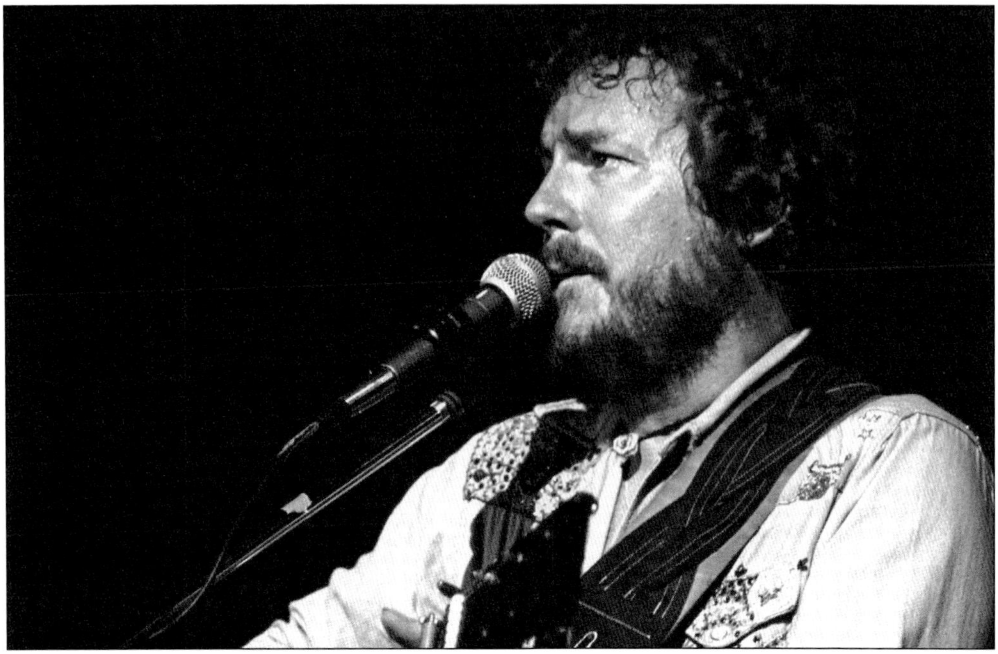

GORDON LIGHTFOOT. Canadian folksinger Gordon Lightfoot came to the festival for the first time on July 16, 1975. He appeared on a bare stage with four backup musicians, playing the guitar and also the piano. Lightfoot included an imitation of Liberace in his performance and also dedicated one number to his daughter. He ended the concert by singing "Cotton Jenny."

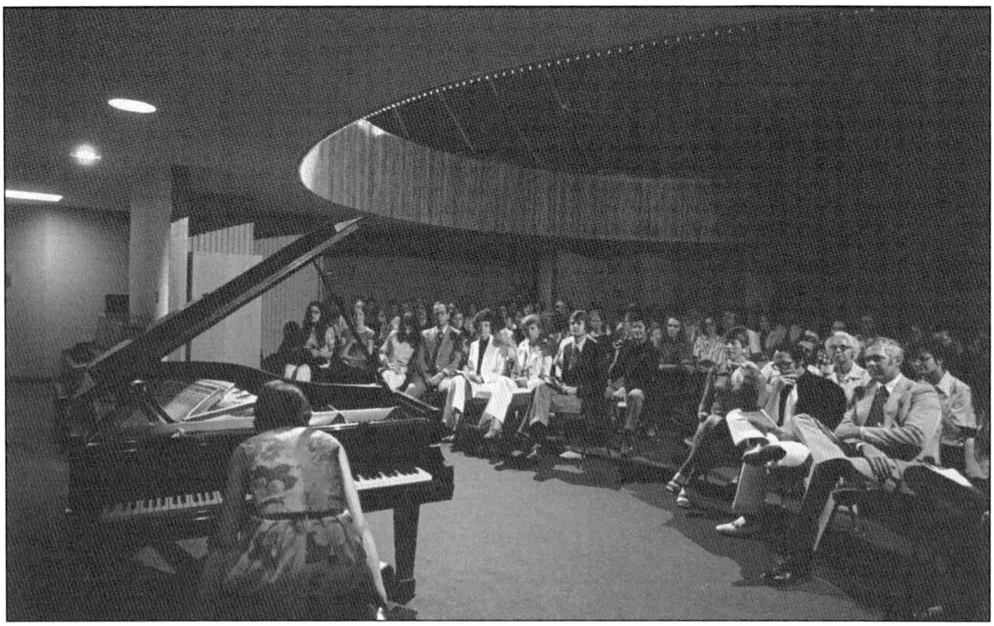

CHAMBER MUSIC. From 1974 through 1977, SIUE faculty members and St. Louis Symphony Orchestra members presented a mini-series of 12 chamber music concerts. In this photograph, taken July 17, 1975, the musicians performed in the SIUE Religious Center, under the geodesic dome designed by Buckminster Fuller. Baritone Dale Moore and pianist Marion Lampe performed as soloists during an all-Beethoven program.

JUDY COLLINS. In her fourth of five visits to Edwardsville, on July 22, 1975, Judy Collins once more delighted her audience. During the first half of her concert, Collins performed with accompaniment on piano, bass, guitar, drums, and harp. For the second half of the evening, Collins took the stage alone and sang while playing her own guitar. For her encore she performed "Amazing Grace."

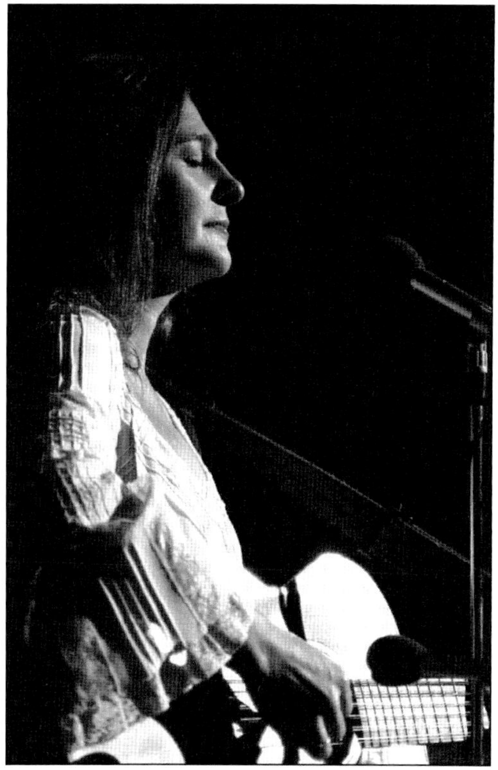

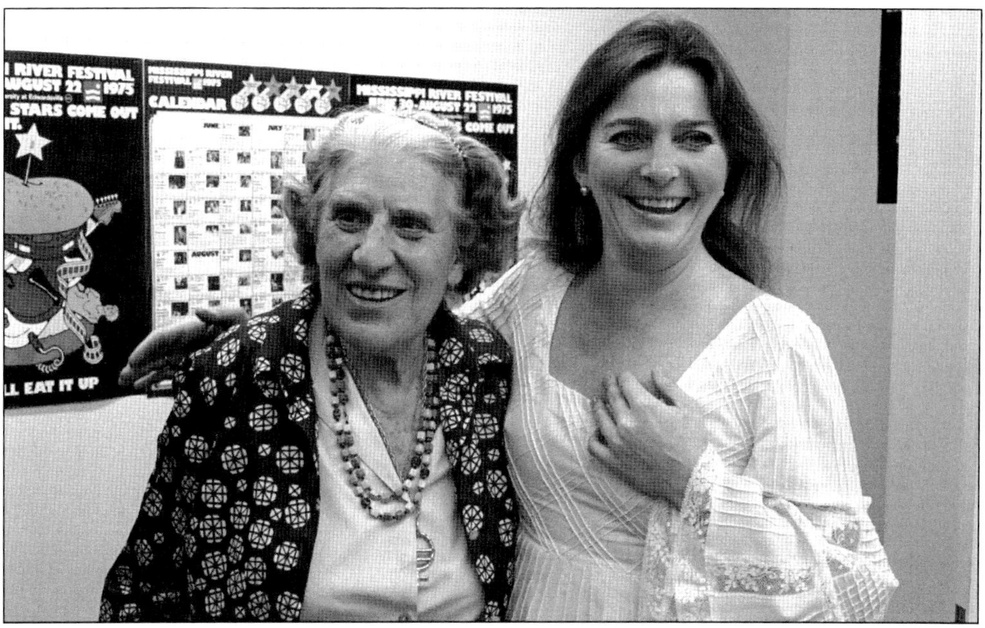

ANTONIA BRICO AND JUDY COLLINS. Antonia Brico, a pioneer female conductor, had given piano instruction to young Judy Collins during the latter's childhood. In 1974, Collins collaborated as the director of a motion picture documentary about the musical career of Antonia Brico. The film had been shown at SIUE on the day before the concert and Brico stayed over in Edwardsville to visit with Collins after her concert on July 22, 1975.

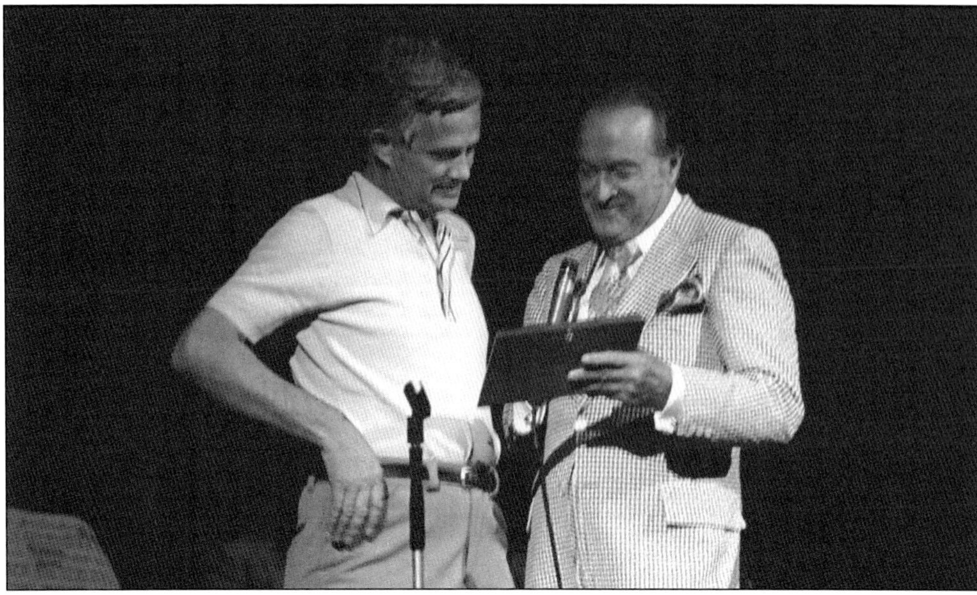

BOB HOPE AND DOLORES HOPE. The festival celebrated a major milestone on July 25, 1975, when John Hugger (left), an insurance salesman from Cahokia, found himself honored as the one-millionth person to attend the MRF. Hugger received an escort onstage to meet the night's featured entertainer, Bob Hope (right), and received a plaque and a free season's pass. The Mercer Ellington orchestra shared the bill with Bob Hope that night, as did his wife Dolores who serenaded the audience with "On a Clear Day."

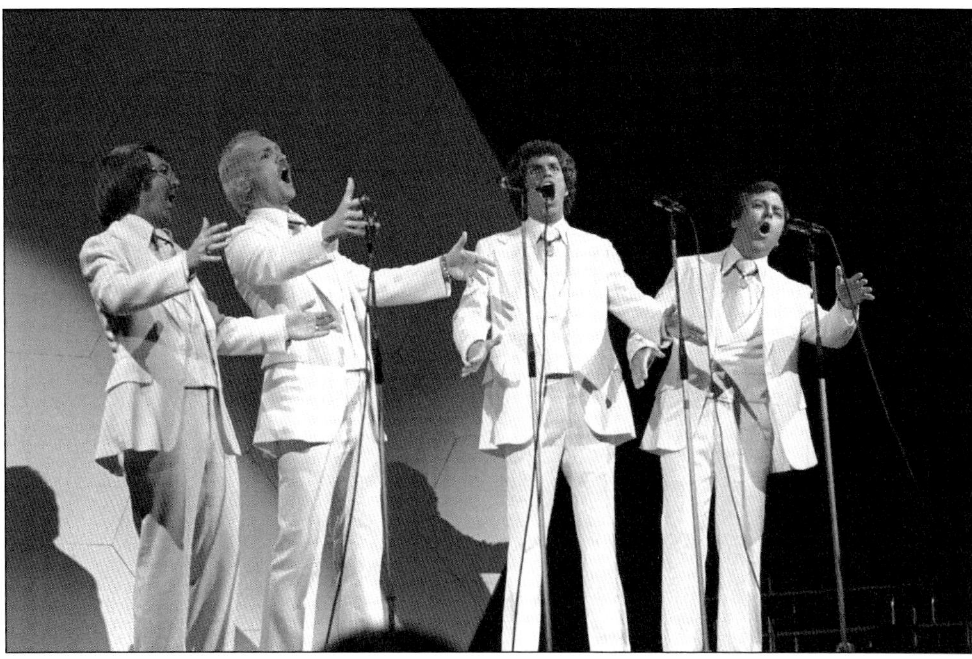

BARBERSHOP MUSIC. In an effort to appeal to diverse audience preferences, the festival included barbershop music on two occasions. On July 26, 1975, as seen here, four barbershop acts entertained: the Chordbusters Chorus, Bron's Tones, Dealer's Choice, and O.K. 4. The other barbershop concert took place on July 23, 1977, and featured three different acts.

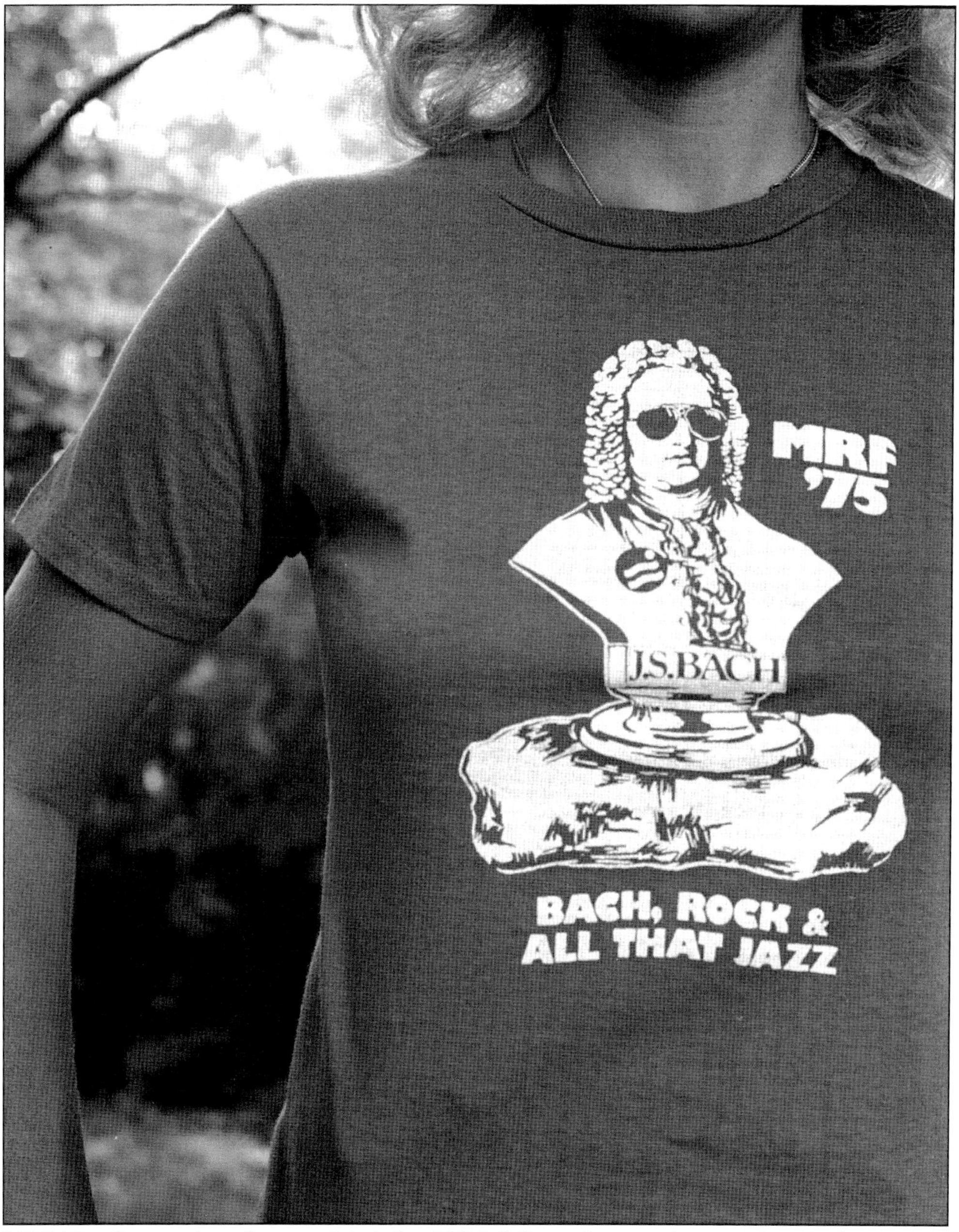

MRF TEE SHIRT. A student modeled the 1975 MRF tee shirt on the eve of an Eagles concert scheduled for July 29, 1975. On that evening, the Eagles (Don Henley, Glenn Frey, Randy Meisner, Bernie Leadon, and Don Felder) attracted the second-largest paid attendance in the history of the festival at 29,491 fans. John David Souther performed as the opening act. The Eagles also appeared at the MRF on July 17, 1974, and August 17, 1978.

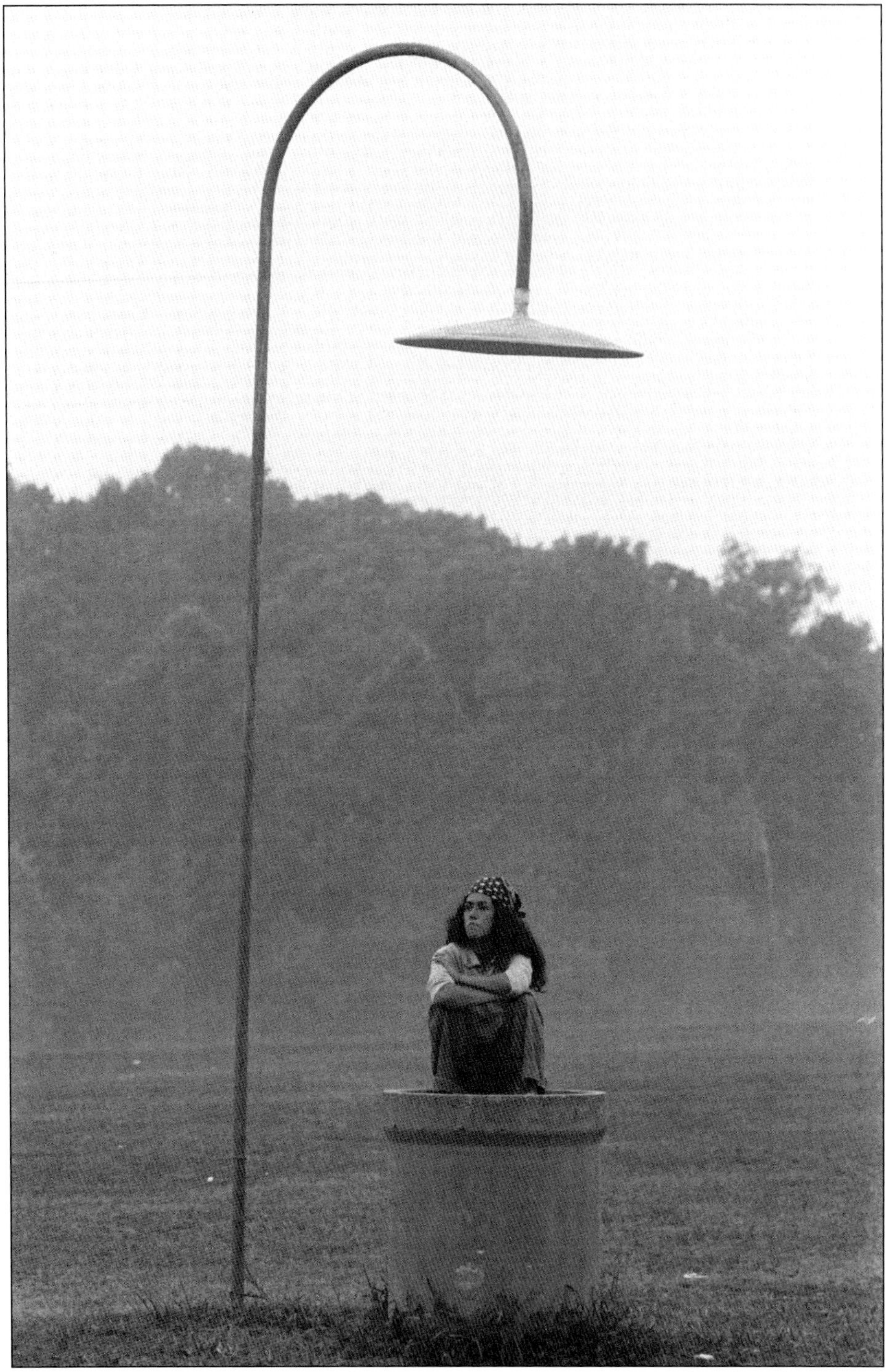

SOLITUDE. Although this photograph of a young woman waiting for her friends conveys an emotion of solitude, the 1975 season actually witnessed five of the largest paid crowds ever to visit the festival. The concerts that drew such substantial audiences included the Eagles (29,491), Yes (25,574), Dave Mason (20,917), Jefferson Starship (18,613), and REO Speedwagon (15,577).

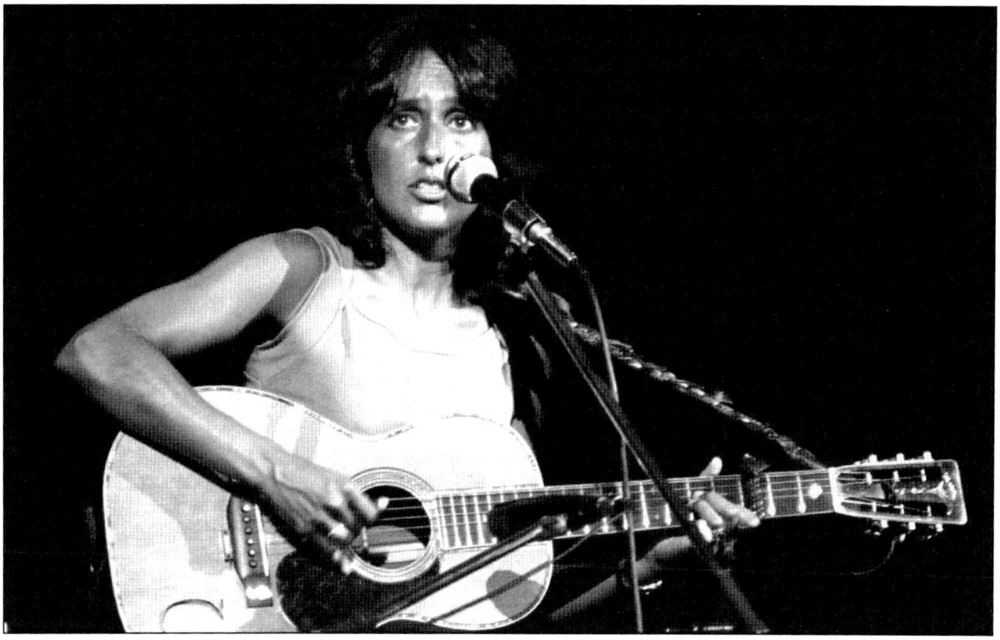

JOAN BAEZ. During her second performance at the festival, on July 30, 1975, Joan Baez included Dan Ferguson (guitar), Jim Gordon (drums), James Jamison (bass), and David Weeks (piano) in her backup group. Baez performed two sets (the first alone) and introduced songs from her new May 1975 album, *Diamonds and Rust*, during the second set. Hoyt Axton, and members of his family, served as the opening act for Baez.

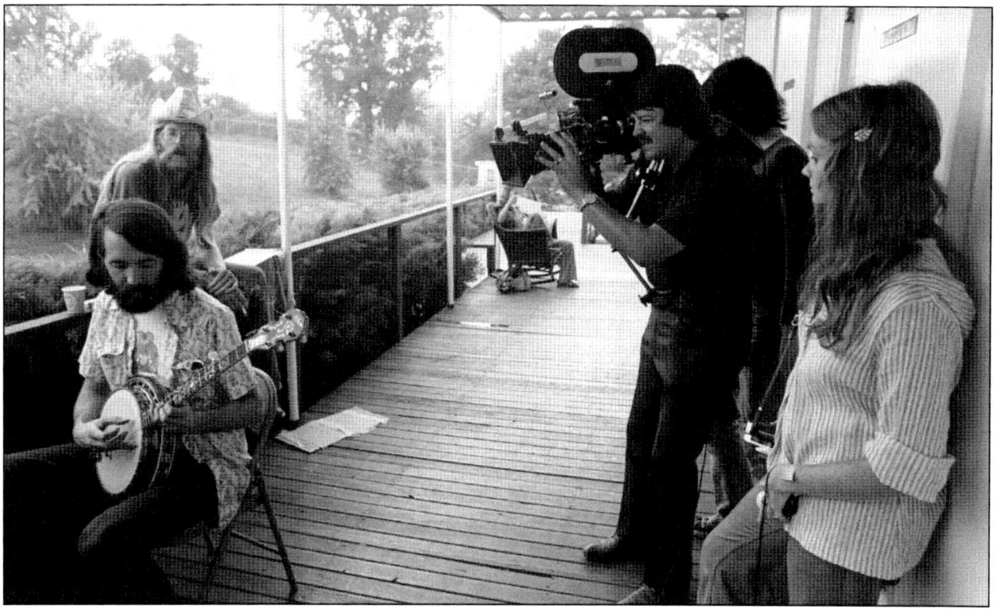

JOHN MCEUEN. The Nitty Gritty Dirt Band made its first of two visits on August 2, 1975, as the headline act following John Hartford's opening appearance. Prior to the scheduled entertainment, John McEuen kindly entertained the MRF crew with an impromptu session on the walkway behind the tent. By the end of the evening, the Nitty Gritty Dirt Band had their fans dancing in the aisles and they received standing ovations after each of their four encores.

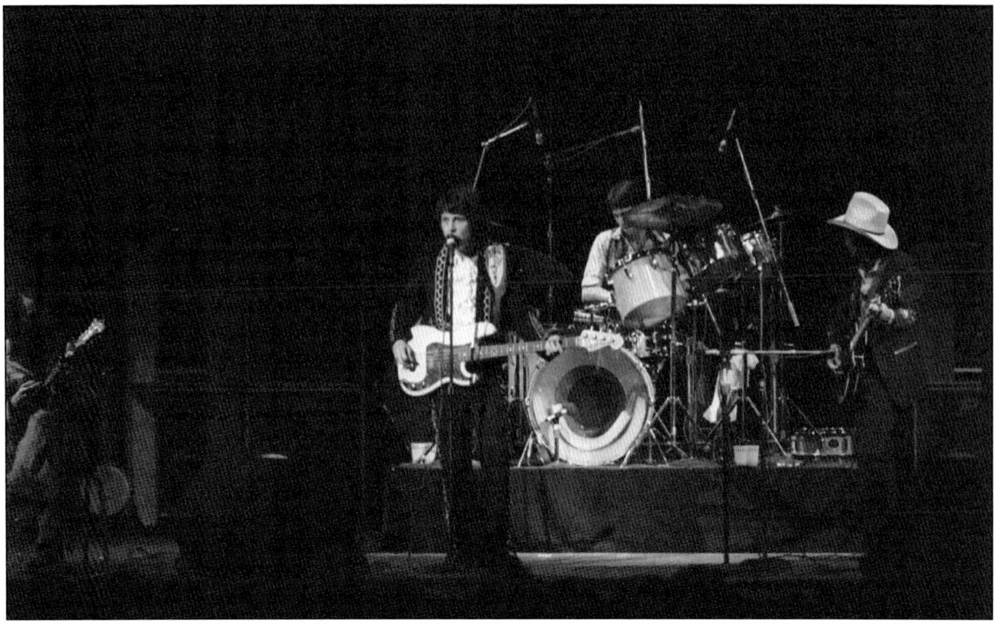

NITTY GRITTY DIRT BAND. The Nitty Gritty Dirt Band performed several of their favorite songs including: "Cosmic Cowboy," "Battle of New Orleans," "Teardrops in My Eyes," "Orange Blossum Special," "Mr. Bojangles," and "Will the Circle Be Unbroken." Formed in Long Beach, California, around 1965, the Nitty Gritty Dirt Band played a significant role in the transformation from folk-rock to country-rock.

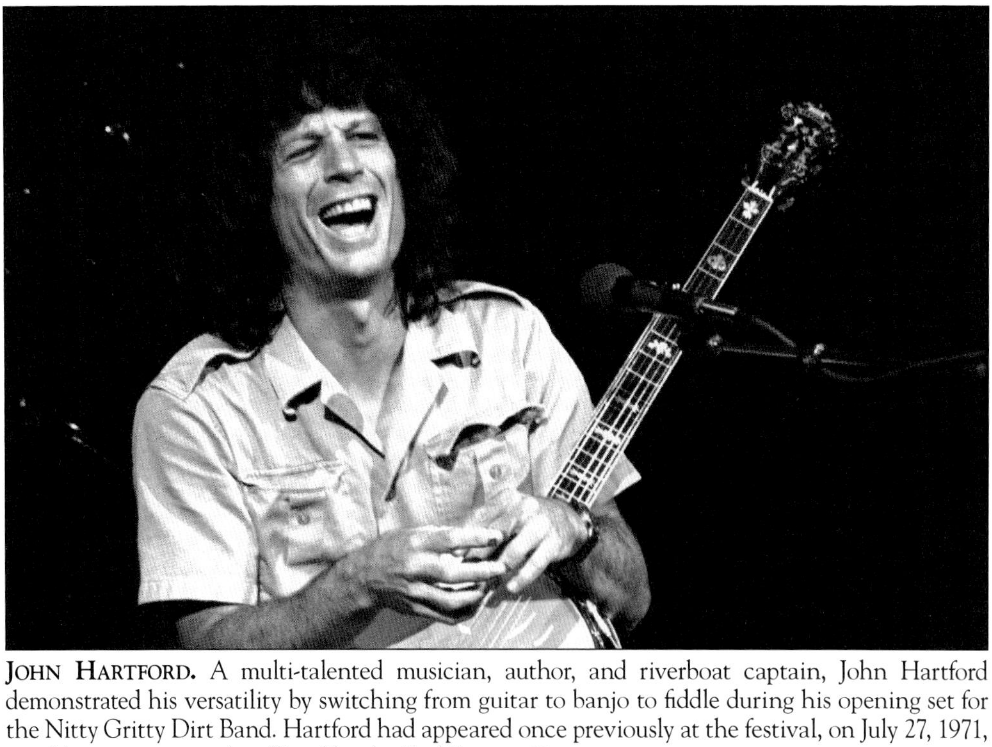

JOHN HARTFORD. A multi-talented musician, author, and riverboat captain, John Hartford demonstrated his versatility by switching from guitar to banjo to fiddle during his opening set for the Nitty Gritty Dirt Band. Hartford had appeared once previously at the festival, on July 27, 1971, in a bluegrass concert headlined by the Earl Scruggs Revue.

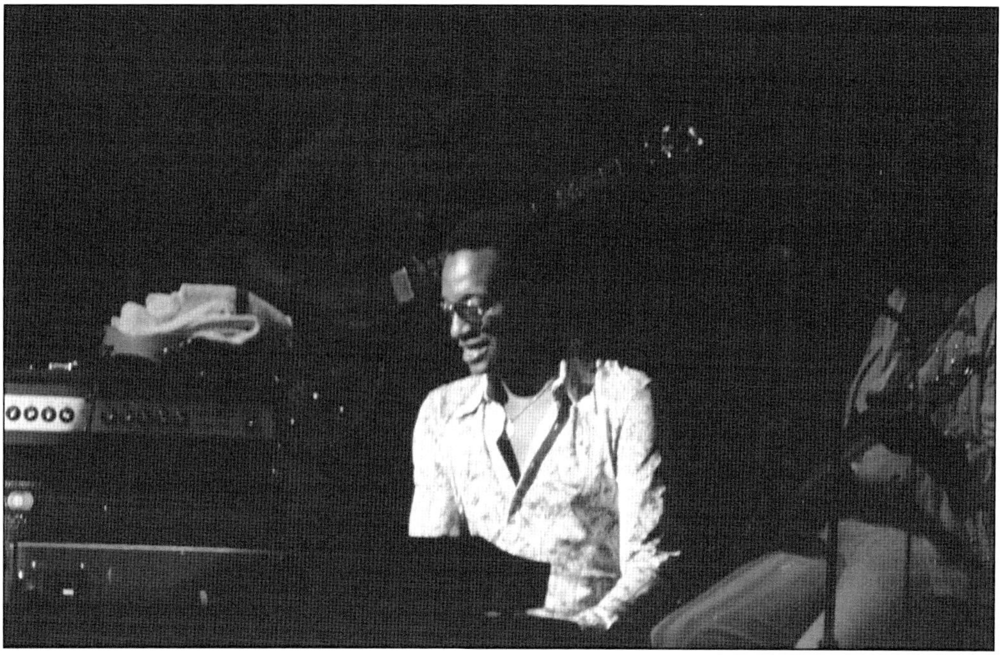

RAMSEY LEWIS. As the opening act for Roberta Flack on a rainy evening, August 5, 1975, Ramsey Lewis made his only visit to the MRF. At this point in his career, the Chicago-born pianist (famed for "The In Crowd") had added an electric keyboard to his act to supplement his work on the grand piano.

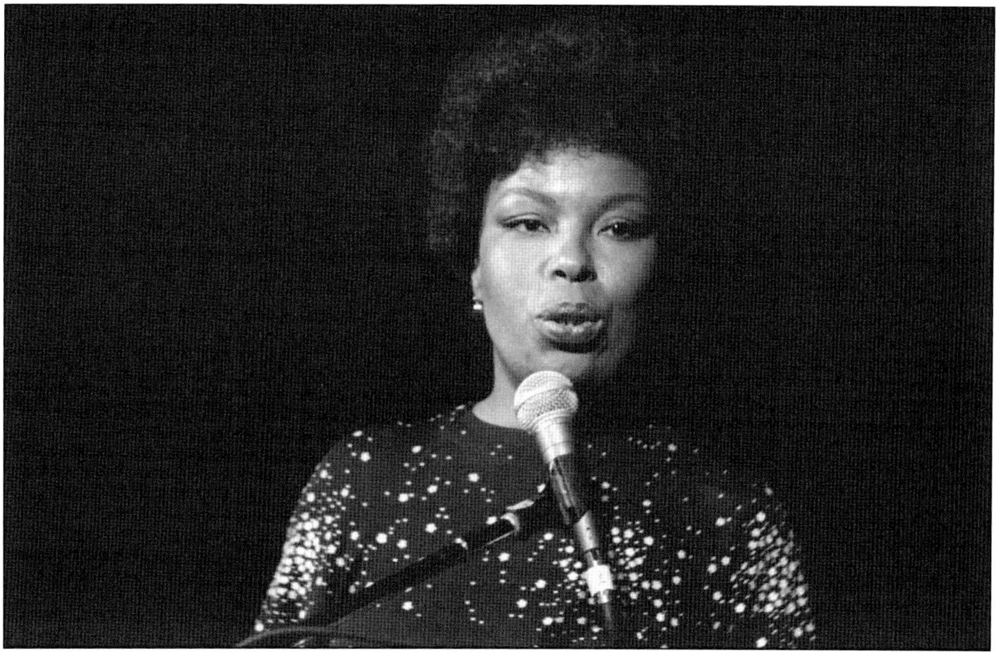

ROBERTA FLACK. An eight-piece orchestra and three singers accompanied vocalist Roberta Flack during her August 5, 1975, concert at the festival. Flack intermixed ballads with a sprinkling of gospel and rock and roll numbers while either playing the piano or walking across the stage. The songstress had performed once previously under the tent on August 10, 1971.

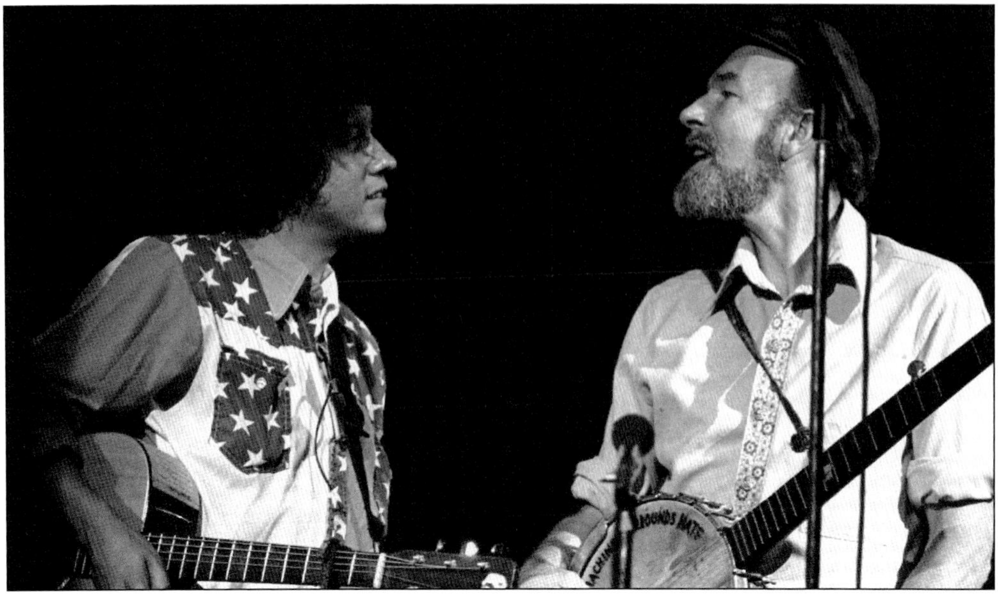

ARLO GUTHRIE AND PETE SEEGER. Arlo Guthrie and Pete Seeger entertained together at the festival for the first time on August 6, 1975. They returned together once more on August 3, 1977. A pioneer in the resurrection of folk singing, Seeger had been a close friend of Guthrie's father, Woody, and indeed served as an artistic forbearer to many of the singers who graced the MRF stage. The artists began the show together and then alternated numbers throughout the evening. They ended with "If I Had a Hammer," "Amazing Grace," and "This Land is Your Land."

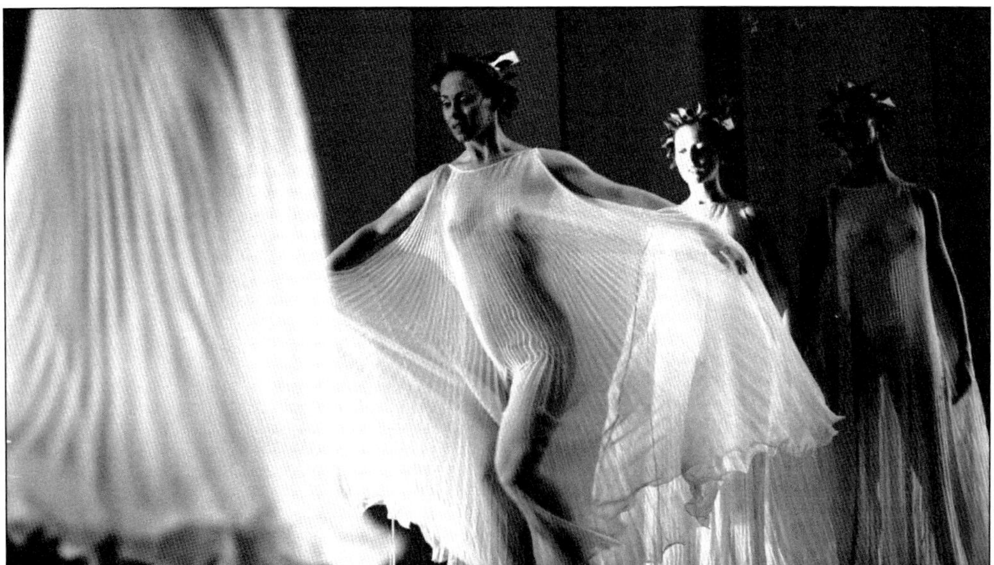

ERIK HAWKINS DANCE COMPANY. A student of Martha Graham, Erik Hawkins brought his modern dance troupe to the festival for performances on August 8, 1975, and the following evening as well. The Erik Hawkins ensemble included Robert Hawkins, Robert Yohn, Nada Reagan, Natalie Richman, Kristin Peterson, Cori White, and Cathy Ward. The dancers spent several days in residence giving instruction on campus in addition to their concert. The program included *Greek Dreams*, *Black Lake*, and *Cantilever.*

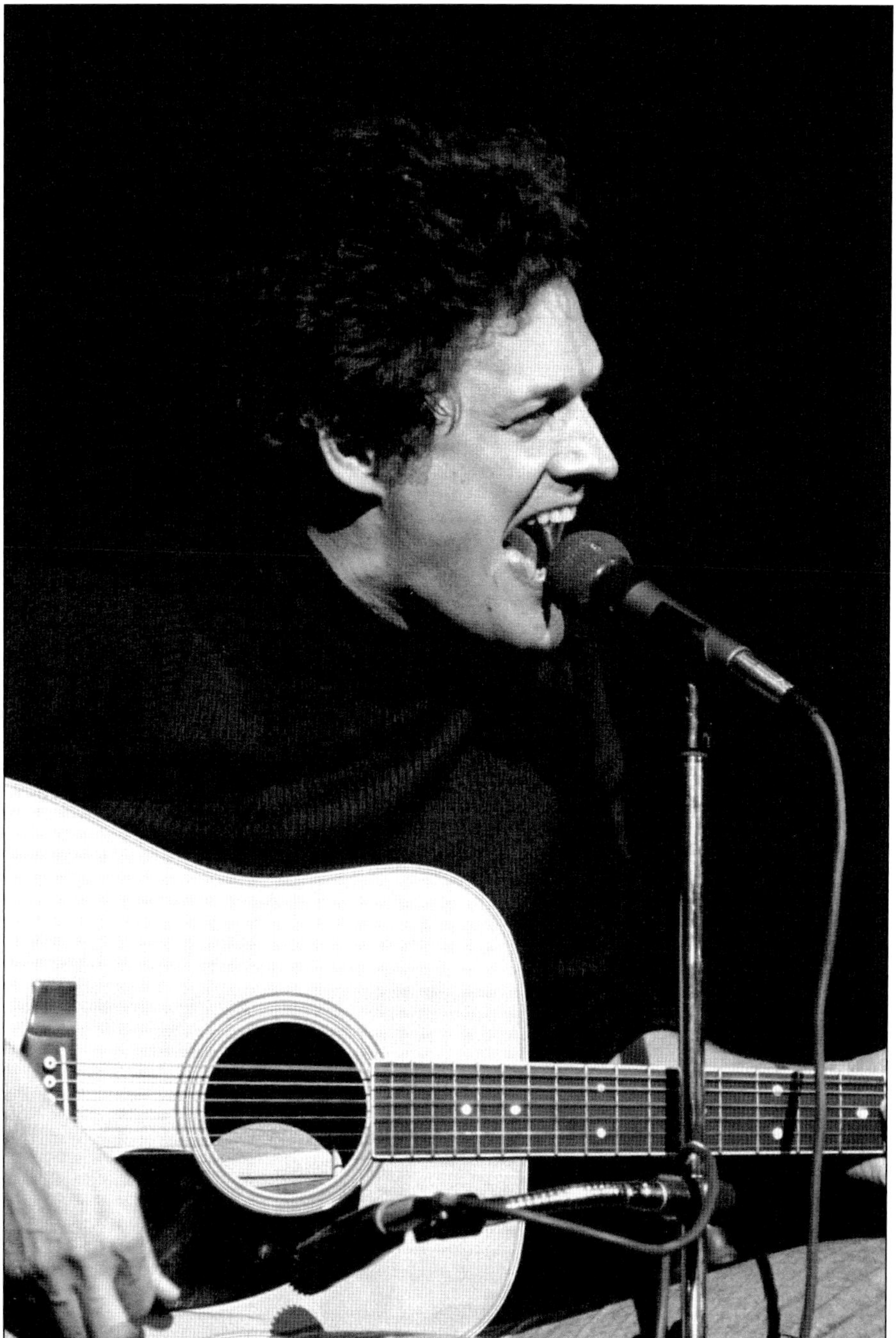

I'VE GOT SOMETHING INSIDE ME. Perhaps the most generous and beloved artist ever to perform at the MRF, Harry Chapin returned to the stage after three encores to oblige his mesmerized audience with three additional songs. He then continued to sign autographs for his grateful fans until 2:00 a.m. In his second appearance, on August 11, 1975, Chapin's supporting cast included his brothers Tom and Steve, Michael Masters (cello), Doug Walker (guitar), Howie Fields (drums), and John Wallace (bass).

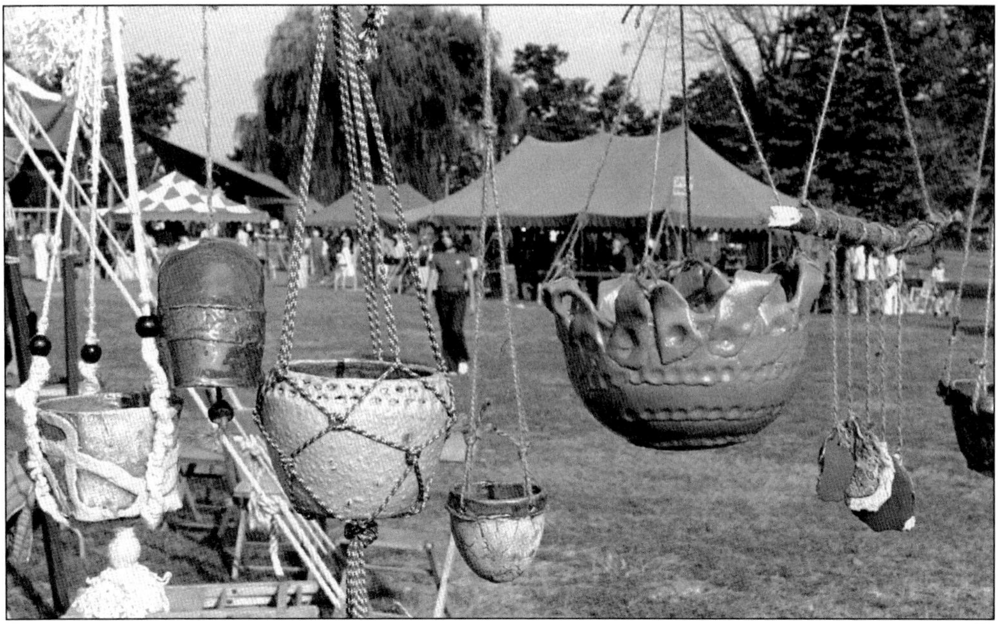

CRAFT SHOW. Beginning in 1973, the MRF included an annual craft show where regional artists and craftsmen might display and sell their handmade wares on the site. By the third time around, on August 15–16, 1975, the craft show had expanded from occupying one tent to six tents and displayed the wares of more than 50 artisans. Pat Sweney, craft shop director, served as manager of the juried fair.

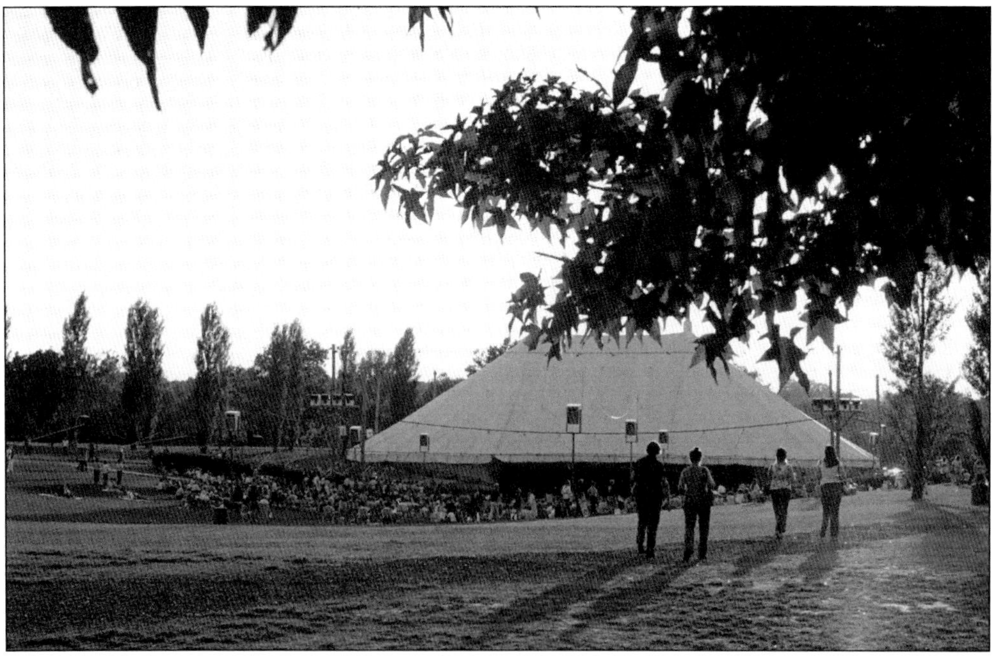

CANVAS CAN DO MIRACLES. Similar to the German exhibit at the international fair Expo '67 in Montreal, Canada, the MRF tent measured 170 feet long by 140 feet wide with a maximum height at the masts of 65 feet. Approximately 7,500 yards of 42-inch-wide, soil-resistant duck canvas had gone into its construction.

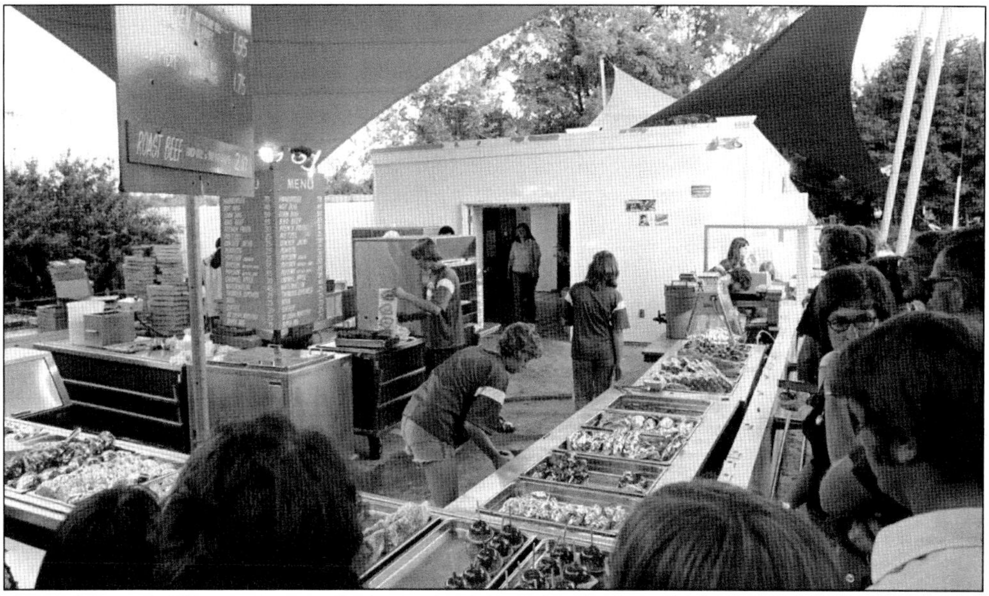

Food Service. The university food service operated two main food stations inside the festival entrance and two beverage stations staffed by a manager, a student manager, an assistant manager, four concessions supervisors, and approximately 50 student workers. Customers could purchase box lunches containing chicken, fish, shrimp, rib-eye, or roast beef, with French fries, coleslaw, and a roll. On an average night, the food service staff might sell 300 burgers, 500 hot dogs, 1,300 bags of popcorn, 1,000 boxes of Cracker Jack, and 2,000–3,000 sodas.

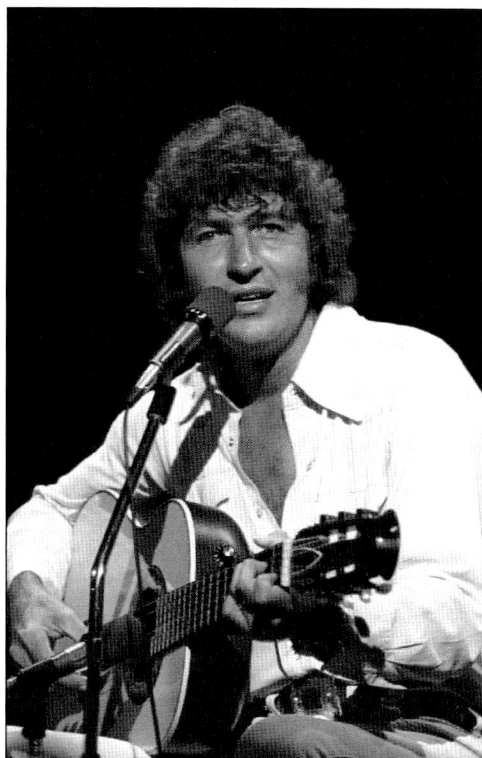

Mac Davis. After a relaxing round of golf, composer/singer Mac Davis took the stage for the second time on August 18, 1975. Davis presented a varied show. At one point he recited *The Creation*, a poem by James Weldon Johnson. He also performed two of his own most famous compositions: "The Ghetto" and "Watching Scotty Grow." Captain and Tennille preceded Davis's entrance. Davis had appeared once before with Anne Murray on August 2, 1974, and later returned for a third time on August 25, 1978.

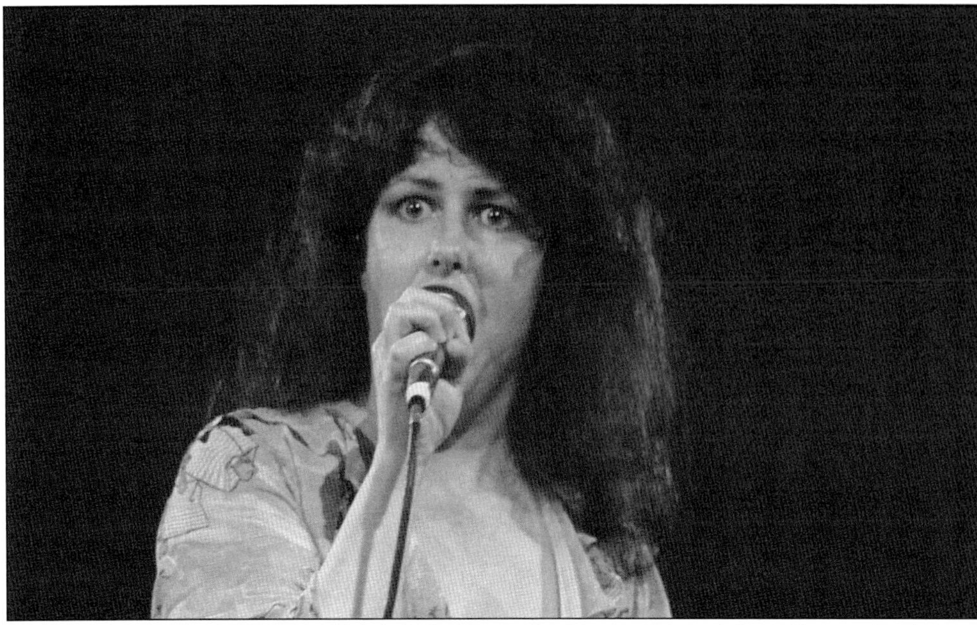

GRACE SLICK. Vocalist Grace Slick left the Great Society and joined the Jefferson Airplane in time to sing "Somebody to Love" and "White Rabbit" on the 1967 album *Surrealistic Pillow.* The success of the album significantly contributed to public fascination with psychedelic music, the hippie lifestyle, and the San Francisco music scene. The group changed its name in 1970 to the Jefferson Starship.

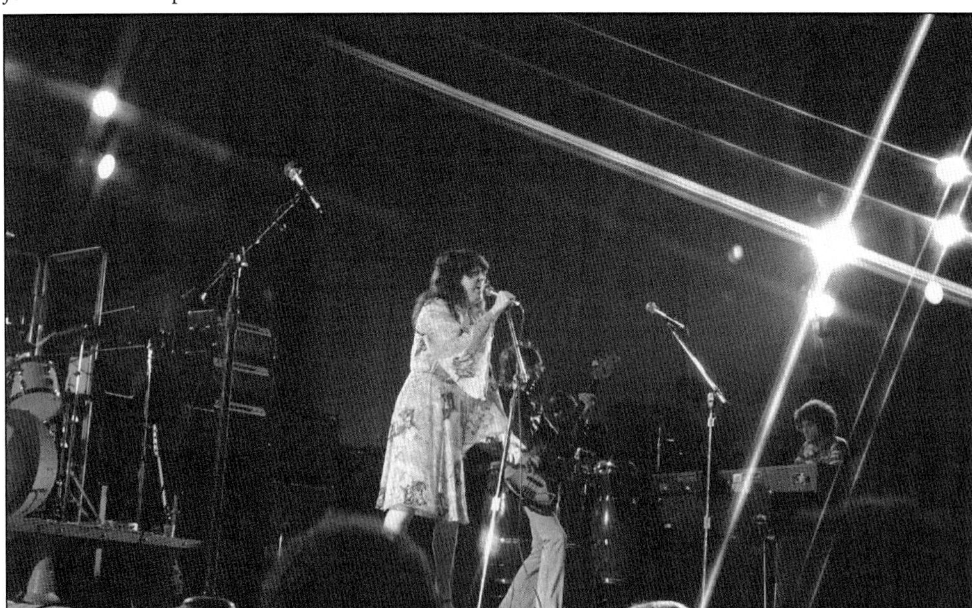

JEFFERSON STARSHIP. On a night with a full moon, Grace Slick, Paul Kantner, Marty Balin, Craig Chaquico, Pete Sears, David Freiberg, and John Barbata performed with the Jefferson Starship on August 19, 1975. Their song list included "Ride the Tiger," "White Rabbit," and "Somebody to Love." Papa John Creech had left the Jefferson Starship by this time. Flo and Eddie (Mark Volman and Howard Kaylan) had been booked as the opening act.

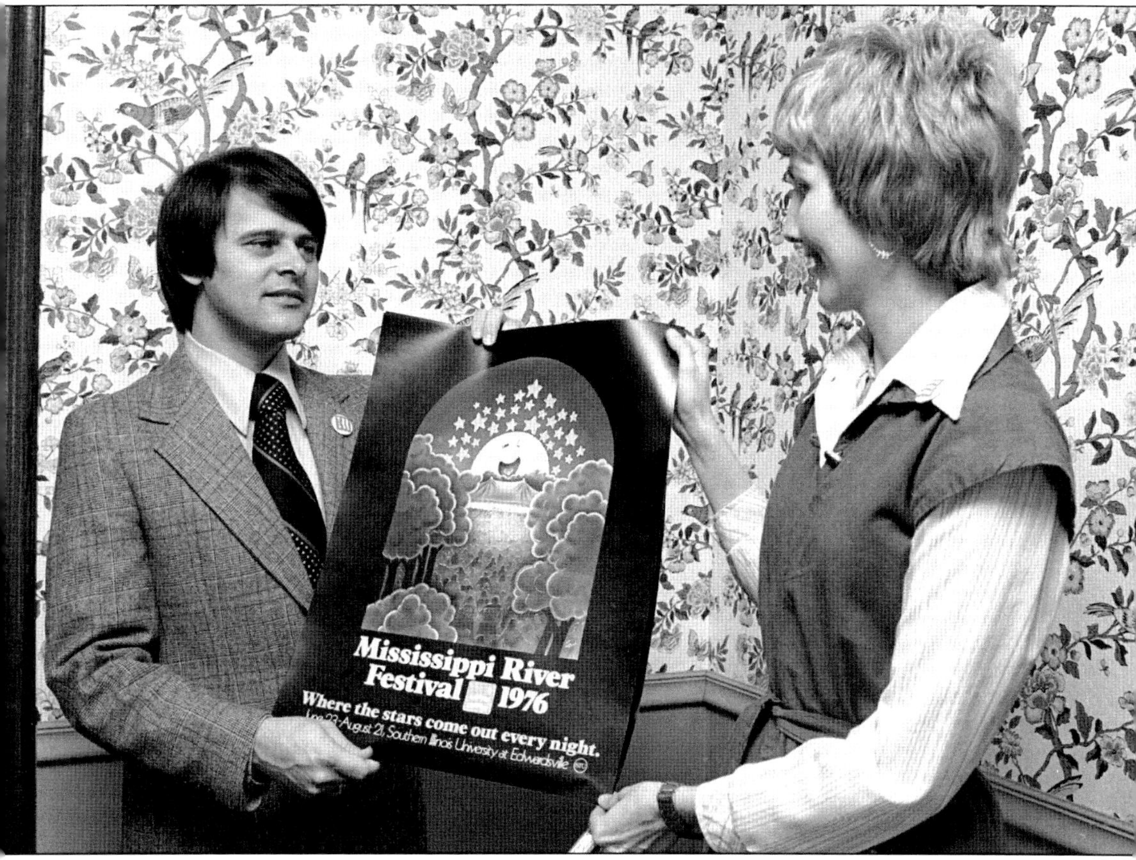

Lyle Ward. A graduate of SIUE, Lyle Ward served an extensive apprenticeship with the MRF. In 1975, Ward advanced from the position of concert manager to become the managing director of the festival when Peter Pastreich of the symphony relinquished that essential role. Always an articulate advocate for the festival, Ward subsequently enjoyed a long and very distinguished career with the university as a senior administrator of the University Center. In this photograph, taken on December 23, 1975, Ward displays new artwork for the forthcoming 1976 MRF season.

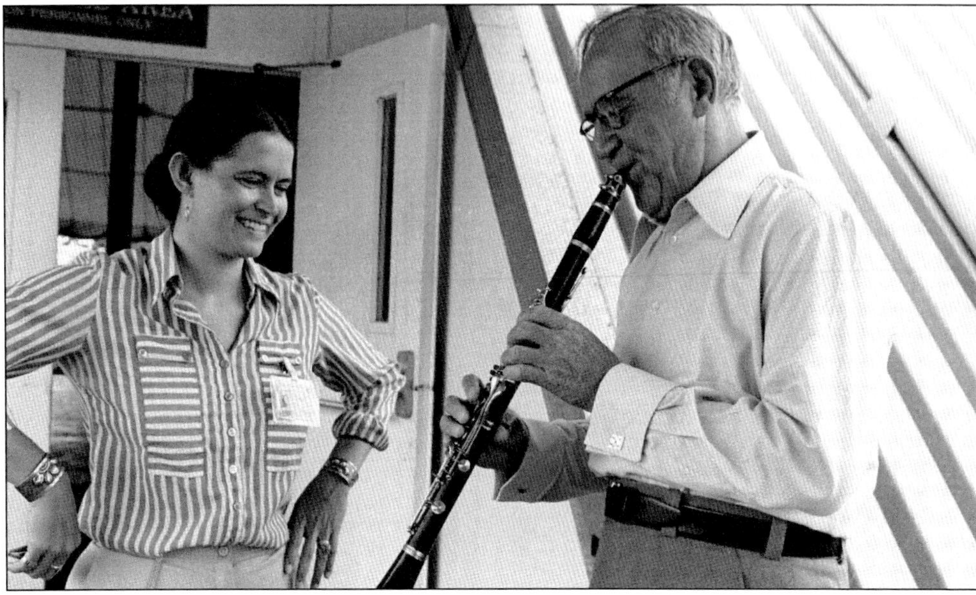

Benny Goodman and Vicky Holt. Concert manager Vicky Holt poses with legendary clarinetist Benny Goodman at the festival site on June 24, 1976. Goodman and his band performed a mix of swing-era songs in a tribute to Duke Ellington and Fats Waller. Connie Kay, Tom Fay, Michael Moore, Peter Appleyard, and Warren Vache performed with the Benny Goodman Sextet for two and a half hours. Later in the summer, Goodman returned to accept an honorary degree from SIUE.

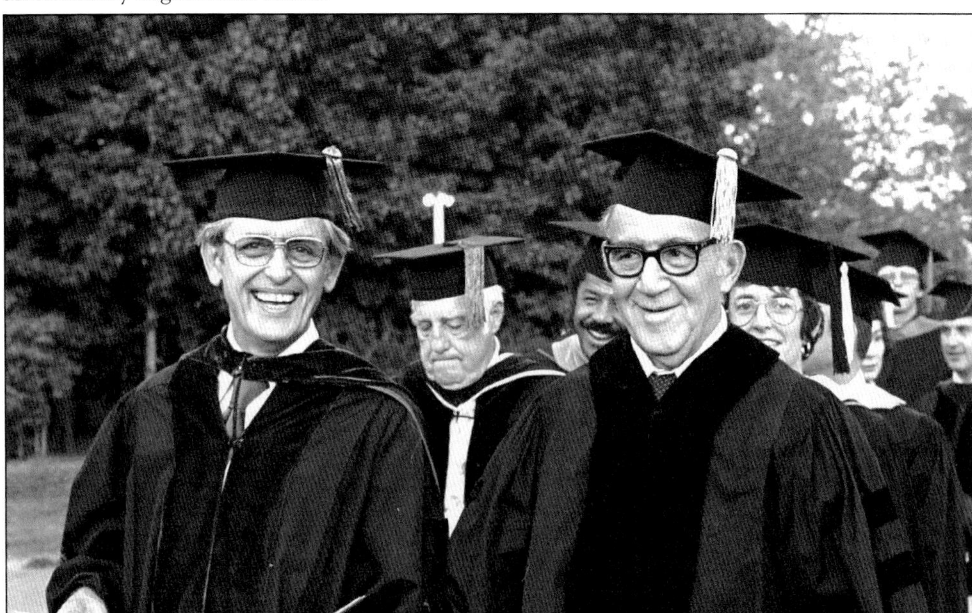

Andrew Kochman and Benny Goodman. Provost Andrew Kochman became acting president of the university after the death of John Rendleman. Although he did not assume the office on a permanent basis, Kochman presided over subsequent university planning for the 1977 festival. In this photograph he is seen marching next to Benny Goodman who received an honorary doctorate during the September 2, 1976, commencement ceremony at the MRF site.

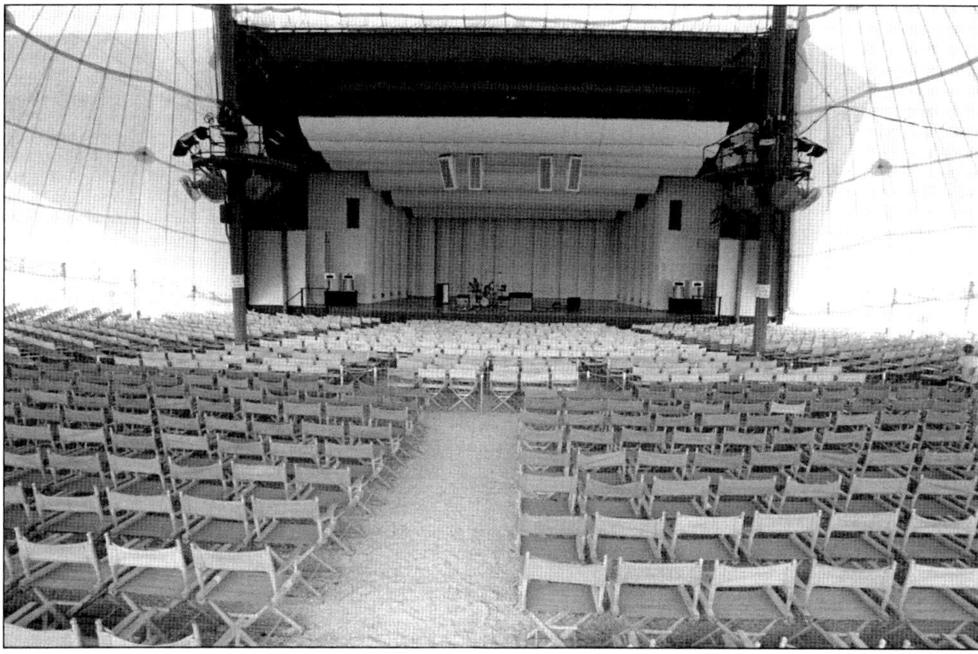

CHUCK MANGIONE. Jazz artist Chuck Mangione made his first appearance on June 25, 1976, backed by Joe LaBarbera (drums), Chip Jackson (bass), Chris Valvado (woodwinds), and vocalist Esther Satterfield. Early in his career, Mangione had played with Woody Herman and Maynard Ferguson. Mangione later returned to the festival for a second time on June 28, 1978.

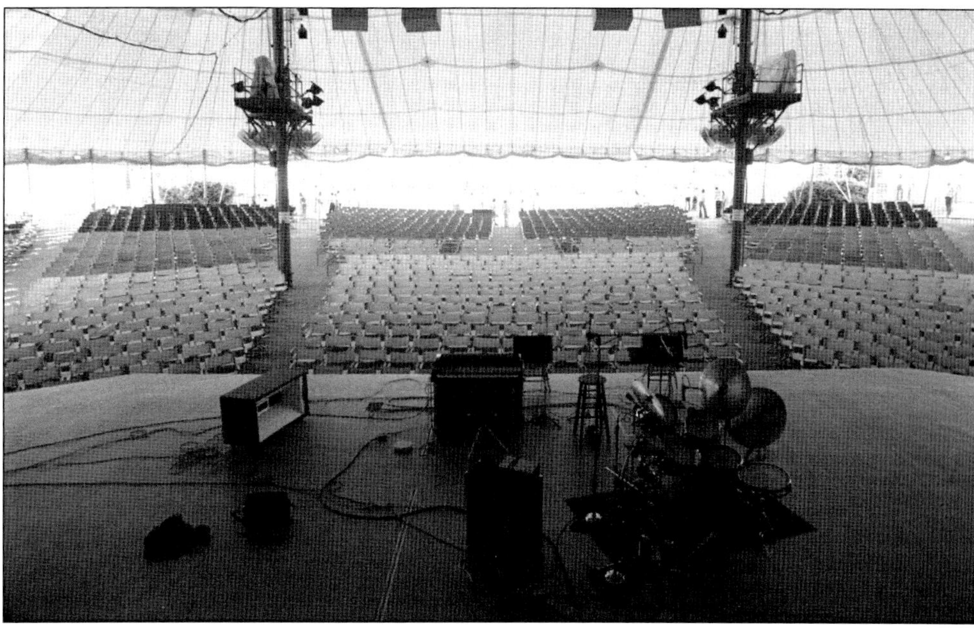

TENT INTERIOR. Prior to the Chuck Mangione concert, the photographer captured the quiet but expectant atmosphere about the empty stage and unoccupied reserved seats under the tent. In addition to providing protection from inclement weather, the tent created a remarkably effective acoustic environment for appreciation of symphonic music. Many expert listeners regarded the acoustics in the tent to be superior to those in Powell Symphony Hall.

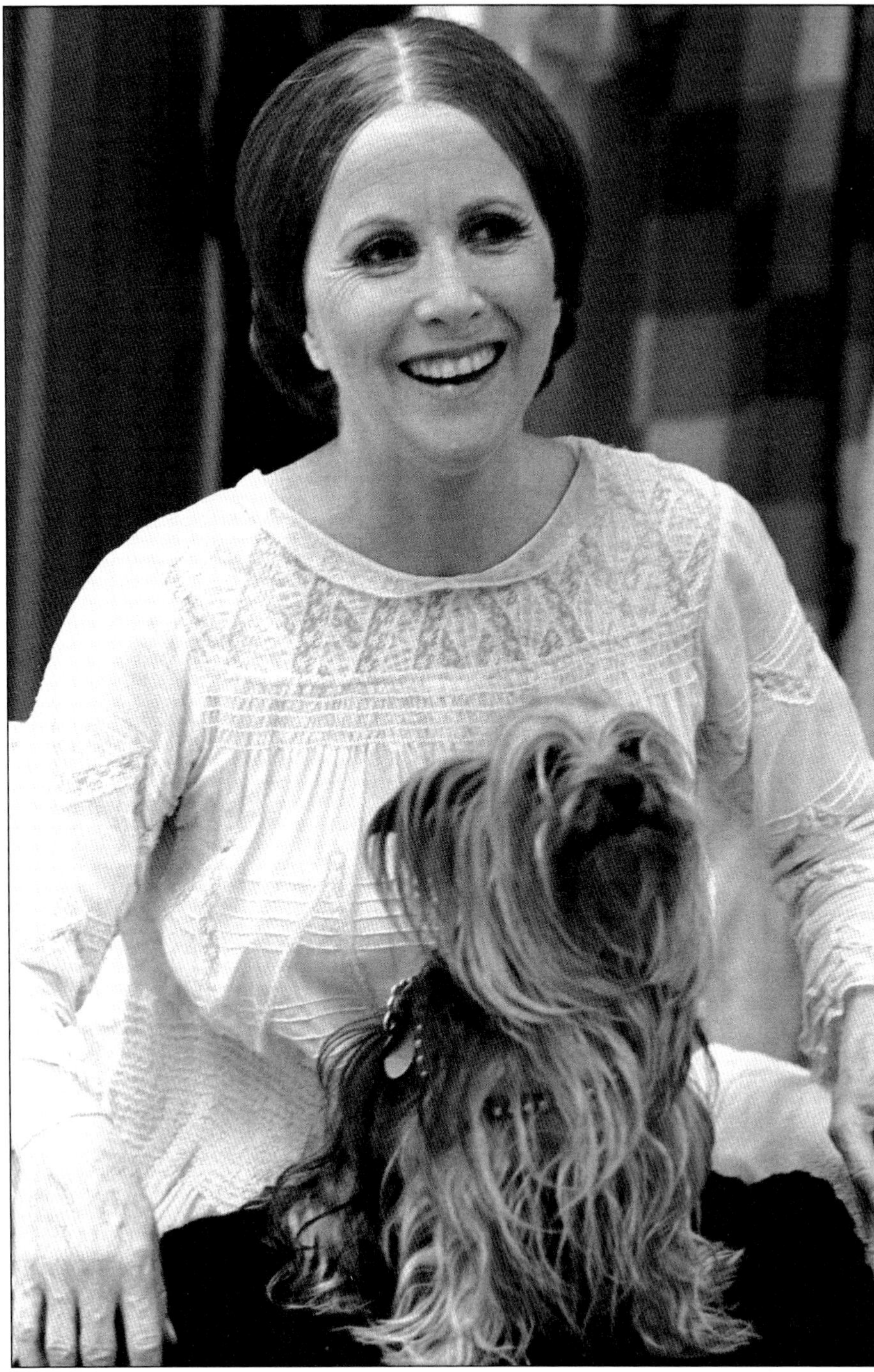

JULIE HARRIS. The festival added the genre of live theater to its offerings for the first time during its eighth season. Julie Harris brought *The Belle of Amherst*, her one-woman Broadway show based on the life of poetess Emily Dickinson, to the tent on June 28, 1976. Directed by Charles Nelson Reilly, the play moved back and forth in time within the setting of the family home in Amherst, Massachusetts, as recreated in different zones of the stage. The written words of Emily Dickinson provided most of the dialogue for the play.

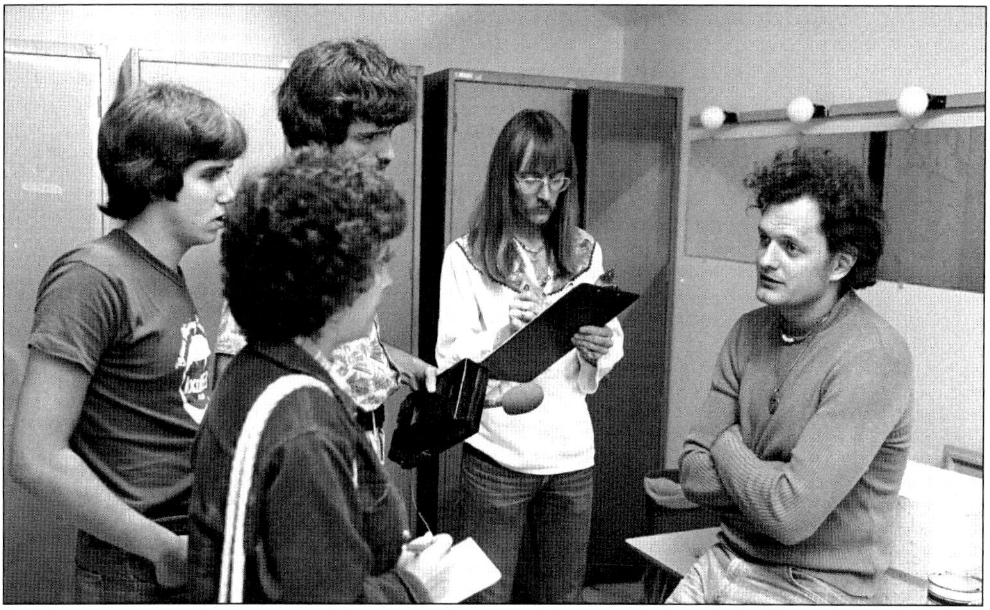

HELICOPTER HARRY. The singer/songwriter/social activist began his career as a documentary filmmaker before recruiting a band and playing in clubs around New York City. His first album, featuring his signature tune "Taxi," became a tremendous success in 1972. Chapin's musical, *The Night that Made America Famous*, opened on February 26, 1975, and earned two Tony nominations. Sadly, Chapin died in an automobile accident on July 16, 1981.

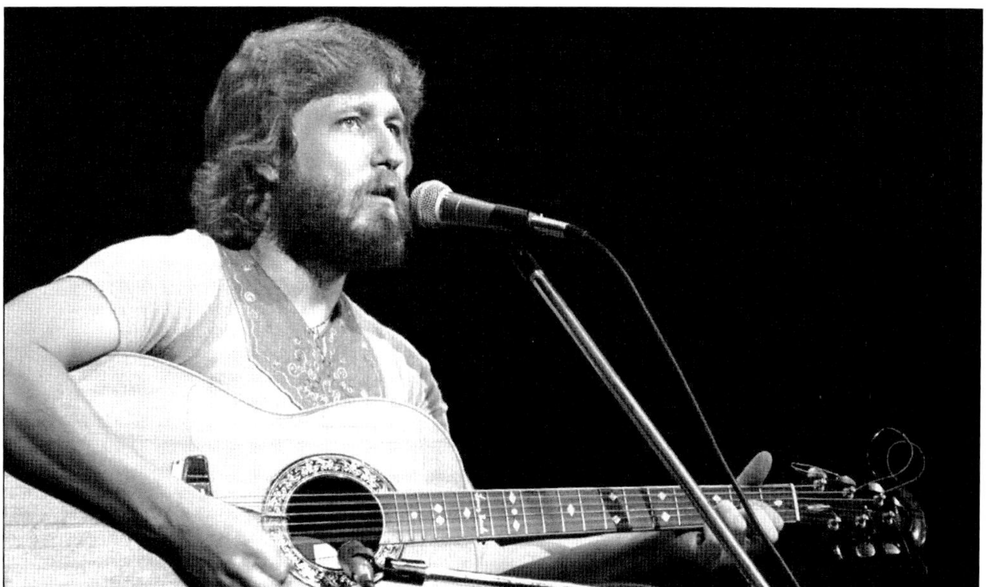

TERRY BECK. When a tornado watch in New York interfered with Harry Chapin's air travel arrangements from LaGuardia Airport to a third MRF concert scheduled on June 30, 1976, festival managers turned to an emergency temporary substitute. Local entertainer Terry Beck, a young performer at area pubs and pizza parlors, filled in on a moment's notice until Chapin could make a spectacular delayed arrival via chartered helicopter. For his efforts, Beck received a standing ovation from the Chapin crowd.

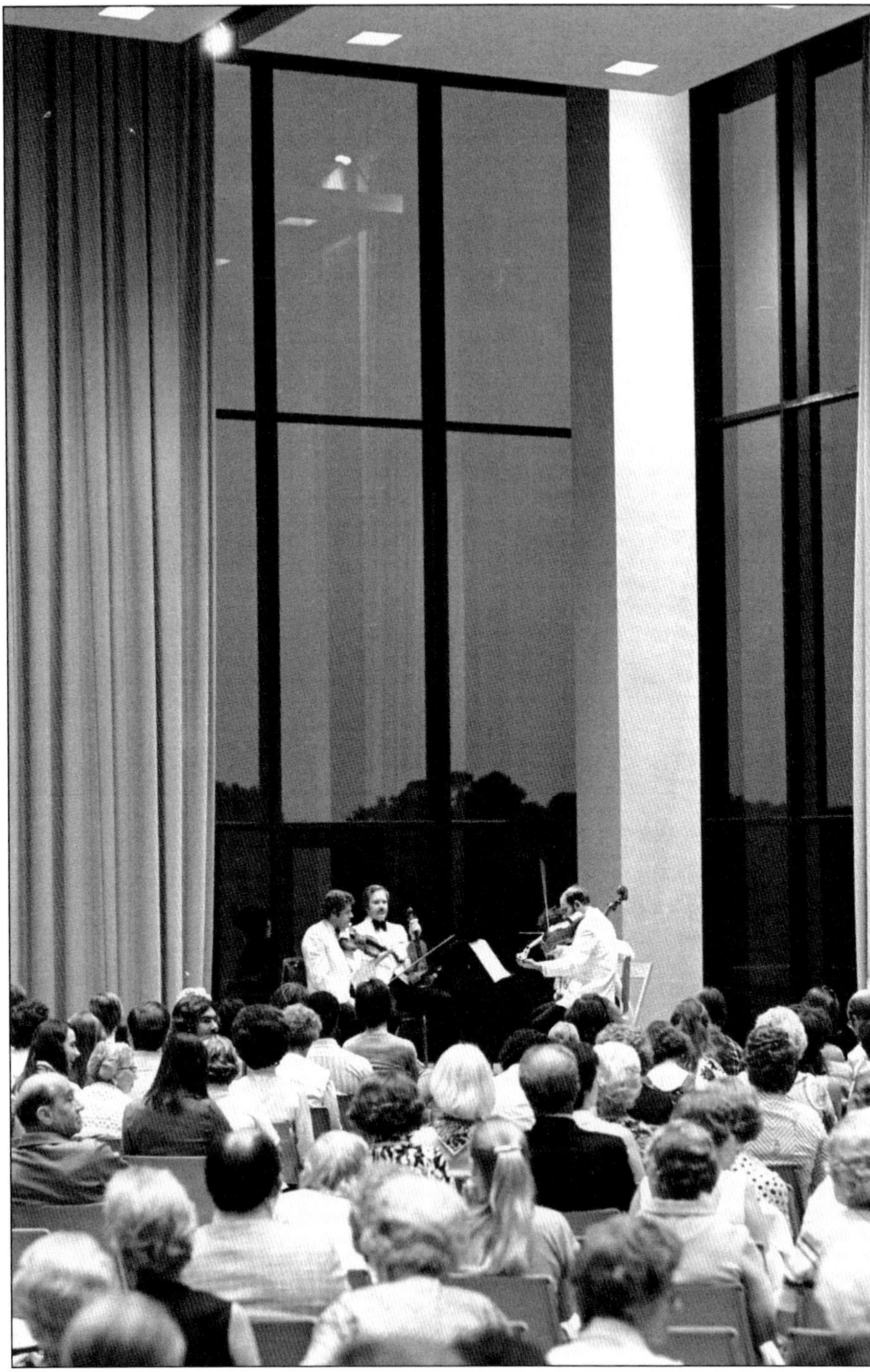

JULLIARD STRING QUARTET. The Meridian Ballroom of the University Center served as the venue when the Julliard String Quartet made an appearance at the festival on July 1, 1976. The program consisted of works by Beethoven and Elliott Carter. Robert Mann, Earl Carlyss, Samuel Rhodes, and Jeff Krosnick made up the quartet who entertained the chamber music enthusiasts gathered for the event.

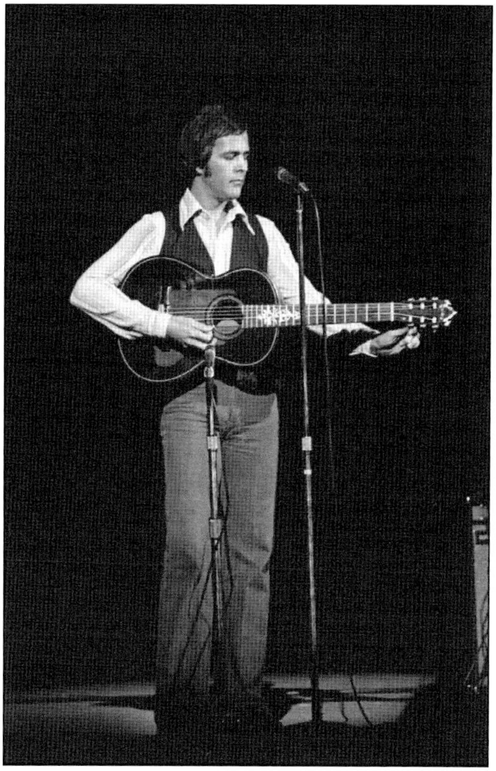

JIM STAFFORD. The July 2, 1976, concert featured country artists Jim Stafford as headliner and Sonny James and the Southern Gentlemen as opening act. The concert marked Stafford's return following his initial 1974 appearance on a program with Helen Reddy. Stafford played both the guitar and the banjo and found himself called back for three encores. Sonny James and his band played several of their golden oldies, including "Only the Lonely" and "Young Love, First Love."

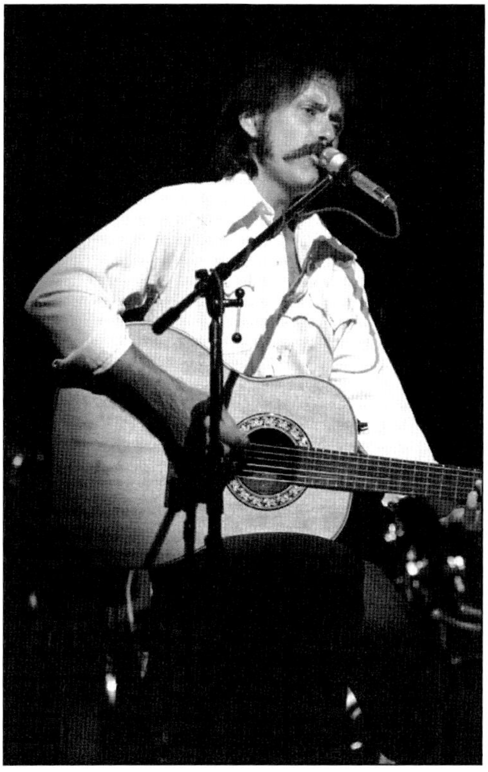

JESSE COLIN YOUNG. On July 6, 1976, Jesse Colin Young made his only visit to the festival, performing for 90 minutes. Young had first tasted stardom as the leader of the Youngbloods who achieved success with the generational anthem "Get Together." Young's most beautiful composition may have been "Sunlight."

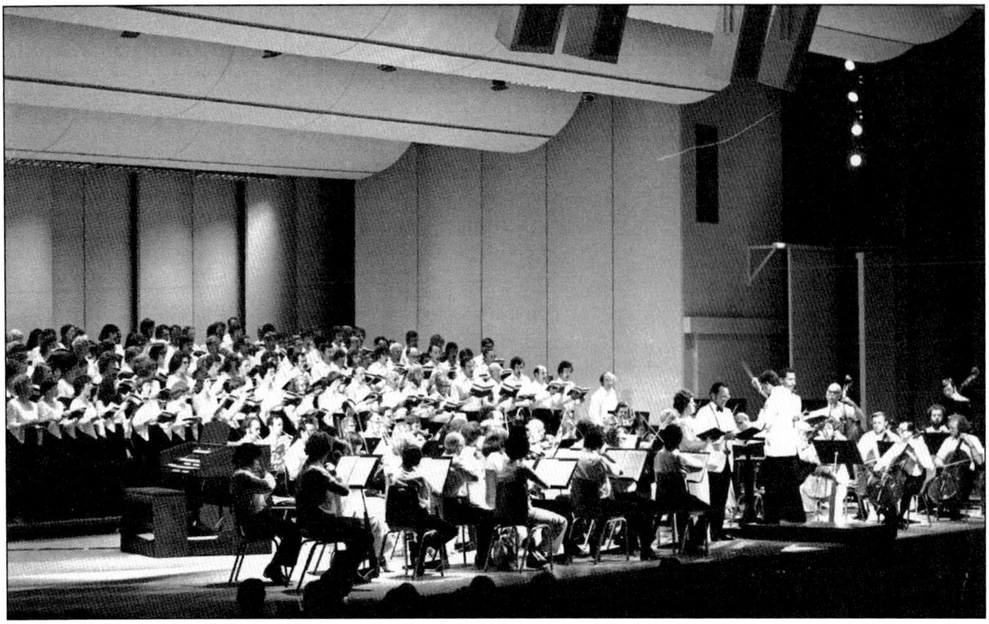

SCOTTISH NATIONAL ORCHESTRA CHORUS. On July 10, 1976, the Scottish National Orchestra Chorus appeared with the St. Louis Symphony Orchestra. Alexander Gibson conducted the concert. John Currie directed the chorus. Together the orchestra and chorus performed Joseph Haydn's oratorio *The Creation*. Gibson began the evening first with the British and second with the American national anthems.

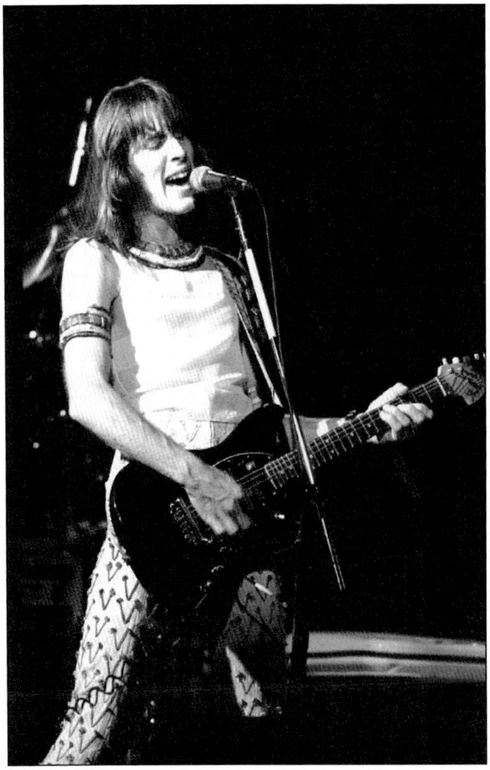

TODD RUNDGREN. The Atlanta Rhythm Section opened the Todd Rundgren and Utopia concert on July 13, 1976. Kasim Sultan (bass), John Wilcox (drums), and Roger Powell (keyboard) performed as Rundgren's sidemen during that appearance. Rundgren later returned to the festival a second time, on July 27, 1980, as the featured act together on a bill with Ambrosia.

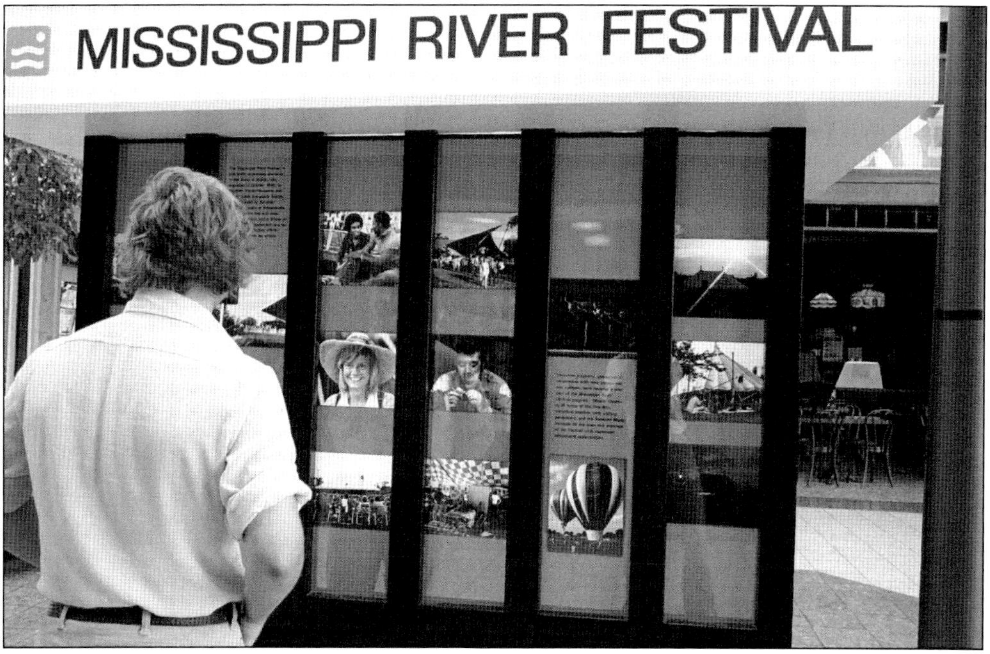

MRF MOBILE DISPLAY. The university prepared a mobile MRF exhibit that could be transported from place to place in order to convey accurate information about the festival to new potential visitors. In this photograph, the exhibit is being viewed by an interested potential patron at a shopping center on the Missouri side of the river.

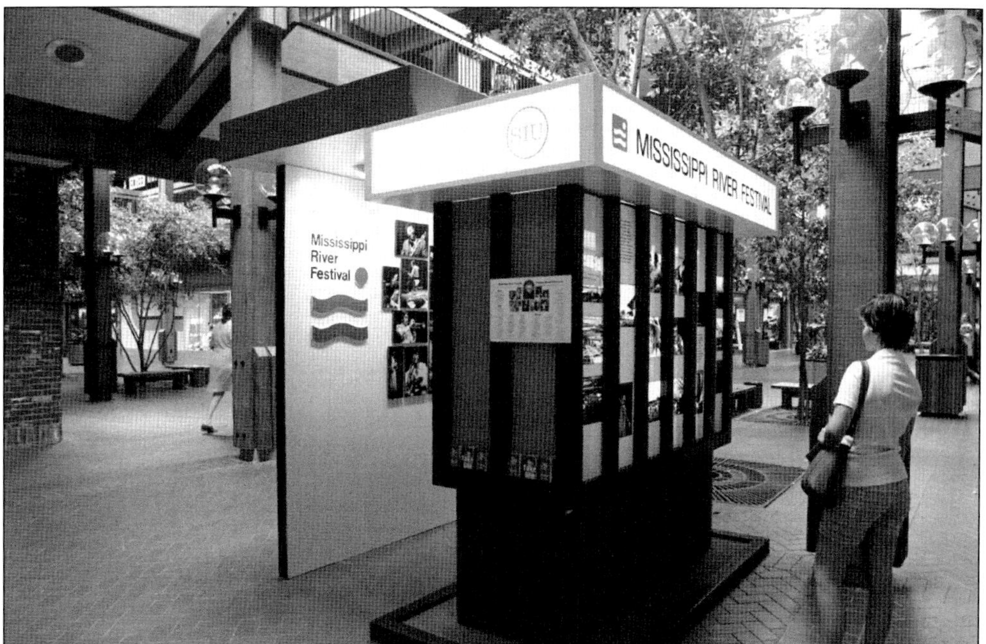

ST. CLAIR SQUARE. A woman examines the MRF exhibit while walking through the new St. Clair Square mall in Fairview Heights, south of Edwardsville. The exhibit featured accurate text and enticing images of performers and of the facilities at the festival site.

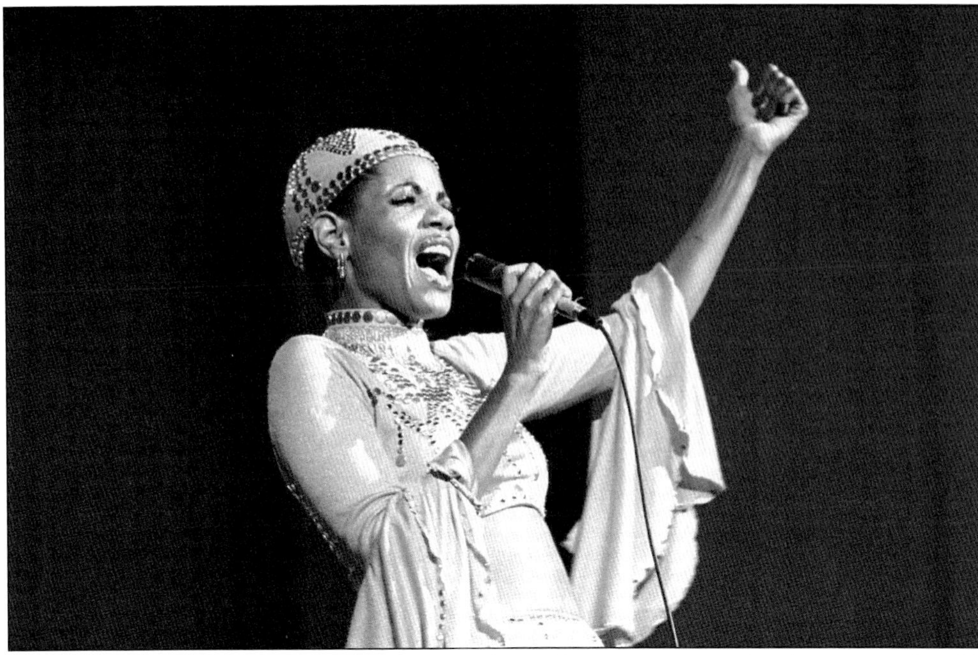

MELBA MOORE. Vocalist Melba Moore made her only appearance under the tent on July 20, 1976, as the headliner on a bill with the Spinners. Moore's hour-long set included songs such as "Summertime," "Brand New," "He Ain't Heavy," "This Is It," and "Lean on Me." Her vocal range, delivery, and stage presence greatly pleased her audience.

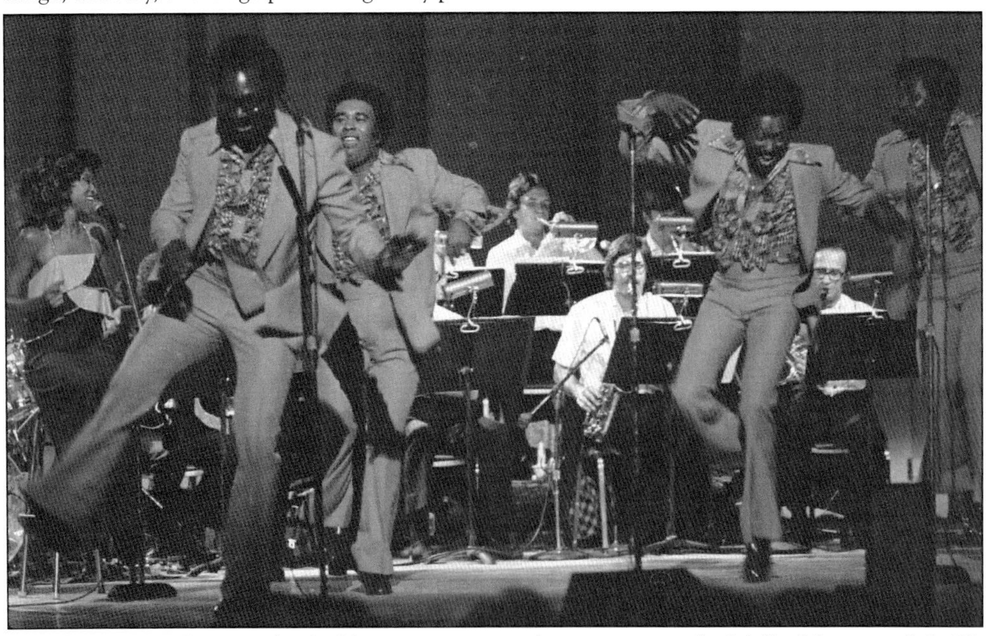

THE SPINNERS. During a lively 90-minute turn as the opening act for Melba Moore on July 20, 1976, the Spinners sang and danced their way through many of their hits. In addition to songs like "Games People Play" and "Could It Be I'm Falling in Love" they finished their performance with "Mighty Love." Perhaps the greatest soul group of the early 1970s, the Spinners featured intricate vocal harmonies.

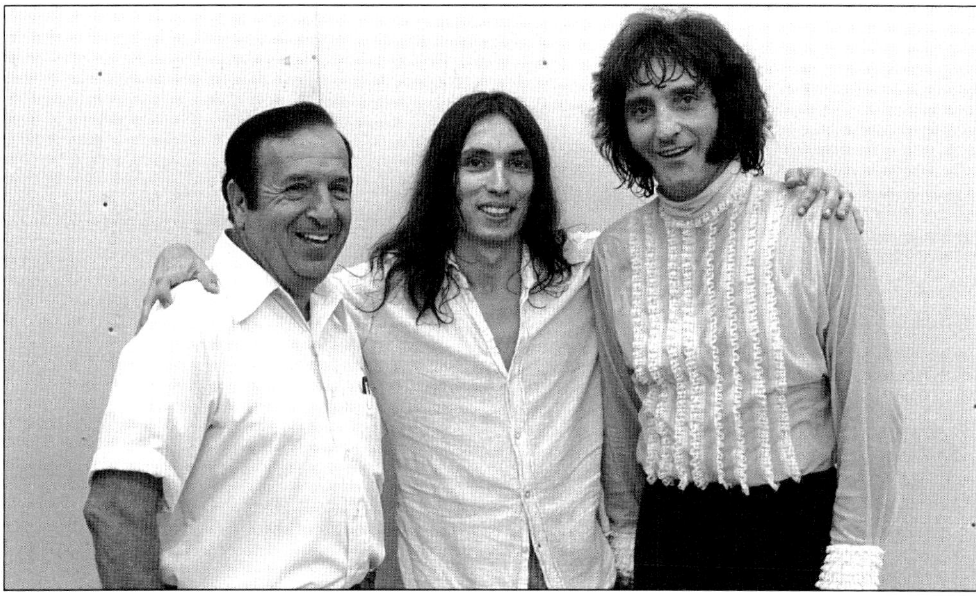

SENATOR SAM AND MARTY VADALABENE. The Ozark Mountain Daredevils visited the festival for the first time on July 24, 1976. Cajun music virtuoso Doug Kershaw and a group called Slidin' Jake opened the concert. Marty Vadalabene, a native of Edwardsville, played the drums for Slidin' Jake. The son of "Senator Sam" Vadalabene, the university's strongest advocate in the Illinois legislature, Marty Vadalabene posed for this photograph between his father and Kershaw during his homecoming appearance.

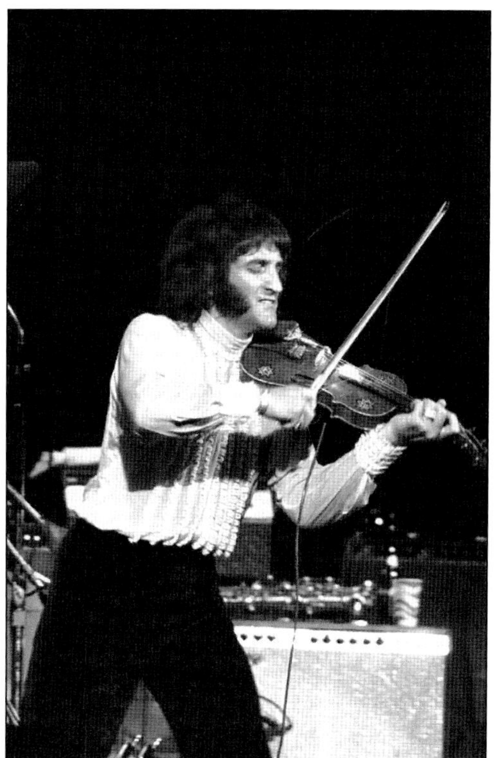

DOUG KERSHAW. A native of Tiel Ridge, Louisiana, the "Ragin' Cajun" combined a pioneering style of Cajun fiddling with exciting live performances. Kershaw began his entertainment career at the age of nine and formed a group together with his brothers at the age of 12. His song "Louisiana Man" became a hit in 1961.

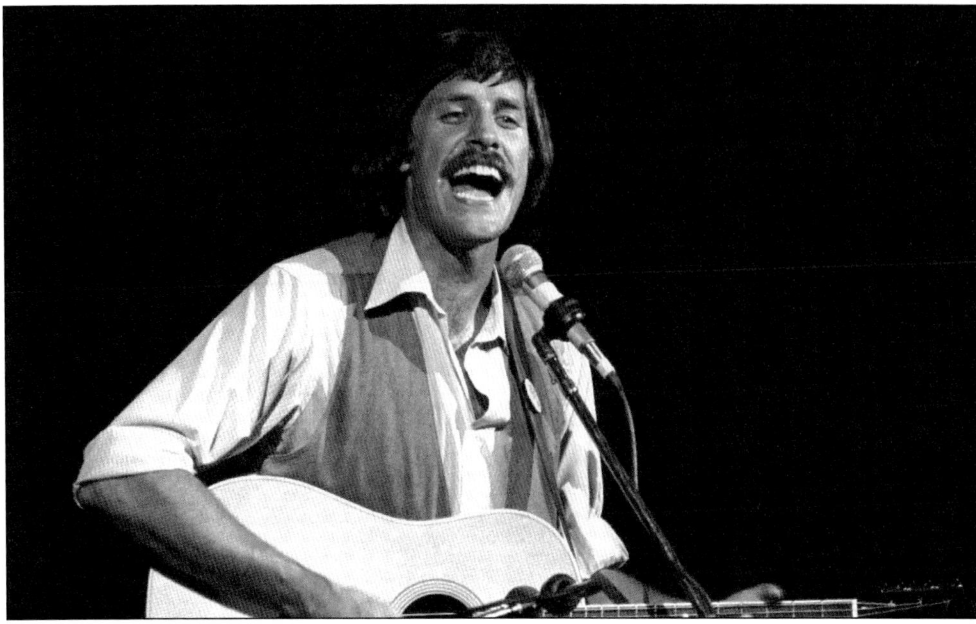

TOM CHAPIN. In addition to appearing with his brother Harry, Tom Chapin hosted *Make a Wish*, an award-winning television show for children between 1971 and 1976. Tom had worked with Harry once before at the MRF on August 11, 1975. Working as a single act, but with a great deal of audience participation, Tom opened the concert for Gordon Lightfoot when the Canadian returned to the festival for the second time on July 27, 1976.

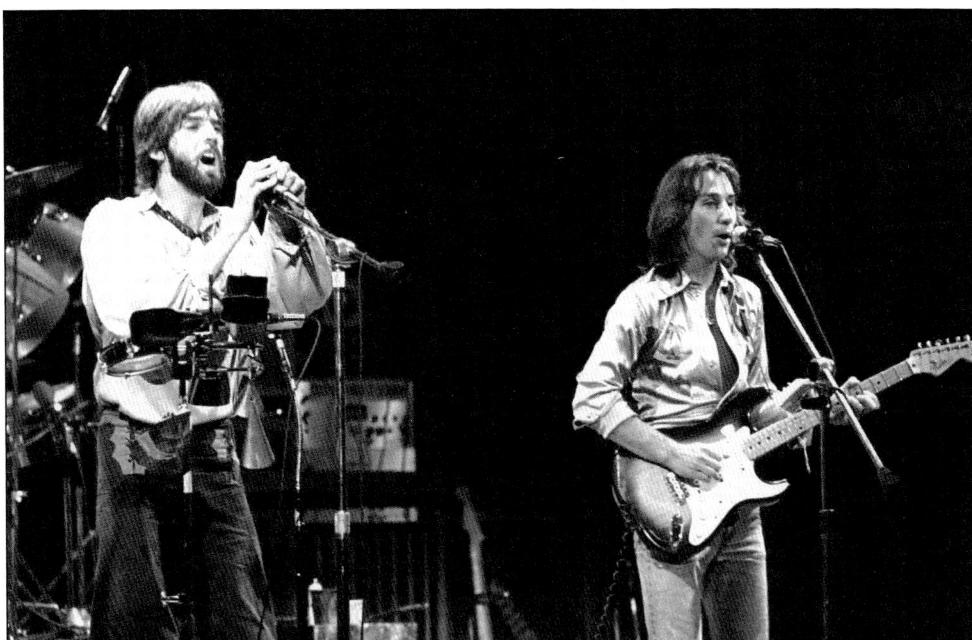

KENNY LOGGINS AND JIM MESSINA. Lightning, thunder, and rain heralded the farewell tour concert by Kenny Loggins and Jim Messina on July 28, 1976. The duo had earlier announced their intention to conclude their musical partnership. Because Loggins had sustained a hand injury, Woody Chrisman had to cover Loggins's part on the guitar.

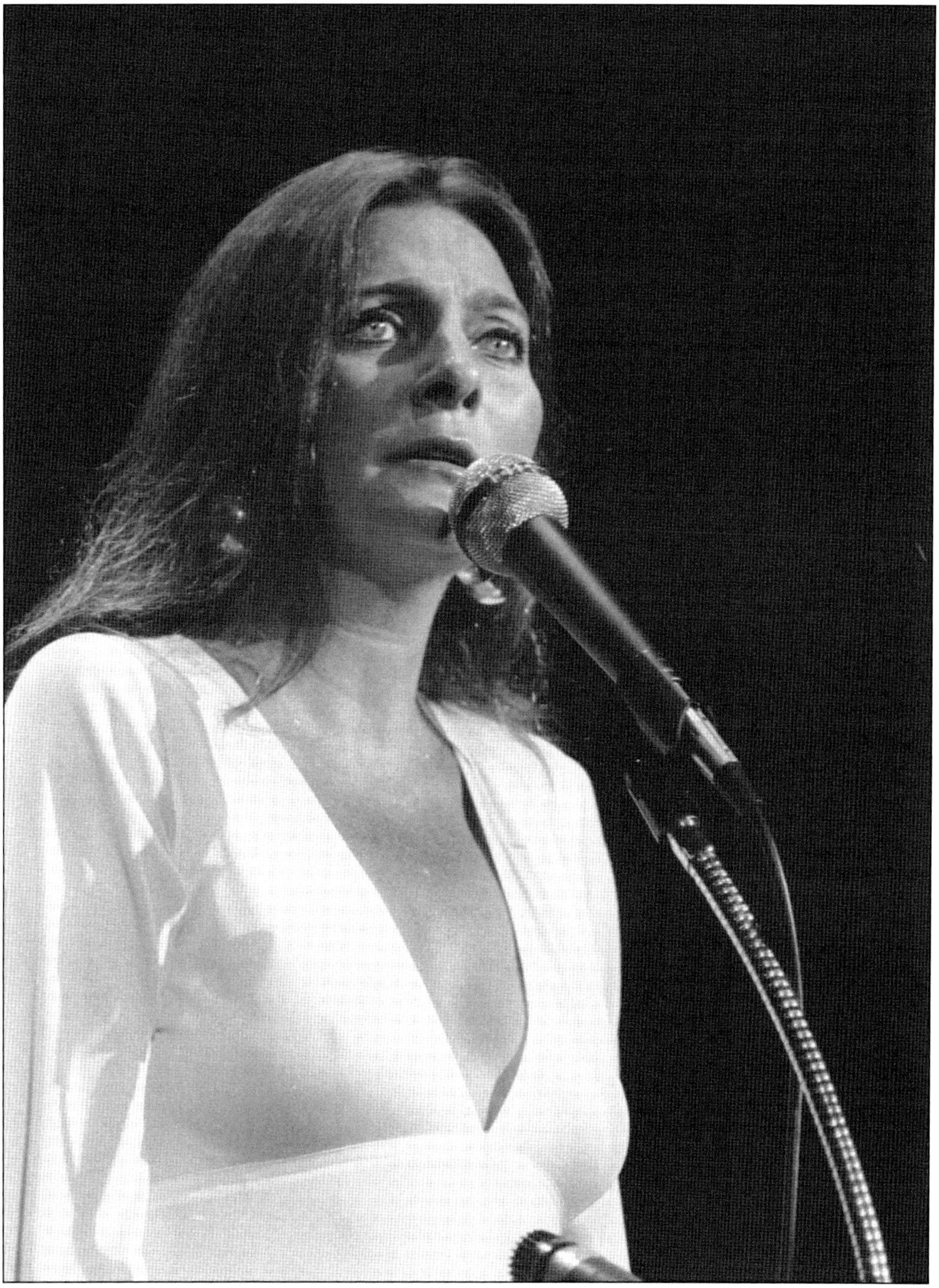

JUDY COLLINS. The festival audience welcomed Judy Collins back to the tent for her fifth and final appearance at the MRF on August 3, 1976. Collins thus became the only popular music artist to work beneath the MRF tent five times, since the tent would no longer exist by the time of Harry Chapin's subsequent 1979 concert. Collins sang for two hours and included among her vocalizations a version of Mimi Farina's "Bread and Roses" accompanied by the recorded voices of singing, marching women.

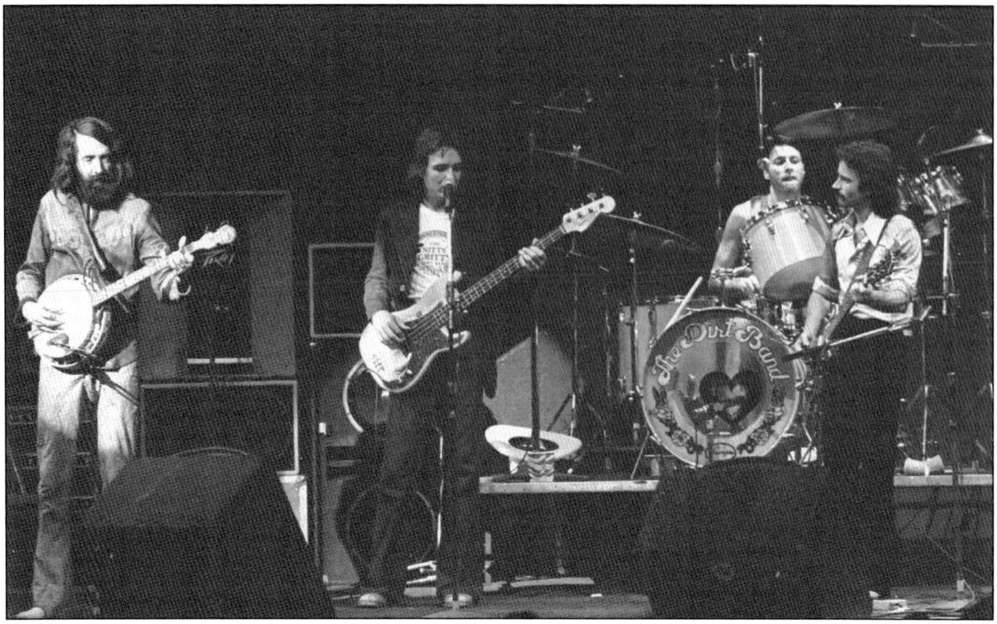

RETURN OF THE NGDB. Jackie Clark (a new addition), John McEuen, and the Nitty Gritty Dirt Band returned to the festival for a second time on August 4, 1976. Canadian folksinger Valdy (Valdemar Horsdad) and his Home Town Band opened the show for the Nitty Gritty Dirt Band while making their first and only appearance in Edwardsville. Together the two acts drew a very respectable crowd of 9,496 paying customers.

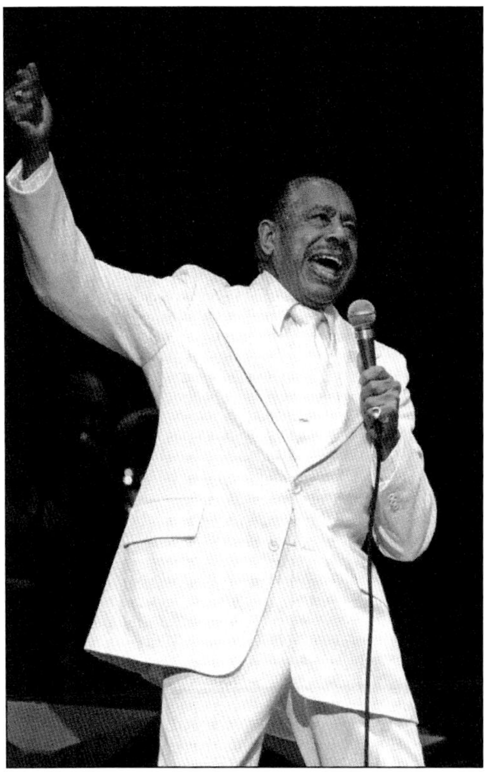

CAB CALLOWAY. Paula Kelly and the Modernaires, Cab Calloway, and Ray McKinley and his orchestra had been booked for a program dedicated to the music of the 1940s on August 6, 1976. Cab Calloway began his career as a singer and band leader during the 1920s. The motion picture *Blues Brothers*, released in 1980, featured Calloway in a significant supporting role that introduced him to a new generation of music fans.

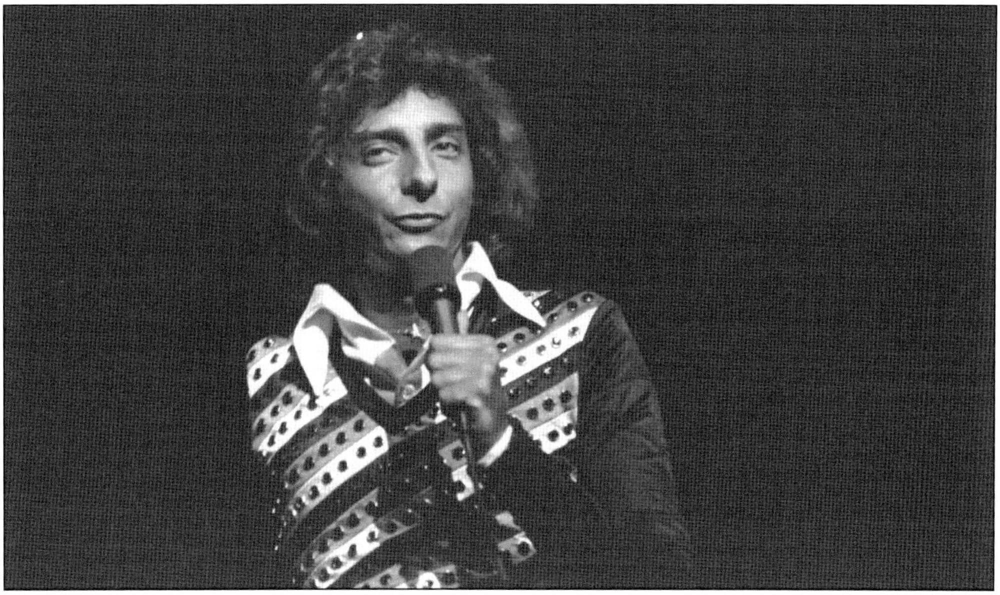

BARRY MANILOW. One of the most prolific composers of advertising jingles and popular songs in his era, Barry Manilow came to the festival as a performer for the only time on August 7, 1976. Manilow appeared with three female backup singers billed as "Lady Flash." The Manilow concert marked the first time that reserved seating on the lawn (as distinct from underneath the tent) would be sold. The singer included in the show his trademark number "I Write the Songs" (actually created by Bruce Johnston of the Beach Boys).

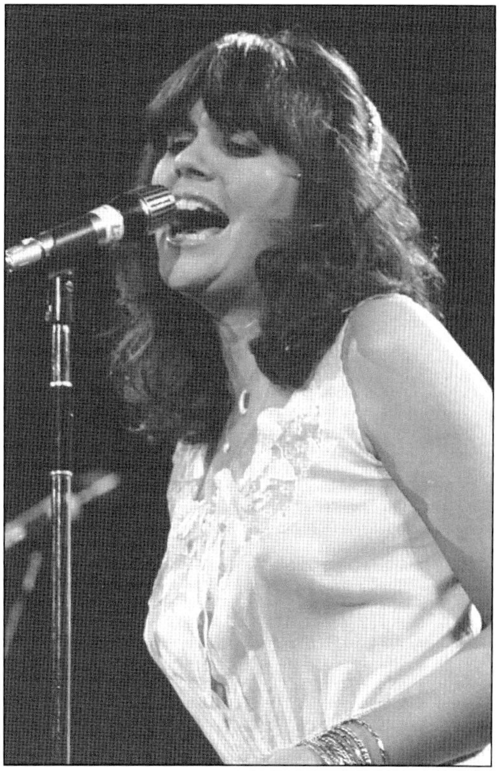

LINDA RONSTADT. Andrew Gold opened the concert for Linda Ronstadt and later joined her act with sidemen Kenny Edwards and Michael Botts. During her one visit to the festival, on August 9, 1976, Ronstadt performed many of her standards including songs such as "When Will I Be Loved," "Tracks of My Tears," "That'll Be the Day," and "Love Is a Rose." Ronstadt spent much of her time onstage standing alone by the microphone and singing song, after song, after song.

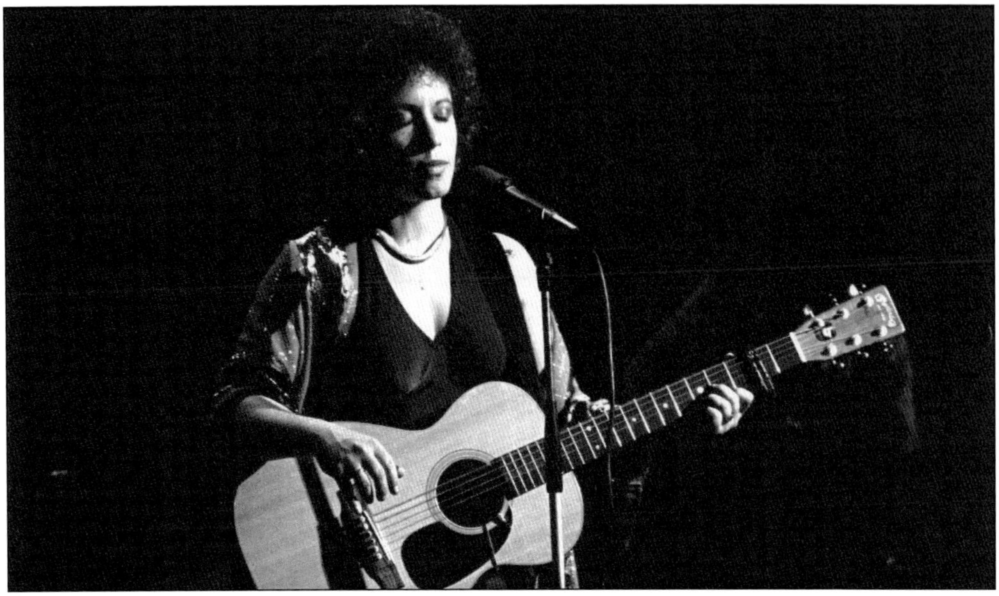

JANICE IAN. Claire Bay, Jeff Layton, Barry Larowitz, and Stu Woods appeared with Janis Ian when the composer/singer made her single visit to the tent on August 17, 1976. Although she did not perform the number that had originally made her famous, "Society's Child," Ian did sing her more recent hit composition, "Seventeen." As Ian's opening act, Richie Furay appeared at the festival for a second time. Furay had appeared previously, on August 14, 1974, together with John David Souther and Chris Hillman.

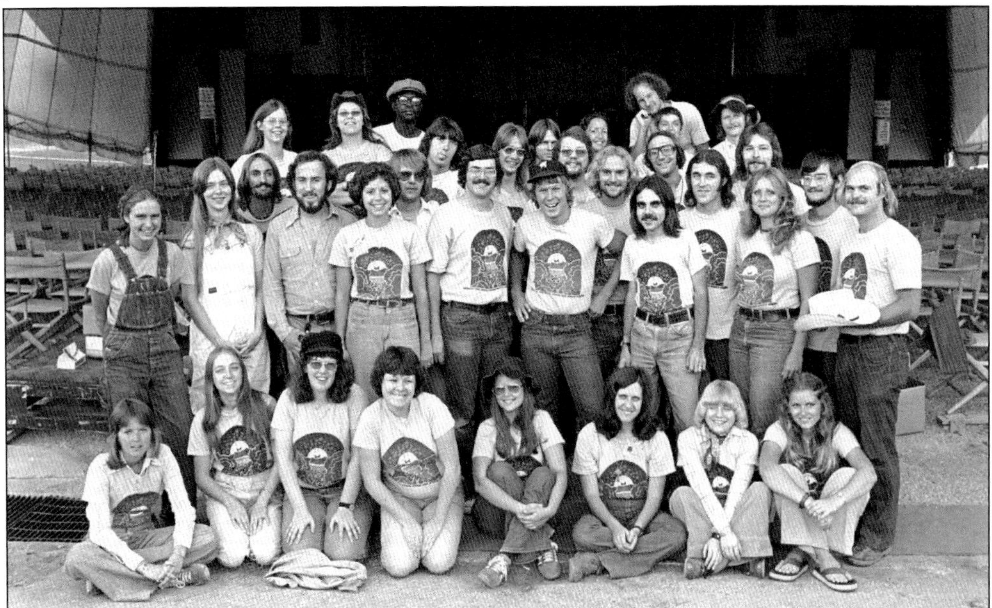

USHERS. The MRF ushers posed for this photograph prior to the Crosby and Nash concert on August 18, 1976. The student ushers and the other student workers consistently received praise from concertgoers and newspaper critics for their enthusiasm, courtesy, and professionalism. Over the years, employment opportunities provided by the festival enabled many SIUE students to finance their college degrees.

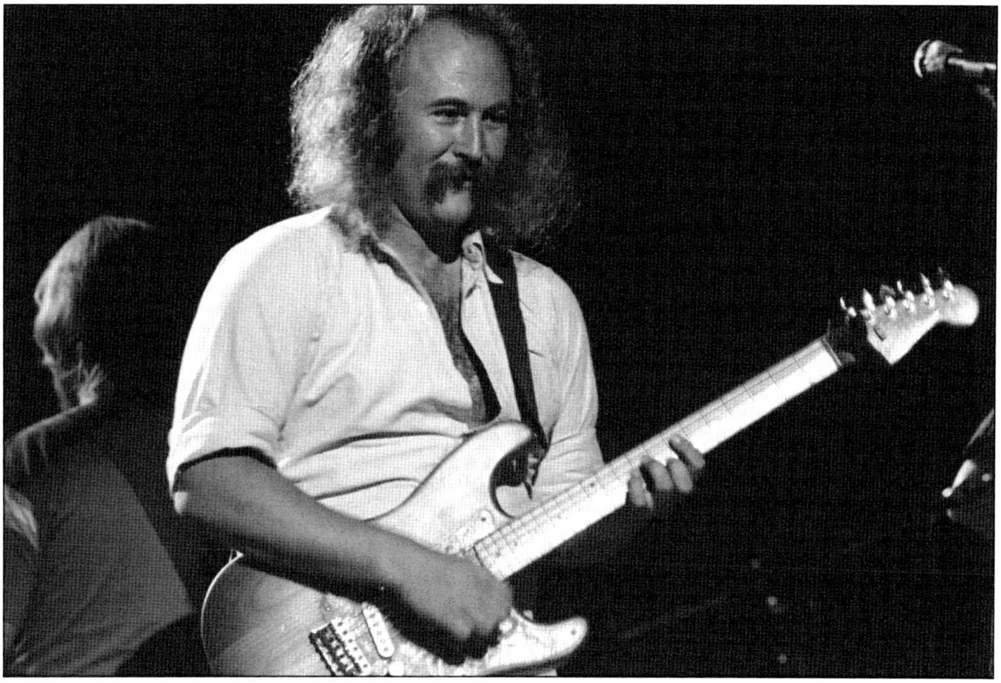

DAVID CROSBY. In the second of their two MRF concerts, on August 18, 1976, David Crosby and Graham Nash employed David Lindley, Danny Kortchmar, Russ Kunkel, Craig Degree, and Joel Bernstein as their sidemen. Crosby and Nash performed two sets, with a 20-minute intermission, and returned for two encores: "Teach Your Children" and "Chicago."

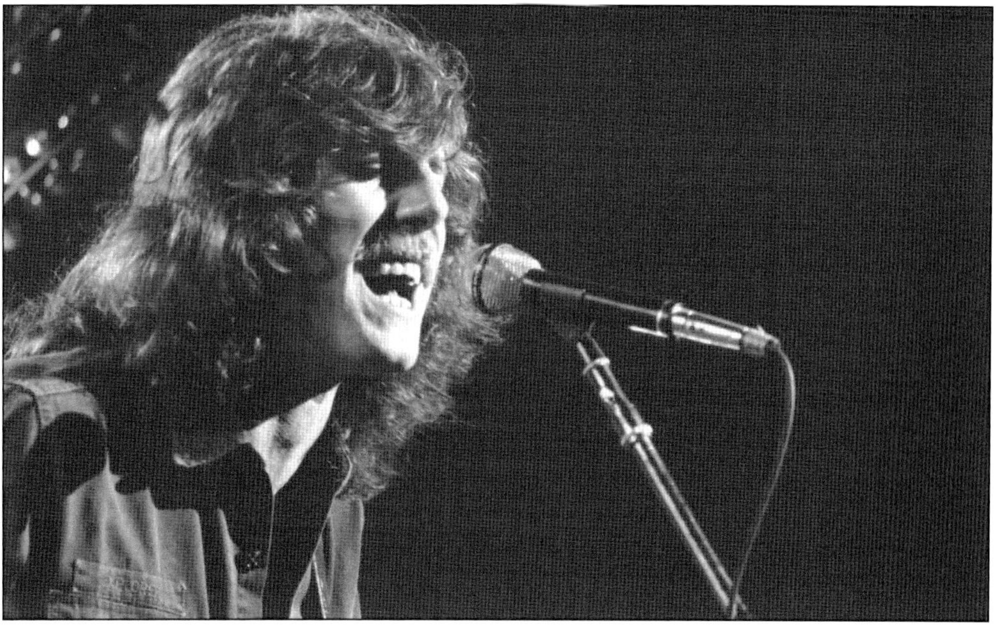

GRAHAM NASH. With or without participation by Neil Young, the trio of David Crosby, Stephen Stills, and Graham Nash constituted one of the most successful studio and touring acts of the 1960s, the 1970s, and the early 1980s. No other American group came as close to approximating the musical impact of the Beatles. Crosby had belonged to the Byrds and Nash to the Hollies.

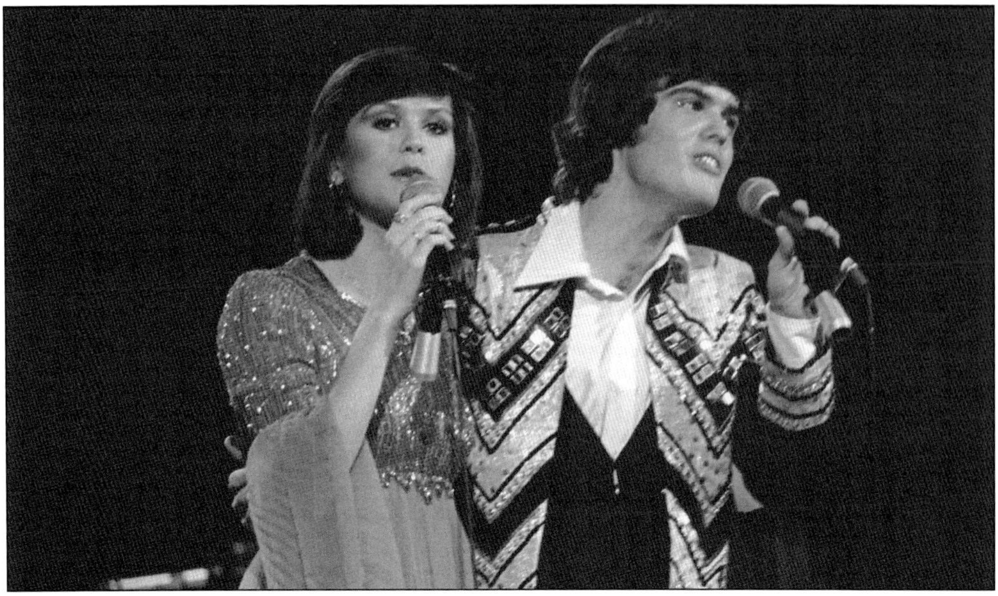

The Osmonds. Merrill, Donny, Wayne, Alan, Jay, Jimmy, and Marie Osmond brought their family song-and-dance act to the festival a second time on August 19, 1976. Marie had been absent from their previous appearance on August 20, 1975. The highlight of the program came when Donny, seated at the piano, sang several of his hit songs like "Go Away Little Girl" and "Puppy Love." Munch, the opening act, had evolved from another family named Muench that had also called itself Brothers Pride up to 1974.

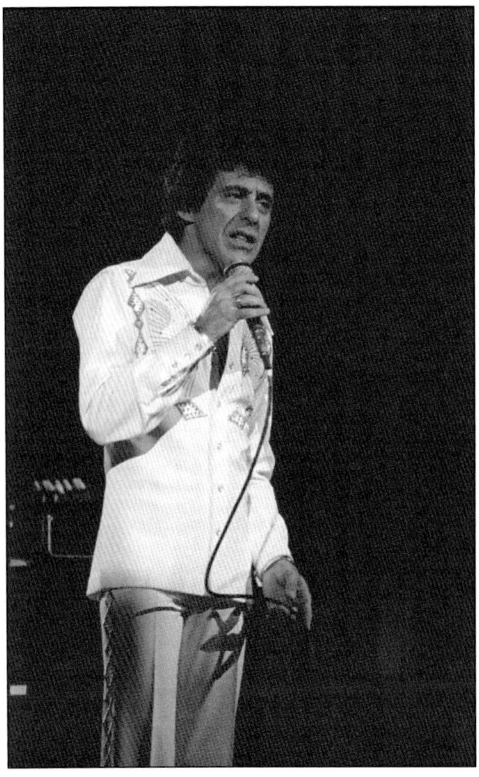

Frankie Valli and Four Seasons. The Four Seasons (Dan Ciccone, John Paiva, Lee Shapiro, and Gerry Polci) and leader Frankie Valli made their only appearance at the festival on August 22, 1976. Drummer Gerry Polci sang the lead on "December '63 (Oh, What a Night)." Ciccone played bass; Paiva, guitar; and Shapiro, keyboard. Comedian Stewie Stone opened for Frankie Valli and the Four Seasons.

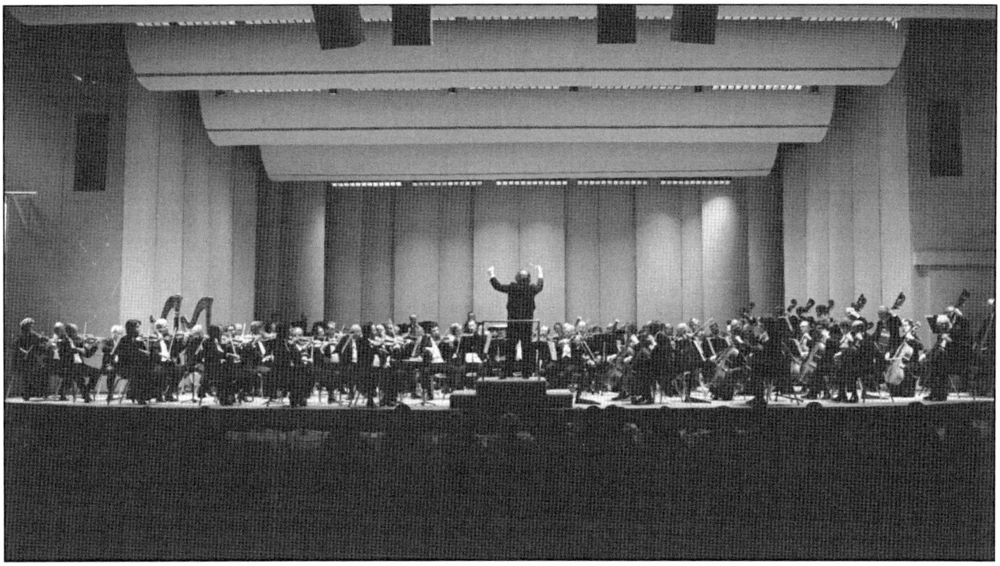

CHICAGO SYMPHONY. After years of effort, and with outside financial support, festival administrators finally succeeded in scheduling the Chicago Symphony Orchestra for an MRF concert on September 15, 1976. Leonard Slatkin of the St. Louis Symphony Orchestra presided as conductor for the Chicago Symphony appearance. The program on this occasion included works by Berlioz, Barber, Strauss, and Prokofiev. The visit by the Chicago Symphony marked the only time that a major orchestra other than the St. Louis Symphony appeared as part of the festival.

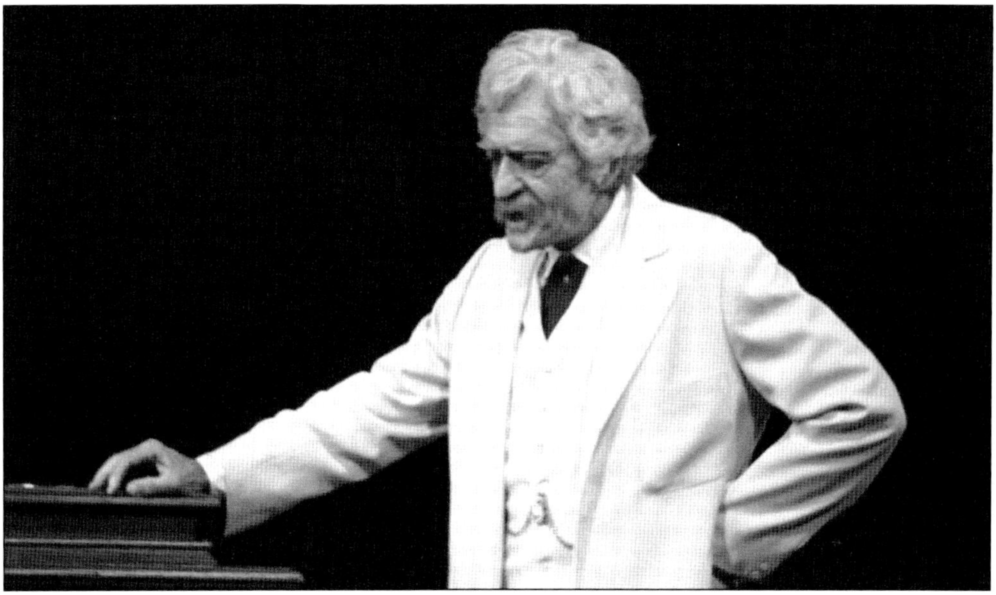

HAL HOLBROOK. On the evening following the Chicago Symphony visit, September 16, 1976, actor Hal Holbrook brought his one-man show *Mark Twain Tonight* to the festival. Holbrook initiated the show as a college honors project, opened it off-Broadway in 1959, and then on Broadway in 1966, winning a Tony award as best actor in a dramatic role. In 1967, CBS presented a 90-minute televised version of the play that attracted an audience of 22 million persons. Holbrook would continue to enact the role of Twain well into the 21st century.

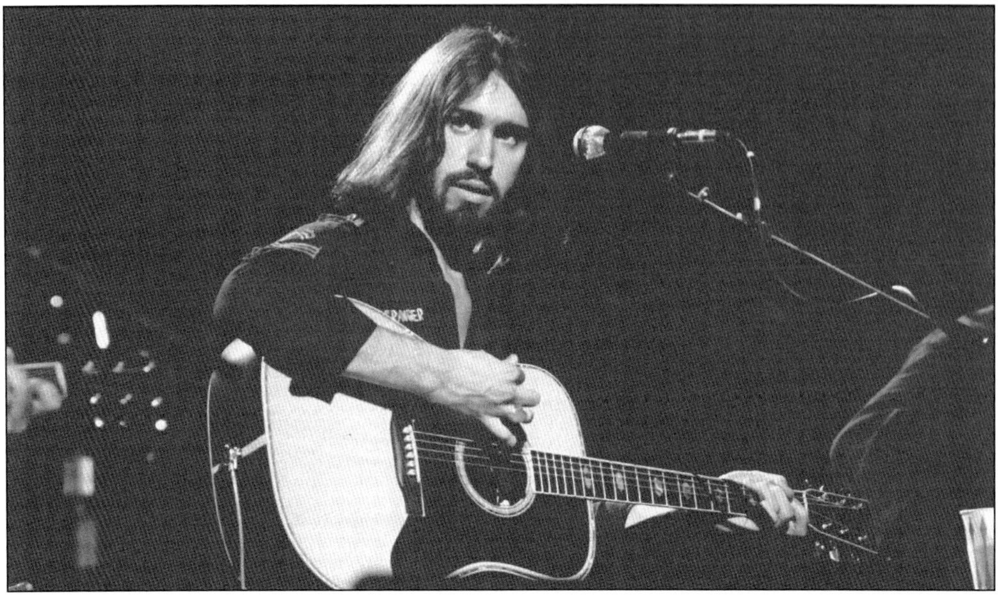

DAN FOGELBERG. The 1977 season, the ninth and last one produced by the university, began with an appearance by Dan Fogelberg on June 22. Fogelberg performed a 50-minute solo set and then brought out his associates, Fool's Gold, for some soft rock numbers. Fool's Gold included, besides Kenny Hatch, Geoffrey Leiv, David Pearlman, and Scott Shelly, two additional musicians from Southwestern Illinois. Denny Henson and Tom Kelly had been members of the Guild, a local group that had performed with Sha Na Na at the festival back on July 18, 1973.

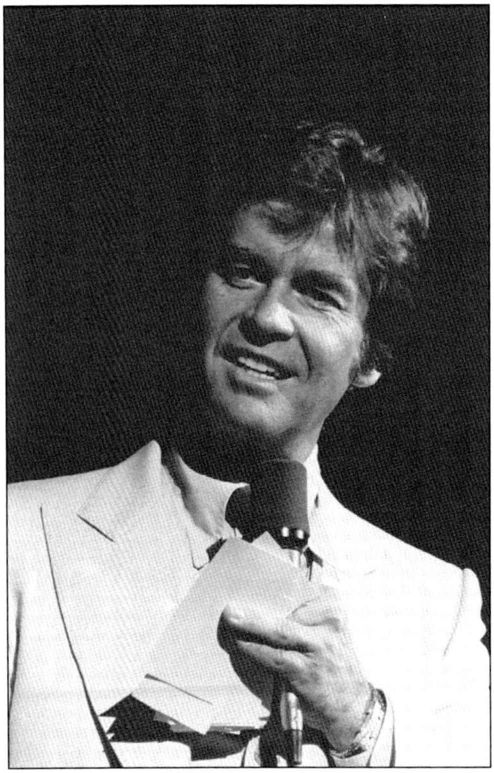

DICK CLARK. The ever-young host of *American Bandstand* brought *Dick Clark's Good Ol' Rock N' Roll Show* to the festival on June 24, 1977. Clark served as master of ceremonies for a four-segment show. The roster for the Clark event included Gary "U. S." Bonds, and his four-man group. It also included Chuck Berry, Bobby Lewis, and Bobby Vee. A similarly themed nostalgia concert back on July 29, 1971, had featured Bonds, Berry, Bo Diddley, and Jerry Lee Lewis.

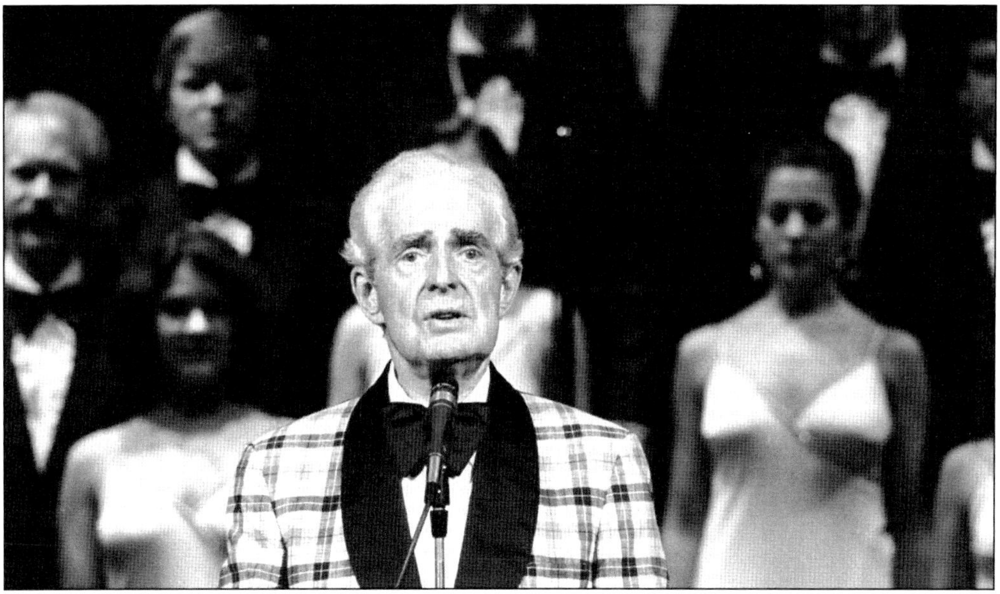

FRED WARING. The Fred Waring Singers arrived at the festival on July 15, 1977. Waring and his "Pennsylvanians" had been involved in the popular music field for more than half a century when the latest incarnation of his orchestra and chorus came to Edwardsville. During the 1960s and 1970s, Waring and his entourage traveled roughly 40,000 miles per year, mostly by bus. The Waring concert opened with his theme song, "I Hear Music" and also included "Sleep," a tune that he had first recorded for the Victor Talking Machine Company back in the 1920s.

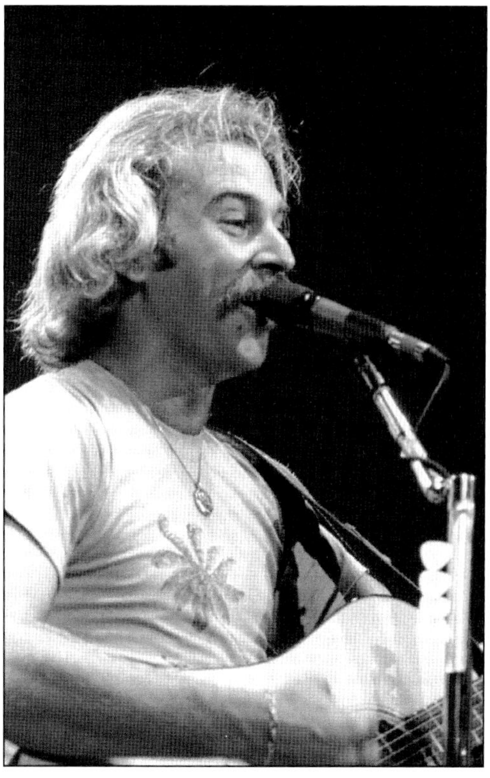

JIMMY BUFFET. A lengthy opening set lasting more than an hour heralded the only festival appearance of Jimmy Buffet on July 20, 1977. Buffet and his Coral Reefer Band played a number of songs from their recent album *Changes in Latitude, Changes in Attitude*, including the major hit "Margaritaville." The length of Buffet's set, plus a 40-minute break, pushed back the start of the featured Ozark Mountain Daredevils appearance until nearly 10 p.m.

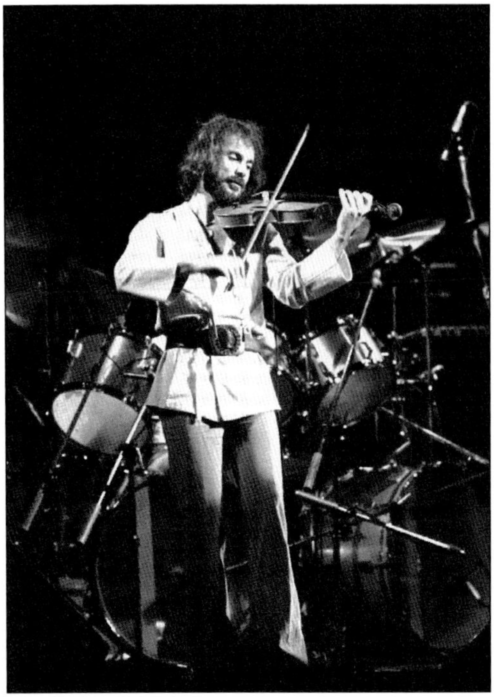

JEAN-LUC PONTY. A pioneer as a jazz violinist and in the use of an electric violin, Jean-Luc Ponty made just one appearance at the festival, on July 27, 1977. Under a nearly-full moon, Ponty played selections from his newest album *Enigmatic Ocean* with the assistance of Allan Zavod, Tom Fowler, Daryl Stuermer, Mark Craney, Steve Smith, and Frank Patterson. Ponty opened for another act making its first and only festival appearance, Renaissance, a band made up of Annie Haslam, Jon Camp, Jon Tout, Terry Sullivan, and Michael Dunford.

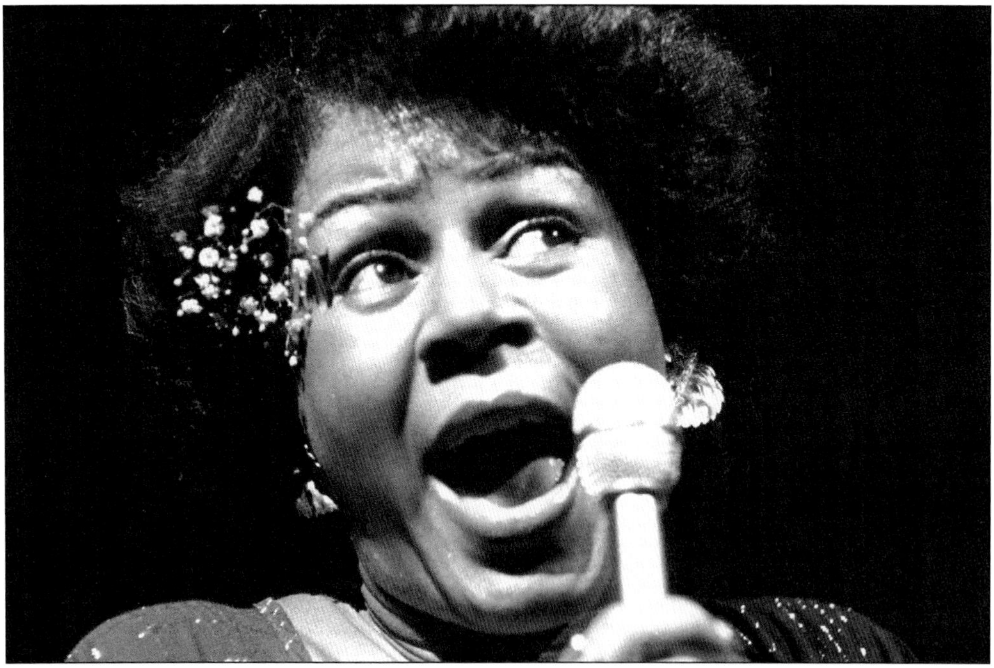

MINNIE RIPPERTON. Prior to the George Benson concert on July 29, 1977, singer Minnie Ripperton displayed her remarkable five-octave vocal range at the festival for the only time. Ripperton included her hit song, "Loving You," in her opening performance. Among other numbers, guitarist/singer George Benson performed "The Greatest Love of All," a song he had composed for a movie about boxer Mohammed Ali. Benson eventually recalled Ripperton to the stage for a dual encore performance of "Misty."

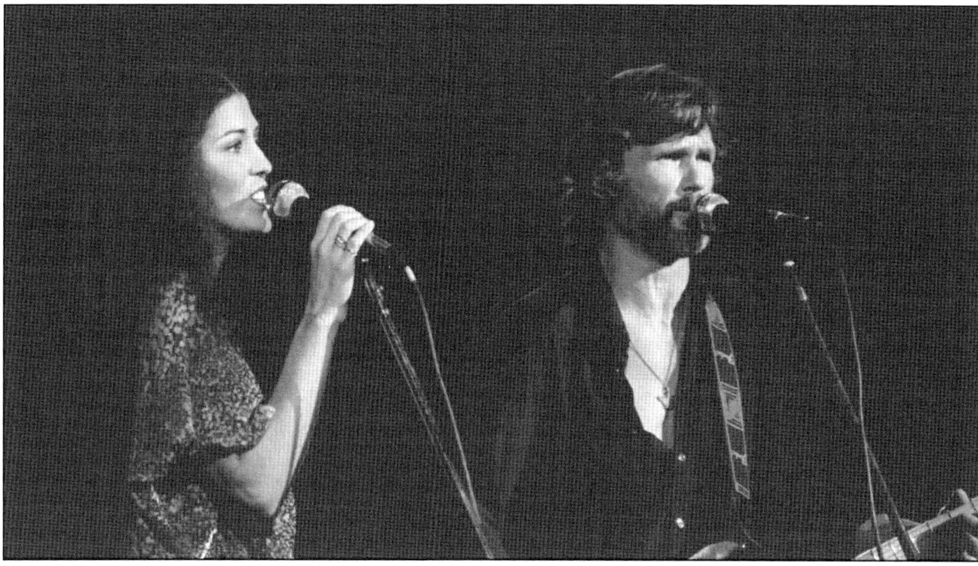

Kris Kristofferson and Rita Coolidge. After an absence of five years, Kris Kristofferson and Rita Coolidge returned to the festival on August 10, 1977. They had previously appeared together on July 11, 1972. Long-time Kristofferson friend Billy Swann sang and played the piano before being joined by Kristofferson. During the first set, Donnie Fritts, Steve Burton, and Jerry McGee also joined the act. The second half of the show introduced and featured Coolidge. Finally Kristofferson joined Coolidge for duets on songs such as "Help Me Make It Through the Night" and "Me and Bobby McGee."

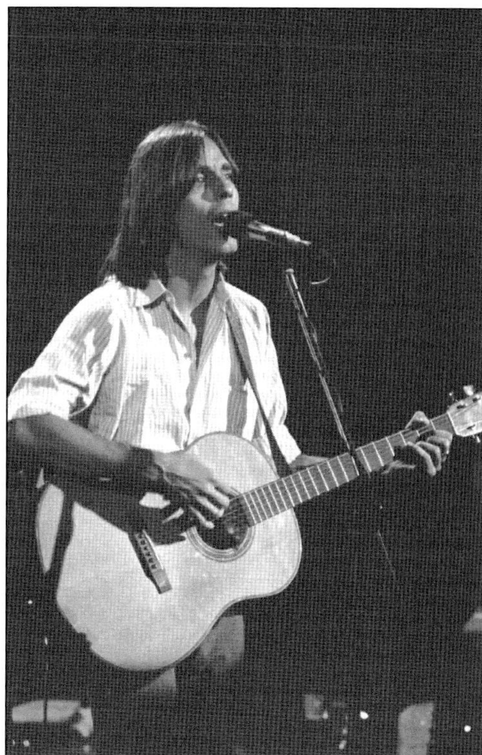

Jackson Browne. For the first time, on August 17, 1977, Jackson Browne appeared at the MRF as a headliner. Browne had opened for Yes on August 21, 1972, and for America on August 8, 1973. David Lindley again accompanied Browne during his third visit. Section, Browne's opening act, had earned the reputation as one of the best backing bands in the business. Russ Kunkel, Leland Sklar, Craig Doerge, and Danny Kortchmar comprised Section.

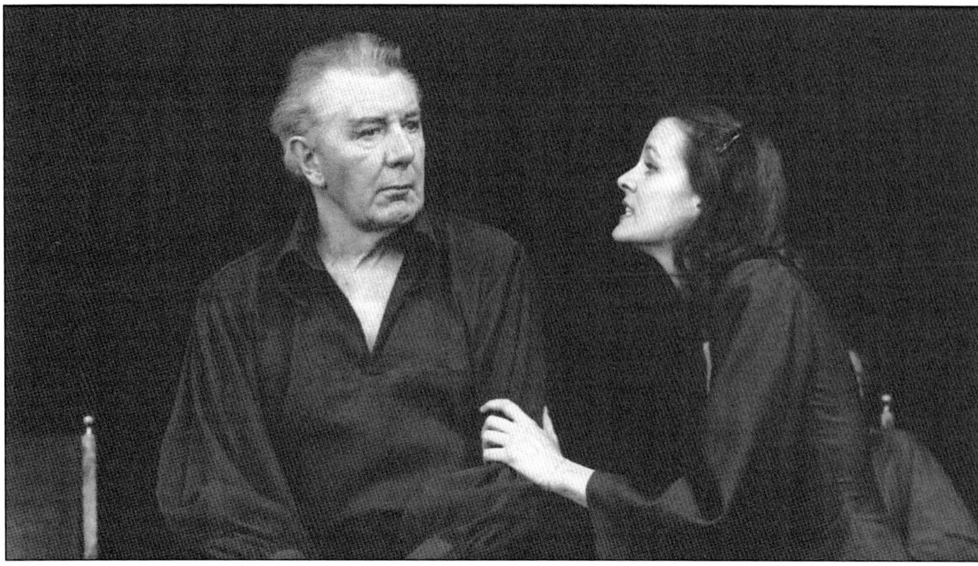

SIR MICHAEL REDGRAVE. *Shakespeare's People*, a compilation of selections from the works of the Bard devised and directed by Alan Strachan, appeared at the festival on August 18, 19, and 20, 1977. Featuring Sir Michael Redgrave, the British production included David Dodimead, Hope Alexander-Willis, George Ceres, and Stephen Schnetzer. When a vital dyed-linen backdrop representing the Globe Theatre disappeared, SIUE scenery artist Larry Bogdan and three students—Sue McKinna, Rodney Masinelli, and Ken Bryant—quickly prepared an emergency replacement.

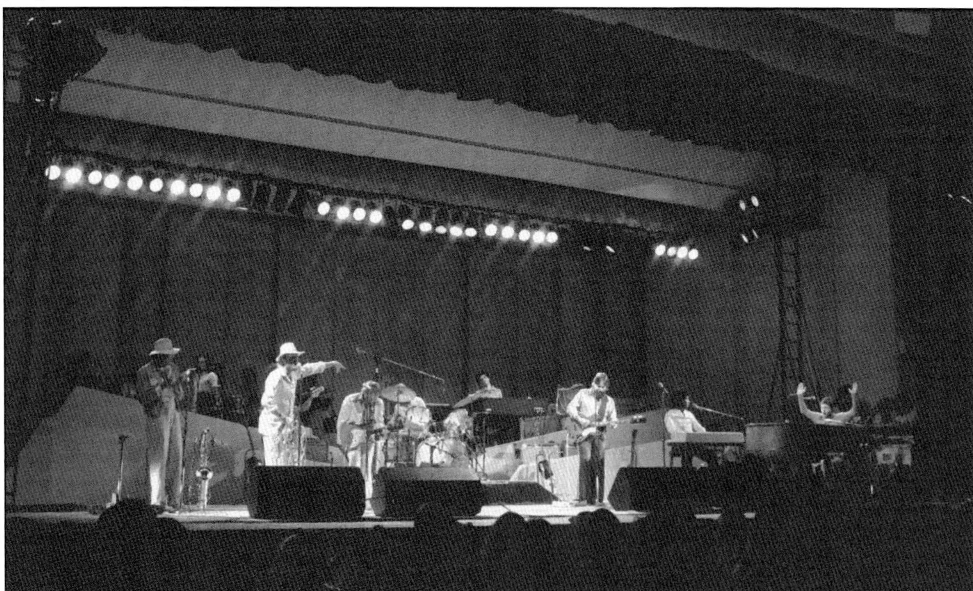

THE BEACH BOYS. Brian Wilson had been unavailable when the Beach Boys first played the MRF on August 16, 1972. But Brian appeared together with Carl and Dennis Wilson, Mike Love, Al Jardine, and Billy Hinsche for the group's second visit on August 21, 1977. For their encores, the band played "You Are So Beautiful;" "Barbara Ann;" "Rock N' Roll Music;" and "Fun, Fun, Fun." The Beach Boys came back again twice, on August 19, 1979, and on August 7, 1980.

Three

ESTRANGEMENT
1978–1980

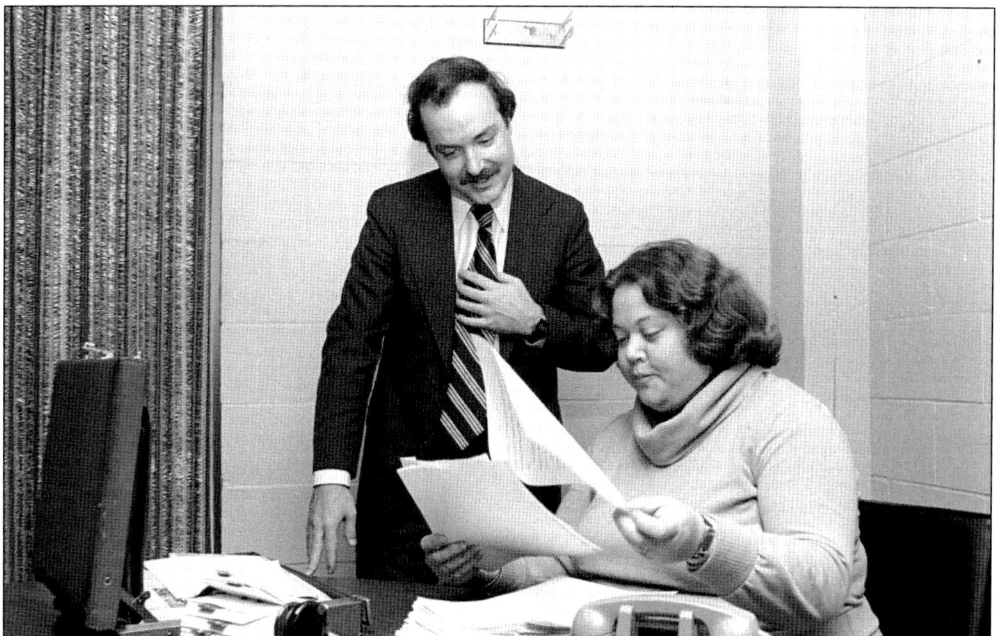

WAYNE NEDERLANDER AND PEGGY WELLS. Following the 1977 season, new SIUE president Kenneth "Buzz" Shaw decided to search for an experienced show business management firm to lease the MRF site and to produce the festival. He believed that he had found one when he announced on April 6, 1978, the signing of an agreement with the Nederlander organization, a major enterprise in theatrical entertainment. Wayne Nederlander, an executive with the family firm, and Peggy Wells, newly-named site manager, attended a news conference on May 3, 1978.

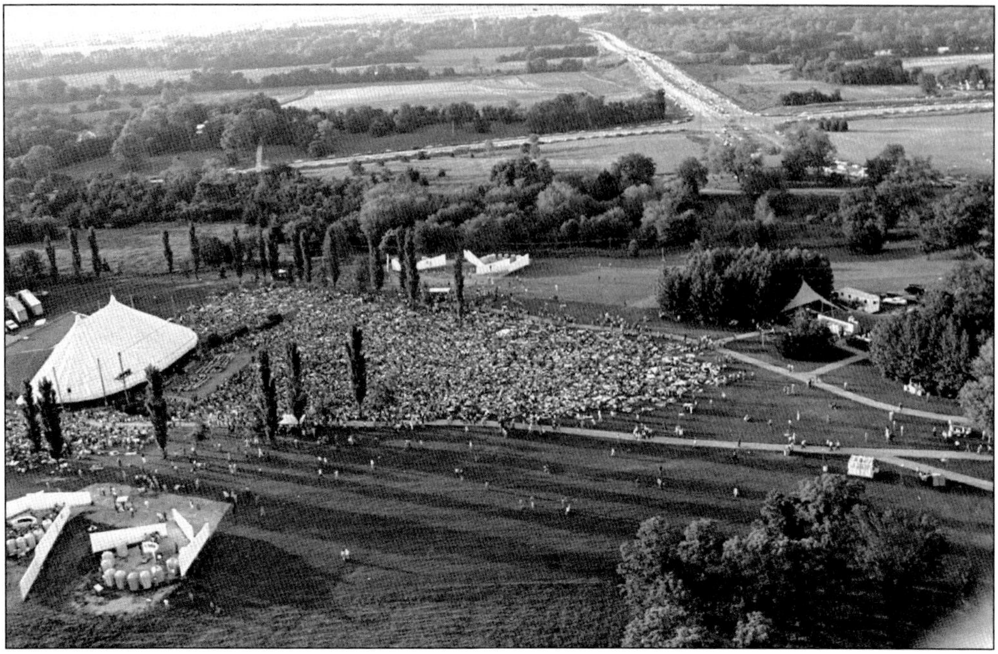

SOUTH TO NORTH. This photograph provides a view of the MRF site looking from south to north. It is possible to see both rest areas, the intersection of North University Drive and Poag Road, and automobiles parked along the side of the roads. The image documents the site at the start of the 1978 season during a June 3 concert by the Marshall Tucker Band.

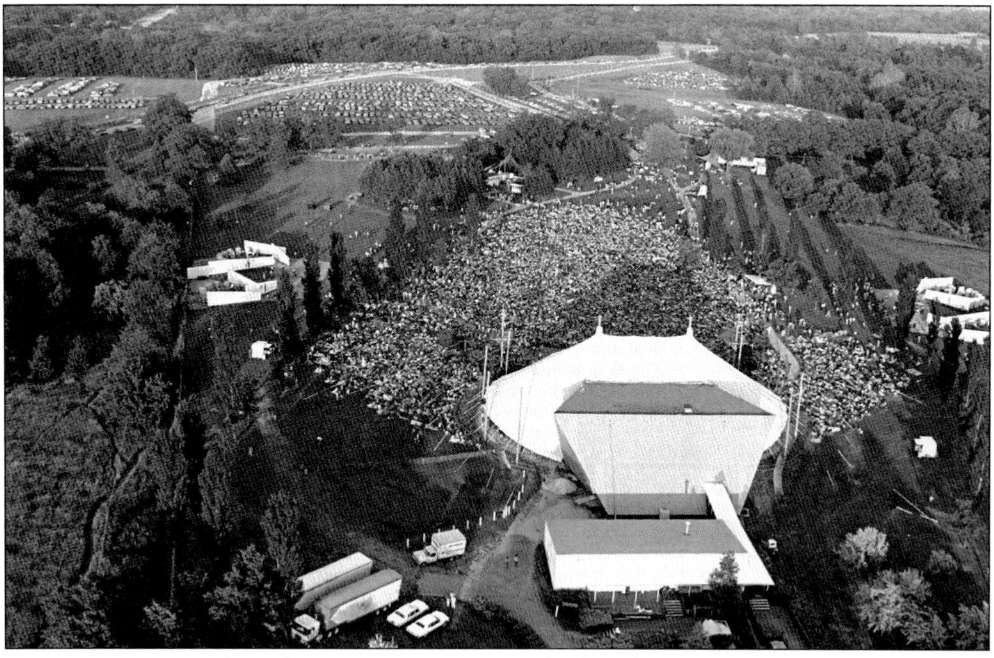

WEST TO EAST. Looking from west to east, toward Edwardsville, this photograph describes the dressing rooms and protective shell behind the tent. Parked trailers used to transport the equipment used by the bands or the symphony are visible in the lower left portion of this image.

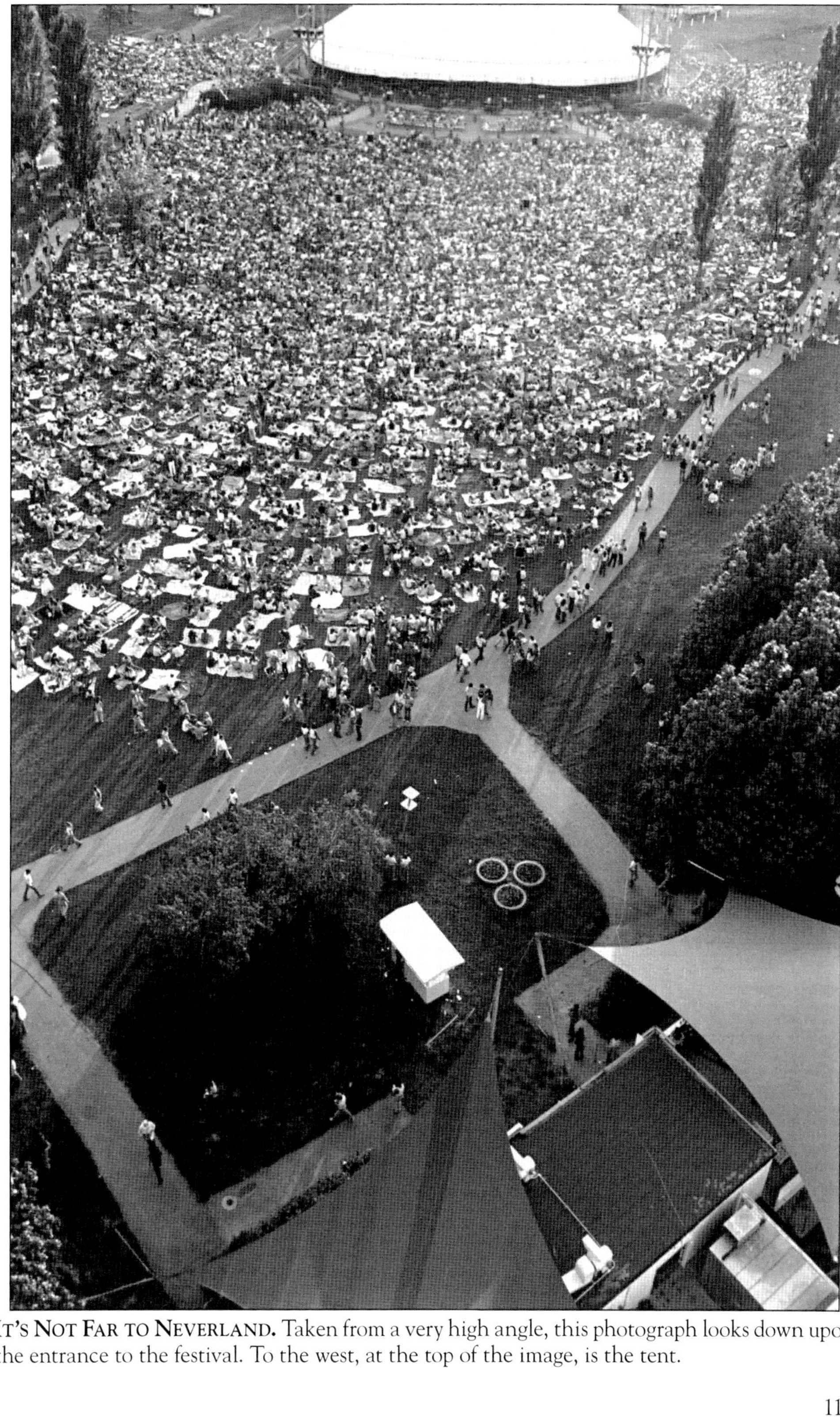

It's Not Far to Neverland. Taken from a very high angle, this photograph looks down upon the entrance to the festival. To the west, at the top of the image, is the tent.

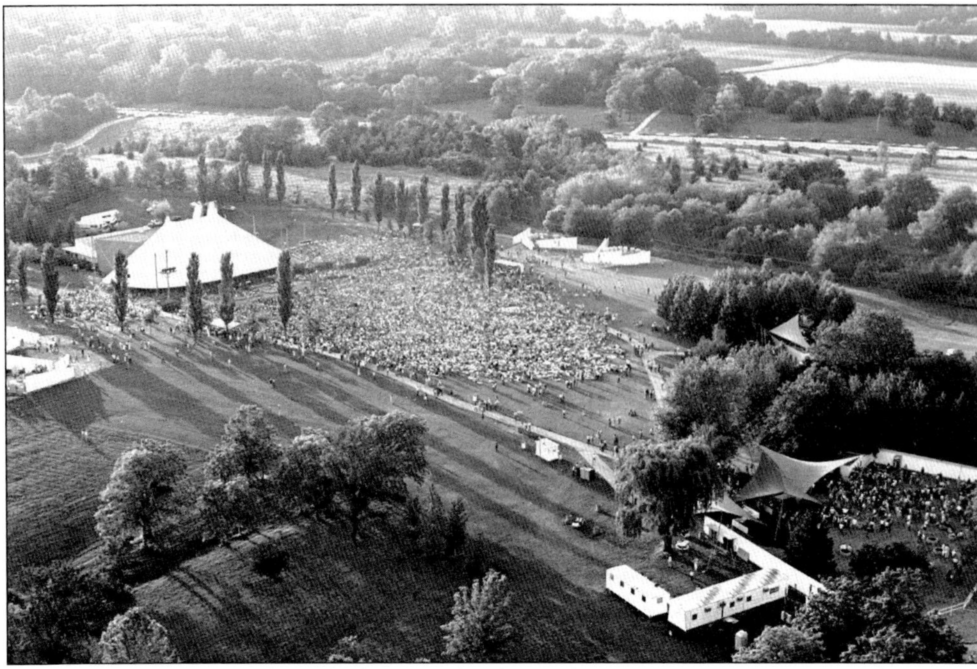

Poplar Shadows. The long shadows cast by the poplar trees on a sunny evening distinguish this photograph of the festival site. The photographer is looking from the southeast to the northwest across the site toward Poag Road at the top of the image.

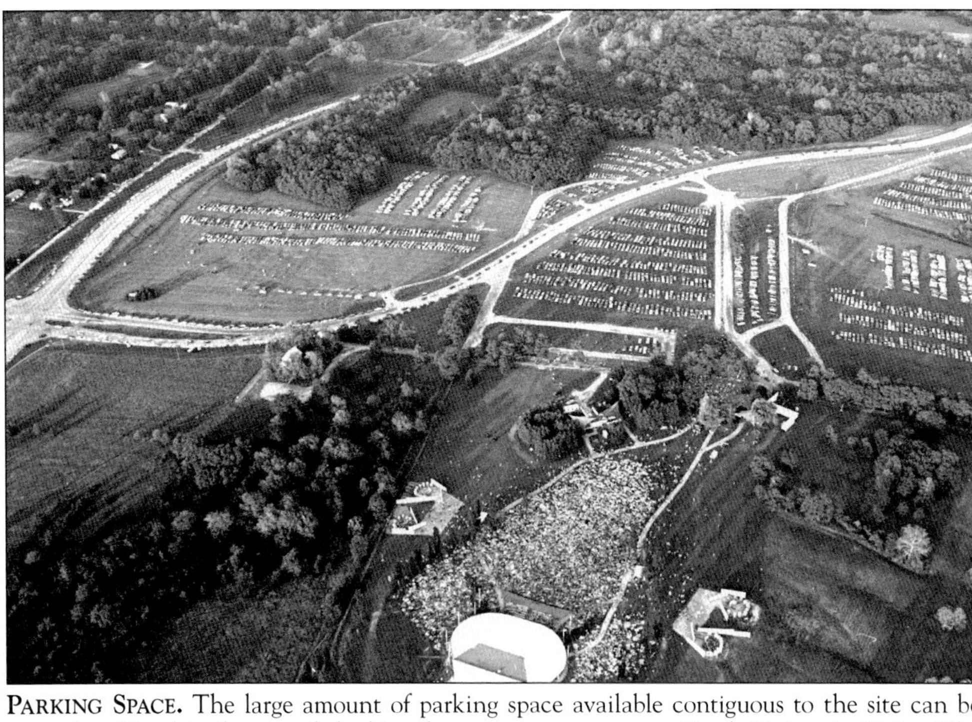

Parking Space. The large amount of parking space available contiguous to the site can be appreciated in this photograph looking from west to east across North University Drive. The intersection of North University Drive and Poag Road can be seen on the far left of the image.

STANLEY CLARKE. Master of the acoustic and electric basses, Stanley Clarke consumed 70 minutes of his featured concert on June 8, 1978, with his first three numbers. Clarke relied upon the accompaniment of Ray Gomez, Mike Garson, Darryl Brown, Al Harrison, James Tinsley, Bobby Malach, and Alfie Williams. Roy Ayers Ubiquity had opened the previous year, on July 13, for Stanley Turrentine and also opened for Clarke. Kerry Turman, Phillip Woo, Carla Vaughan, Chano Oferral, Justo Almario, and J. T. Lewis played with Roy Ayers.

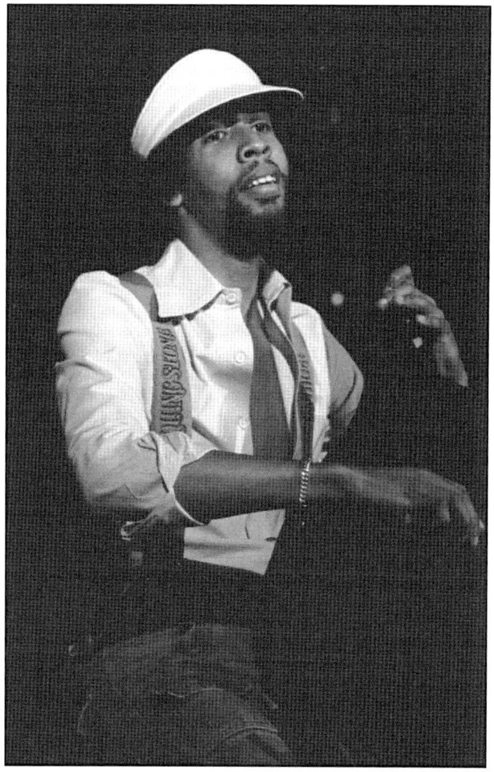

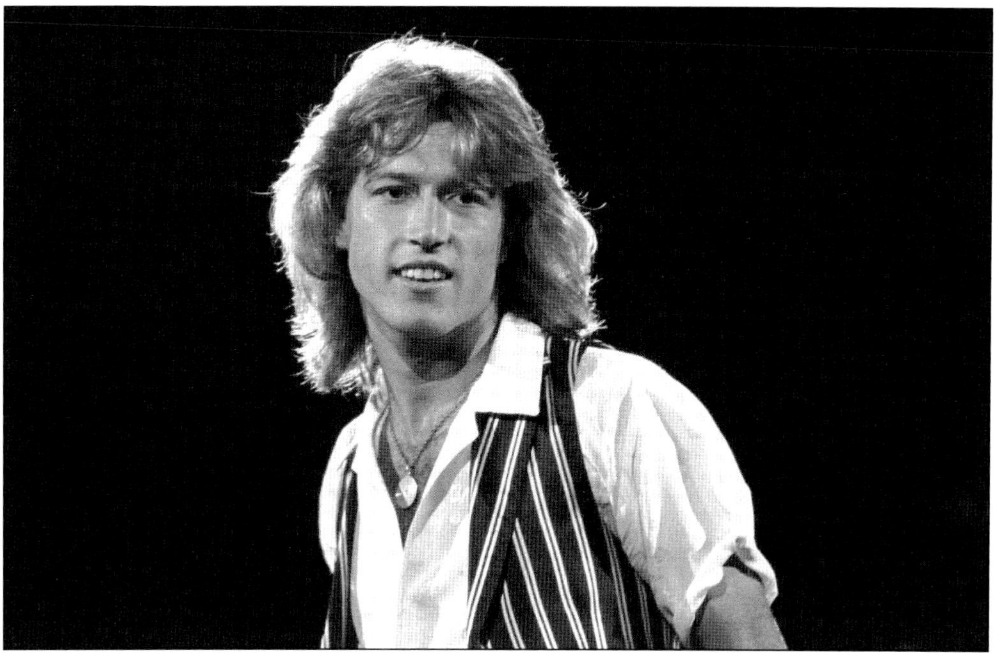

ANDY GIBB. The youngest of the famous brothers Gibb, Andy appeared at the festival only once, on June 15, 1978. Andy delighted his audience, composed largely of teenaged and preteen-aged girls, by singing his emerging hit "I Just Want to Be Your Everything," a song written by his brother Barry. Bobby and Billy Alessi, the Alessi Brothers, opened the Andy Gibb concert.

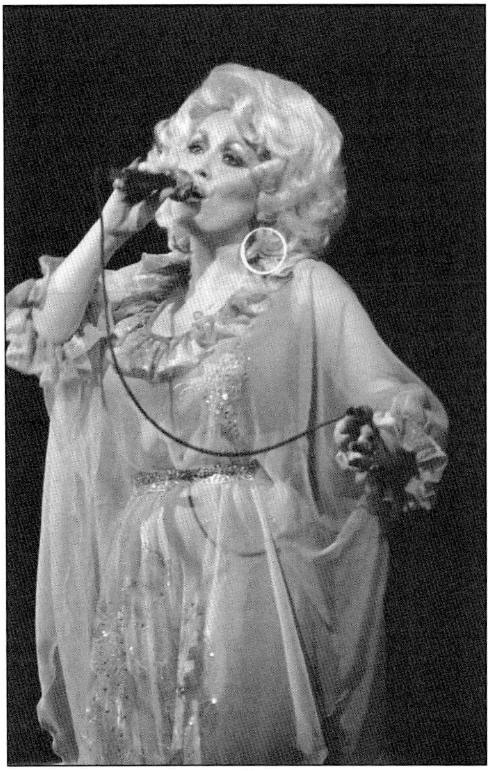

Dolly Parton. Eddie Rabbitt appeared on the bill just once, on June 24, 1978, as the opening act for Dolly Parton. During her pop numbers, Parton included an eight-piece band made up of six instrumentalists and two singers. For her country songs, Parton often sat alone on a stool accompanied only by her own guitar or banjo playing.

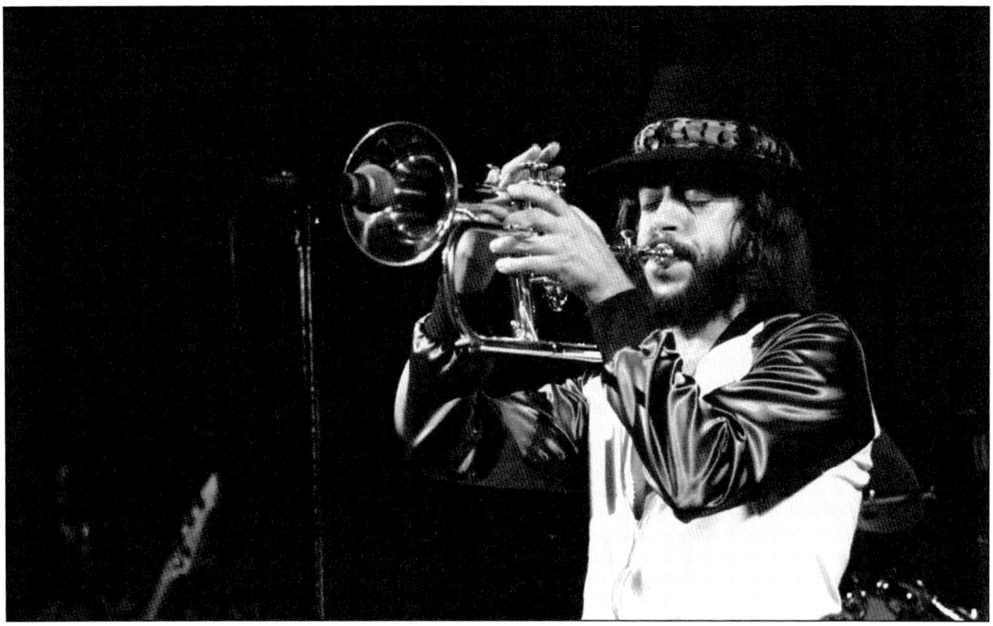

Chuck Mangione. Composer and flugelhorn artist Chuck Mangione came to the festival on June 28, 1978, for the second time. Previously, on June 25, 1976, Mangione had headlined a concert opened by vocalist Esther Satterfield. For his return visit, Mangione brought along Chris Vadala, Charles Meeks, James Brantley Jr., and Grant Greissman. Woodwind artist Vadala subsequently became a professor of music at the University of Maryland.

WILLIE NELSON. In his solitary festival appearance, on July 6, 1978, Willie Nelson shared the bill with opening act Emmylou Harris. Among many songs, Nelson performed "Mommas, Don't Let Your Babies Grow Up to Be Cowboys," a tune he recorded with Waylon Jennings in 1978 and that he sang while acting in the motion picture *Electric Horseman* with Robert Redford and Jane Fonda in 1979.

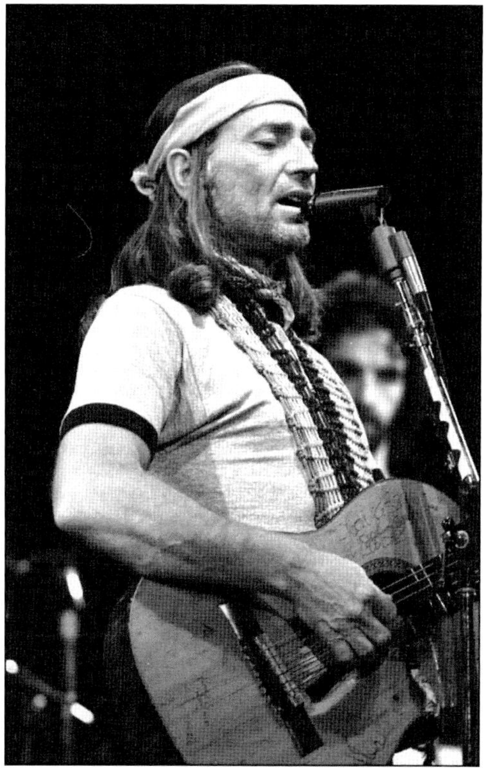

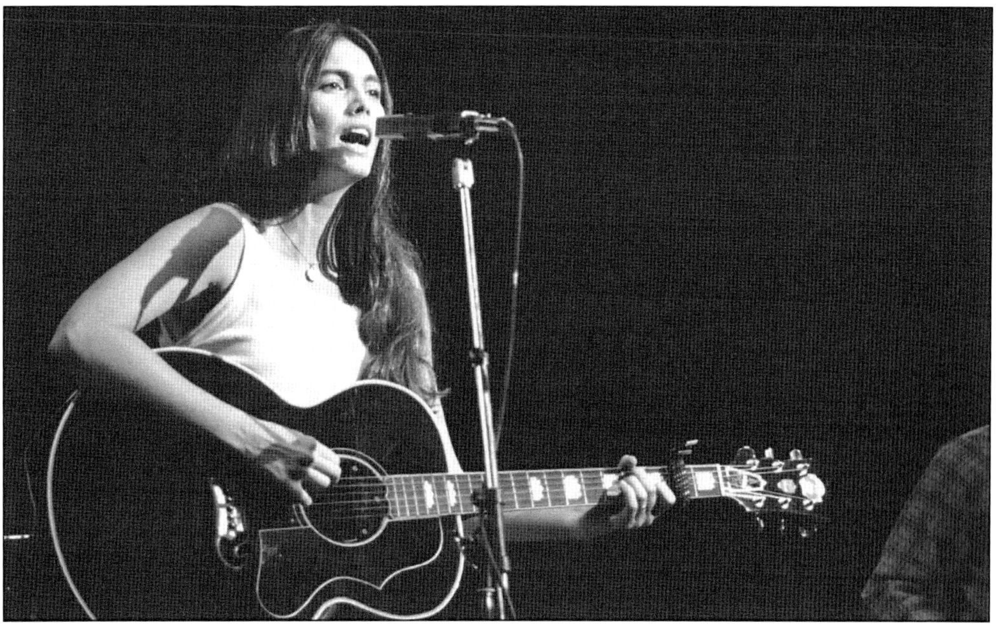

EMMYLOU HARRIS. Born in Birmingham, Alabama, Emmylou Harris possesses a restless creative spirit and abundant musical talent. Moving from country through many other musical genres, Harris continued to be a successful performer for several decades. During her appearance with Willie Nelson, on what had been expected to be a very hot night, she apologized to the audience for wearing shorts.

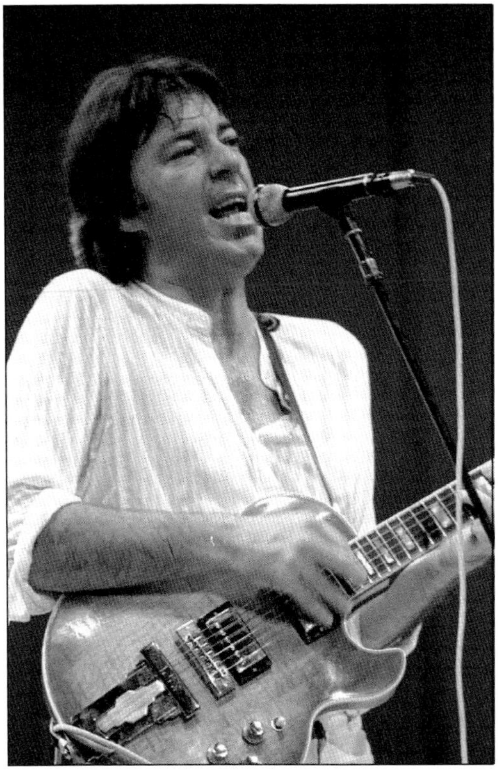

Boz Scaggs. On July 8, 1978, Boz Scaggs appeared at the MRF for a second time. He wore an all-white costume quite similar to the white clothing he had worn the previous year on June 29. During his show, Scaggs performed selections from his *Silk Degrees* album, including "Harbor Lights." A group called Coal Kitchen opened for Scaggs.

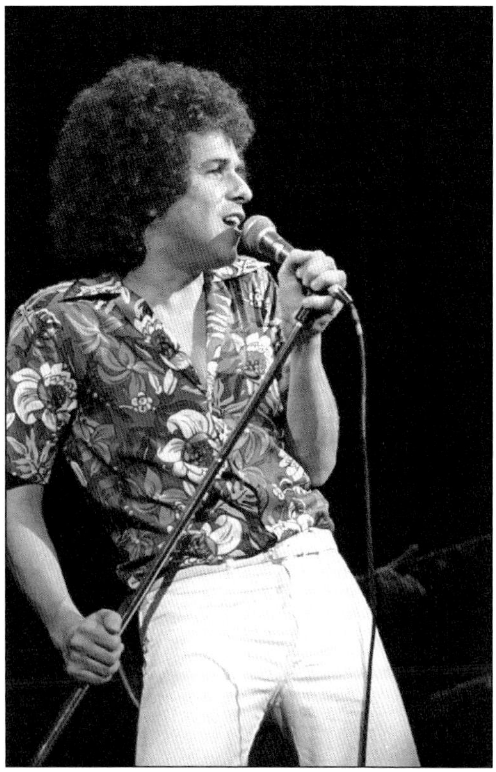

Leo Sayer. Yvonne Elliman served as the opening act for a Leo Sayer concert on July 9, 1978. Elliman had sung the role of Mary Magdalene in *Jesus Christ Superstar* and had recorded the Bee Gee's "If I Can't Have You" for the motion picture *Saturday Night Fever.* This concert constituted the only festival performance by Sayer or Elliman.

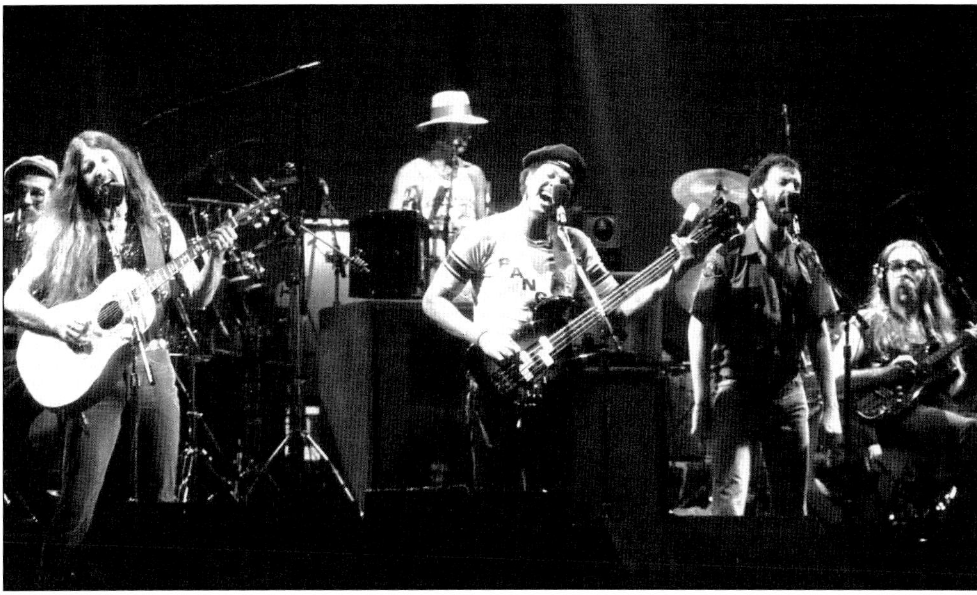

Doobie Brothers. John Hartman, Michael McDonald, Tiran Porter, Patrick Simmons, Jeff Baxter, and Keith Knudson made up the group when the Doobie Brothers returned to the festival for a second time on July 14, 1978. A Texas band named Toby Beau preceded the Doobie Brothers this time around. Although accurate attendance statistics for 1978 are not available, the Doobie Brothers sold 16,695 tickets on July 21, 1976, when they appeared with Heart. The Doobie Brothers came back to the MRF once more on July 13, 1979.

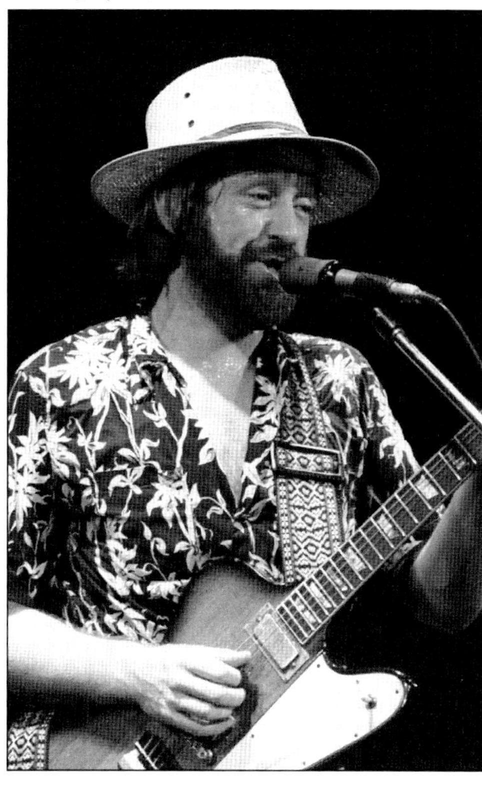

Dave Mason. Les Dudek, Mike Finnigan, and Jim Krueger appeared on July 21, 1978, prior to the performance by Dave Mason. In his only prior festival performance, on July 23, 1975, Mason and Poco had managed to bring in a paid crowd of 20,917 attendees. For his encores in 1978, Mason played "Share Your Love" and "Feelin' Alright."

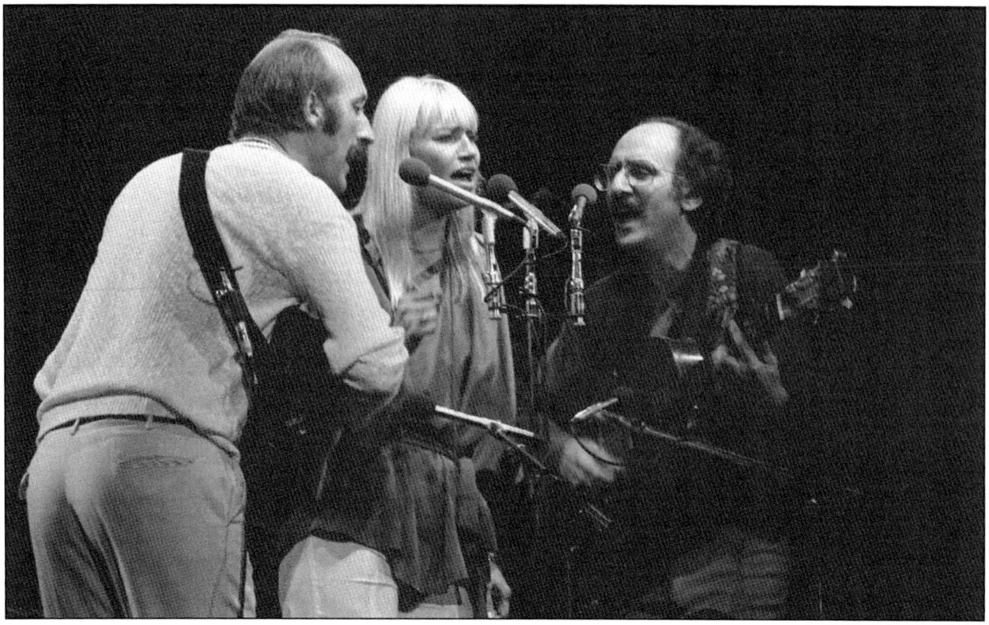

PETER, PAUL, AND MARY. On August 11, 1978, after being apart for eight years, folksingers Peter Yarrow, Paul Stookey, and Mary Travers performed together again at the MRF on the first stop of their reunion tour. Although nervous and slightly uncomfortable, the trio found themselves embraced by an enthusiastic and uncritical crowd. Peter, Paul, and Mary performed a two-set concert that lasted nearly two and a half hours including three encores.

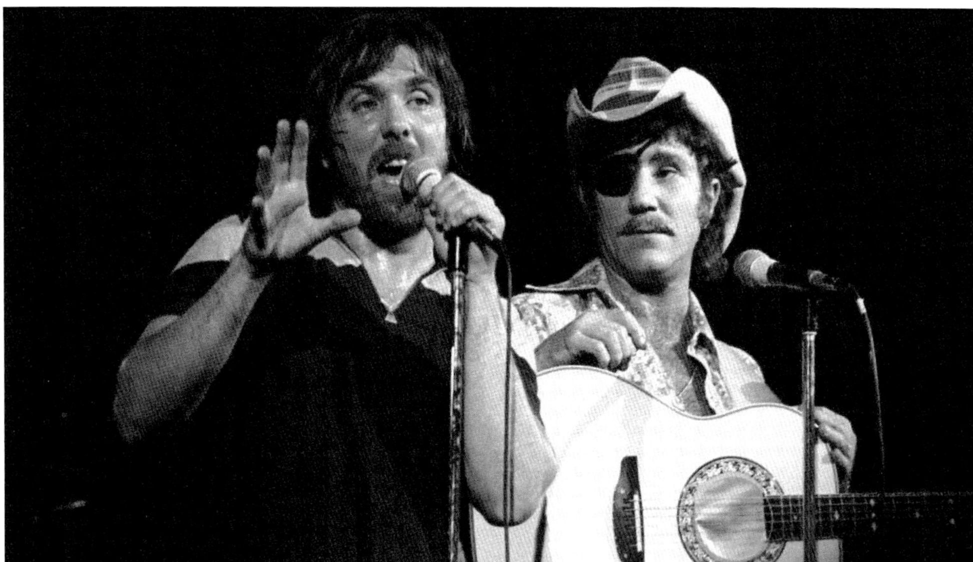

DR. HOOK. On August 18, 1978, Sha Na Na returned to the festival for a fourth time. The motion picture *Grease*, starring Olivia Newton-John and John Travolta and containing an appearance by Sha Na Na, had been released barely two months earlier. John "Bowser" Bauman, Scott Simon, John Contardo, Tony Santini, Lenny Baker, and Denny Greene all participated in the act at this time. Dr. Hook opened the show for Sha Na Na, with performances by Ray Sawyer, Dennis Locorriere, Bill Francis, Rik Elswit, Jance Garfat, John Wolters, and Bob Henke.

CHARLES COX. As official photographer for SIUE beginning in 1961, Charles (Charlie) Cox witnessed and recorded the history of the institution in photographic images for the ensuing 25 years. Prior to joining the university, Cox had published a weekly newspaper in Altamont. Cox and his student assistants faithfully observed and documented the history of the Mississippi River Festival as an integral element of university life. Cox became as familiar a sight around the MRF then as Skip Manley. It is thanks to the dedication and artistry of Cox and his assistants that it remains possible for everyone to continue to experience the MRF visually more than a quarter century after the final concert.

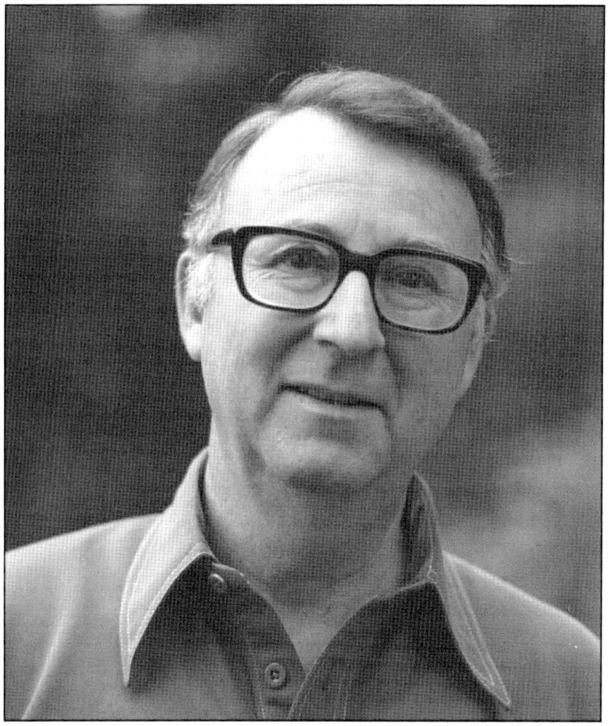

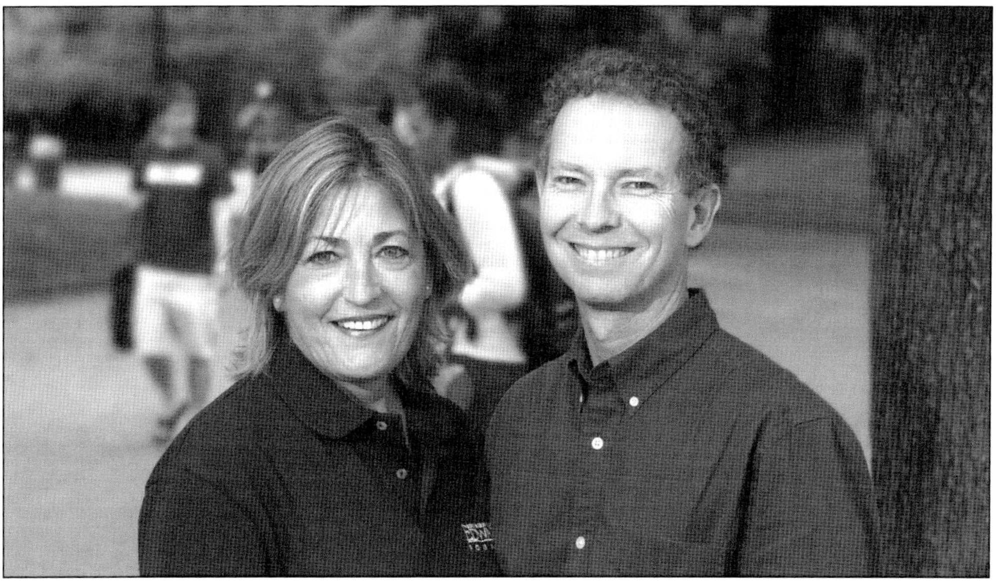

BILL BRINSON AND DENISE MACDONALD. Denise Macdonald began working as an office assistant for Cox in 1984. In response to her interest in his profession, Cox offered her the opportunity to learn from him and mentored her as a professional photographer. Bill Brinson majored in mass communications at SIUE during the 1970s while working as a photographer at the *Collinsville Herald*. As photography editor of the university's student newspaper, the *Alestle*, Brinson also covered the MRF. After graduation, Brinson served as chief photographer with the *St. Louis Globe-Democrat*. Brinson returned to SIUE in 1986 following the retirement Cox. Macdonald and Brinson deserve credit for the digitization of the photographs included in this volume.

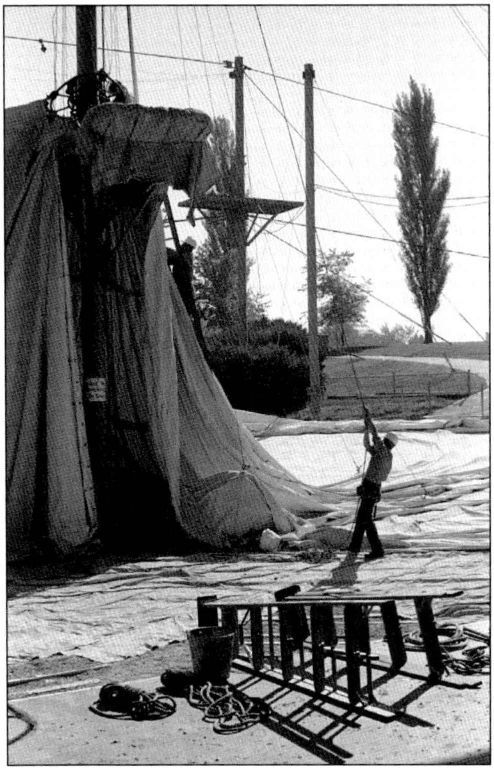

LOWERING THE TENT. On October 20, 1978, the physical plant work crew lowered the famous MRF tent for what would be the very last time. Although no official decision had yet been announced by the Nederlander officials, a decision would be made prior to the 1979 season not to raise the tent again.

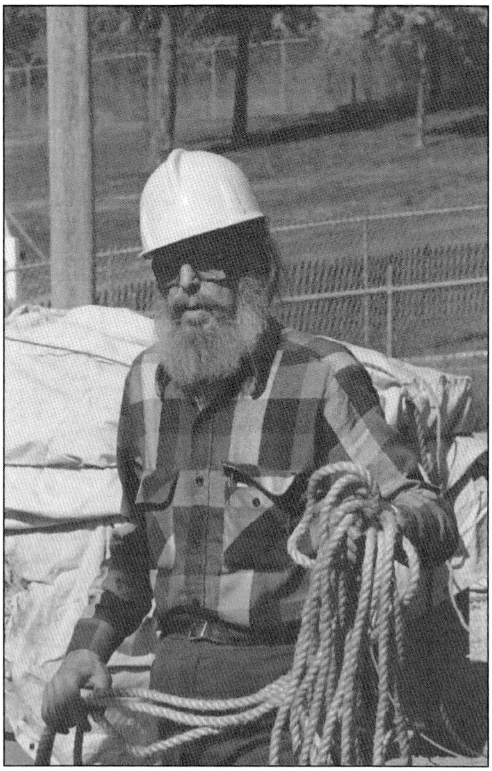

LEADER OF THE BAND. The elimination of the tent meant that Skip Manley would lose his post as tent master after 10 summer seasons. The disappearance of the tent and of Manley symbolized the growing estrangement between the university community and the festival.

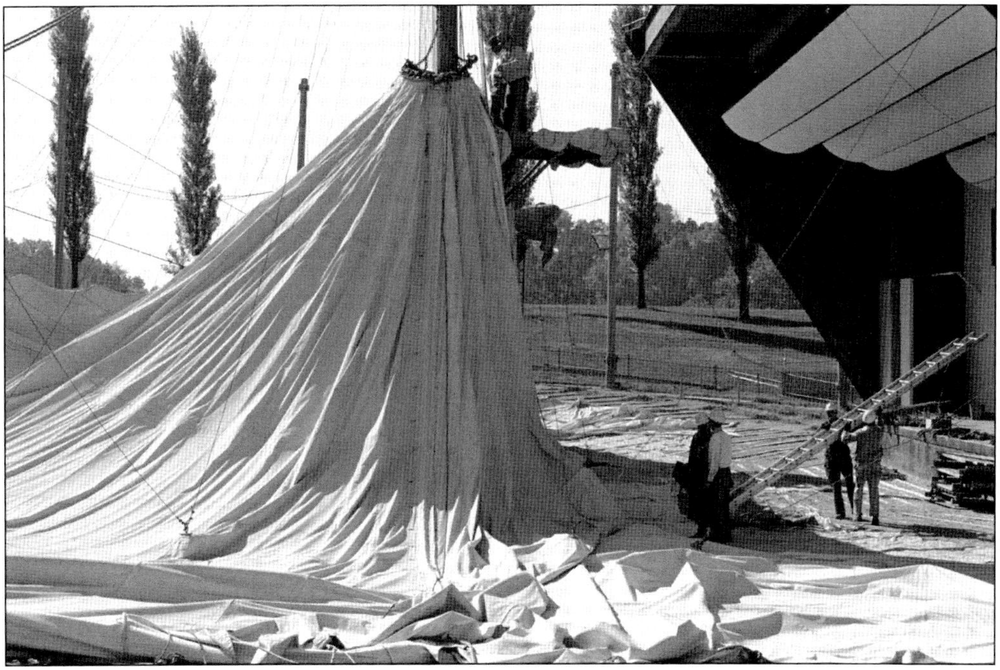

THE SHELL. Although the tent would disappear from the scene, the stage and protective shell would remain. However, the experience of attending the festival would be profoundly and permanently altered by the absence of the tent.

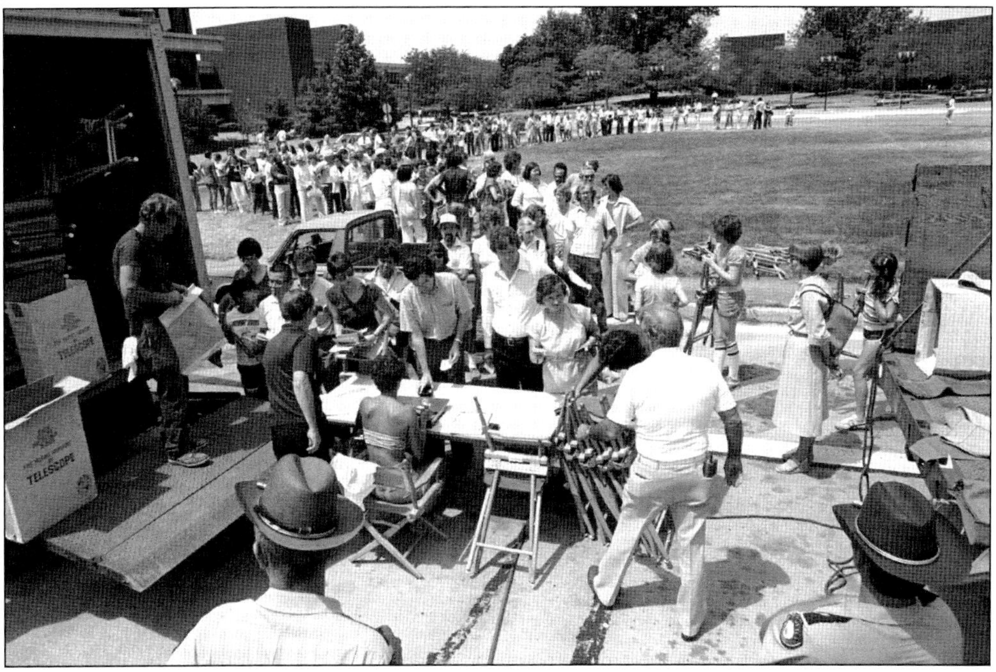

CHAIR SALE. Members of the university community and others who had treasured the experience of attending the MRF during the glory days gathered on the Hairpin to purchase a keepsake during the sale of the reserved seating chairs on July 17, 1979. In this photograph it is possible to view the long line of waiting purchasers winding around in front of the core campus buildings.

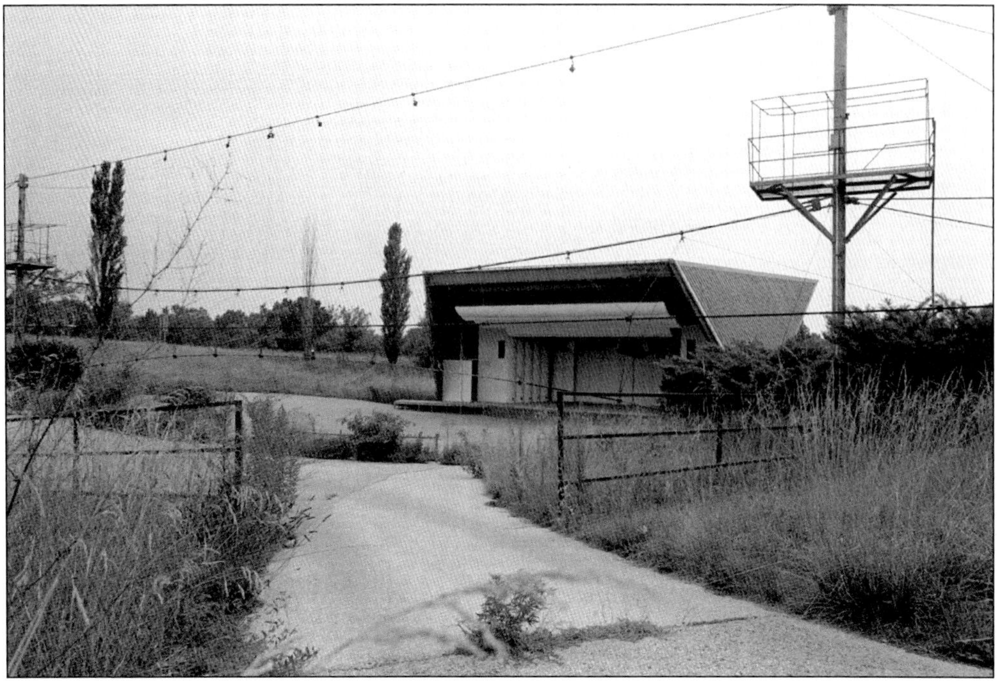

Deteriorating Site. This photograph of the area formerly covered by the tent, taken on August 18, 1983, illustrates the inexorable deterioration of the site. Although the poplar trees continue to dominate the perimeter, grass and weeds had begun to engulf the site in just three years.

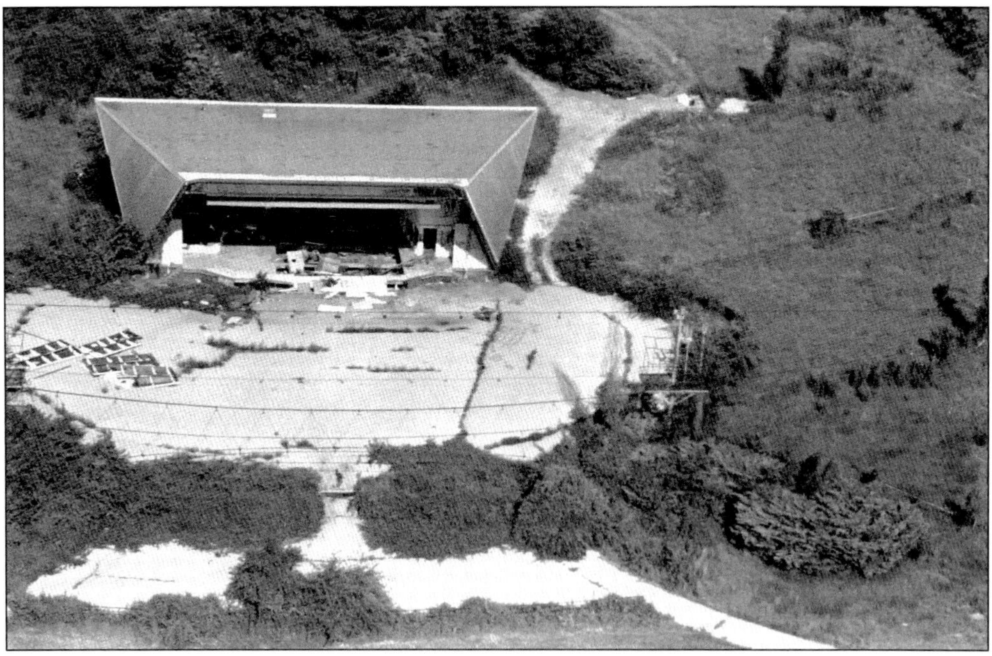

Aerial of Deteriorating Site. The rapid transformation of the site is evident in this aerial photograph dating from July 15, 1988. The plant life surrounding the site has continued to swallow and disguise it. In coming years it would become virtually impossible to recognize the original natural amphitheater as trees took hold and grew there.

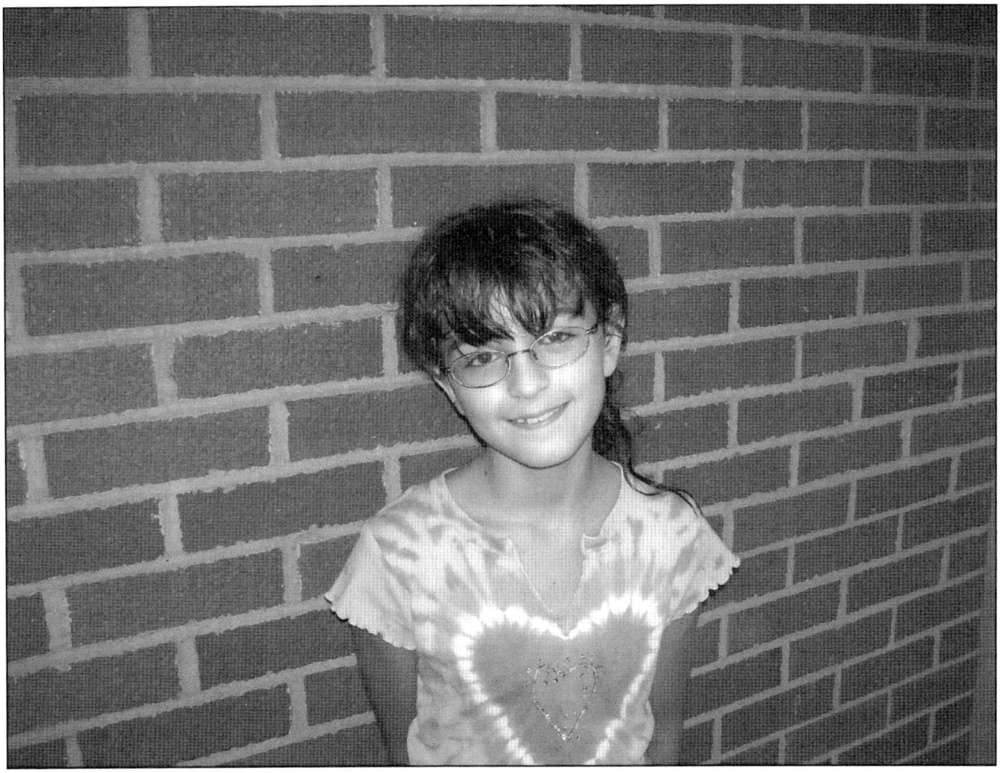

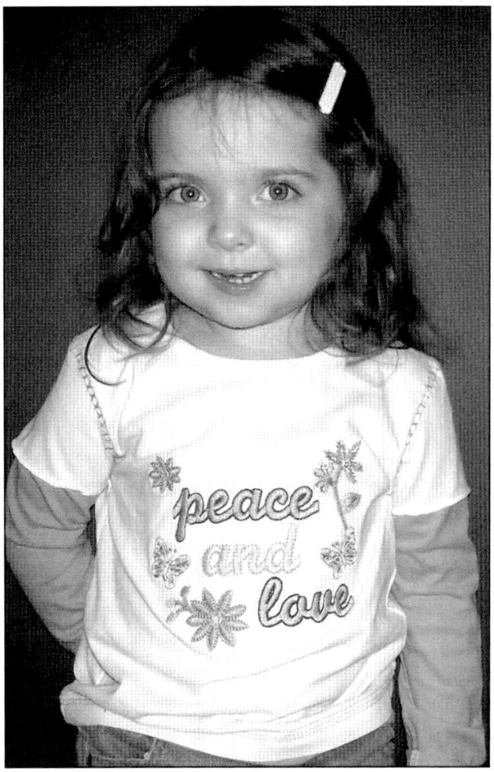

TEACH YOUR CHILDREN WELL. SIUE will celebrate its 50th anniversary with a year-long series of events beginning with the Founders Day Convocation on September 24, 2007. As one part of the 50th-anniversary celebration, the university will be honoring the history and heritage of the MRF. Preparation of this pictorial history about the MRF has been intended as a preliminary step in the ongoing process of honoring the festival. It is the authors' hope that, in some small way, the book will assist those who participated in the MRF to teach their children, and their grandchildren, about the importance of daring to make audacious dreams come true, of pursuing excellence in every realm of intellectual endeavor, and of employing music as a means to communicate, to educate, and to overcome barriers between people. Catherine Kerber (above) and Audrey Evola (right) look forward to the MRF commemorative concert during the 50th-anniversary celebration.